Love in a Time of Slaughters

AnthropoScene
THE SLSA BOOK SERIES

Published in collaboration with the Society for Literature, Science, and the Arts, AnthropoScene presents books that examine relationships and points of intersection among the natural, biological, and applied sciences and the literary, visual, and performing arts. Books in the series promote new kinds of cross-disciplinary thinking arising from the idea that humans are changing the planet and its environments in radical and irreversible ways.

Love in a Time of Slaughters

Human-Animal Stories
Against Genocide and Extinction

Susan McHugh

The Pennsylvania State
University Press
University Park,
Pennsylvania

Library of Congress Cataloging-in-Publication
   Data
Names: McHugh, Susan (Susan Bridget), author.
Title: Love in a time of slaughters : human-animal
   stories against genocide and extinction / Susan
   McHugh.
Other titles: AnthropoScene.
Description: University Park, Pennsylvania : The
   Pennsylvania State University Press, [2019] |
   Series: AnthropoScene: the SLSA book series |
   Includes bibliographical references and index.
Summary: "Explores a narrative pattern in which
   storytellers revisit instances of genocide and
   extinction not simply to reveal historical
   erasures of whole populations but also to
   rearticulate lifeways premised on cross-species
   interdependence. Focuses on recovering a
   sense of affective bonds shared across species
   lines"—Provided by publisher.
Identifiers: LCCN 2019001332 | ISBN
   9780271084619 (cloth : alk. paper) | ISBN
   9780271083704 (pbk. : alk. paper)
Subjects: LCSH: Human-animal relationships in
   literature. | Genocide in literature. | Animal
   welfare in literature.
Classification: LCC PN56.A64 M44 2019 | DDC
   809/.93362—dc23
LC record available at
   https://lccn.loc.gov/2019001332

Published by The Pennsylvania State
University Press,
University Park, PA 16802-1003

The Pennsylvania State University Press is a
member of the Association of University Presses.

It is the policy of The Pennsylvania State
University Press to use acid-free paper.
Publications on uncoated stock satisfy the
minimum requirements of American National
Standard for Information Sciences—Permanence
of Paper for Printed Library Material,
ANSI Z39.48-1992.

There is nothing intelligent to say about a massacre.
Everybody is supposed to be dead, to never say
anything or want to say anything again. Everything
is supposed to be very quiet after a massacre, and it
always is, except for the birds.

And what do the birds say? All there is to say
about a massacre, things like *"Poo-tee-weet?"*

Kurt Vonnegut, *Slaughterhouse-Five*

Contents

Acknowledgments

Love is not just the subject of this book but also its growing medium. My heart swells just thinking of everyone who has been there for me along what turned into a remarkably difficult journey in the making of this book.

When I doubted whether I had the wherewithal to see this book through, it was the confidence that others expressed in me while working on this and related projects—whether as collaborators, contributors, editors, panel organizers, reviewers, respondents, reference providers, students, event hosts, and guests—that inspired much-needed courage in me to carry on. Special love and thanks to my coeditors of various related projects: Giovanni Aloi, Sarah Bezan, Garry Marvin, Robert McKay, John Miller, Robert Mitchell, Ken Shapiro, Nik Taylor, and Wendy Woodward. Our contributors, reviewers, and production staff have taught me way more than they will ever know. Love also to more friends who have helped in so many consummately collegial ways: Joni Adamson, Philip Armstrong, Cecelia Åsberg, Kristin Asdal, Steve and Aly Baker, Karyn Ball, Ang Bartram, Michelle Bastian, Alice Bendinelli, Lynda Birke, Amelie Björck, Kristian Bjorkdahl, Roland Borgards, Sune Borkfelt, Sally Borrell, Ron Broglio, Eric Brown, Jacob Bull, Henry Buller, Jonathan Burt, Erika Andersson Cederholm, Una Chaudhuri, Keridiana Chez, Lucinda Cole, Marion Copeland, Istvan Csicsery-Ronay, Marianne DeKoven, Margo DeMello, Jamie Denike, Jane Desmond, Vinciane Despret, Richard and Karin Dienst, Thom van Dooren, Ben Doyle, Phillip Drake, Kári Driscoll, Tone Druglitrø, Jeanne Dubino, Gunnar Eggertsson, Aden Evens, Leesa Fawcett, Guro Flinterud, Elisabeth Friis, Erica Fudge, Catrin Gersdof, Ty Gowen, Katherine Grier, Lori Gruen, x Lisa Haynes, Donna Haraway, Elina Helander-Renvall, David Herman, Steve Hinchcliffe, Tora Holmberg, Kelly Hübben, Zoe Hughes, Kristina Jennbert, Karen Jones, Daniel Heath Justice, Hilda Kean, Kara Kendall-Morwick, André Krebber, Michael Lawrence, Jacob Leveton, Tobias Linné, Melissa Littlefield, Ann-Sofie Lönngren, Michael Lundblad, Davide Majocchi, Robert Markley, René Marquez, Monica Mattfeld, Seán McCorry, Laura McMahon, Peter Meedom, Frederike Middelhoff, Mara Miele, Brett Mizelle, Kaori Nagai, John Ó Maoilearca, Kira O'Reilly, Anat Pick, Rachael Poliquin, Annie Potts, Jason Price, Ziba Rashidian, Thangam Ravindranathan, David Redmalm, Carrie Rohman, Mieke Roscher, Nigel Rothfels, Kathy Rudy, Joshua Russell, Sebastian Schönbeck, Stephanie Schwandner-Sievers, Julietta Singh, Andrew Smyth, Bryndis Snæbjörnsdóttir, Nathan Snaza, Krithika Srinavasan, Susan Squier, Rajani Sudan, Karen Lykke Syse, Liv Emma Thorsen, Antoine Traisnel, Stephanie Turner, Tom Tyler, Jessica and Martin Ulrich, Sherryl Vint, Harlan Weaver, Kari Weil, Boel Westin, Mark Wilson, and Cary Wolfe. My most sincere apologies to anyone I've forgotten to list. I'm not ungrateful; it's just that my memory is leaking. I'm particularly honored to have worked with Nicolene Swanepoel and Michael Wessels, though their sudden deaths have been difficult to bear.

Many helpfully discussed parts of this project with me at excellent academic events, including those organized by the Animal Studies Roundtable in Africa, Animals and Society Institute, Animal/Nonhuman Workshop at the University of Chicago, Aotearoa New Zealand Centre for Human-Animal Studies, British Animal Studies Network, Centre for Development and Environment at the University of Oslo, Environmental Humanities Laboratory at KTH Royal Institute of Technology, Environmental Humanities Research Workshop at Northwestern University, Environmental Research Group at Cardiff University, the HumAnimal Group at Uppsala University's Centre for Gender Research, Human Animal Studies at the University of Kassel, Leslie Center for the Humanities at Dartmouth University, Living with Animals at Eastern Kentucky University, Minding Animals International, Sheffield Animal Studies Research Centre, Society for Literature, Science, and the Arts, Tufts University Art Gallery, Wesleyan Animal Studies, United Centre for Theological Studies at the University of Winnipeg, and Würzburg Summer School for Cultural and Literary Animal Studies. The organizers are my heroes for doing the difficult but necessary work of holding space for genuine, ongoing intellectual engagements that otherwise would not be happening.

Kendra Boileau gets superspecial affection and appreciation for believing in this project, offering excellent guidance in shaping it, and heading up the great team that wrangled it into production at the Pennsylvania State University Press.

Part of the research for this book was supported by a sabbatical leave from the Department of English, College of Arts and Sciences, and a grant from the Office of Sponsored Research at the University of New England. I appreciate the support of my UNE colleagues, especially Ali Ahmida, Stephen Burt, Elizabeth De Wolfe, Teresa Dzieweczynski, Cathrine Frank, Cathleen Miller, and Halie Pruitt. I am also indebted to the kind indulgence of students in several of my undergraduate courses—the Animal Humanities Seminar, Postcolonial Ecocriticism, Dog Stories, Indigenous Film and Literature, Nature Films, and Animals, Literature, and Culture—who joined me in reading, discussing, and writing about many of the narratives and some of the theories at the core of this book. Their curiosity and enthusiasm remain deeply inspiring.

I'm ever most obliged to the world's best physician and my beloved friend Hetty Carraway, who guided me through successful cancer treatment care at the Dana Farber Institute and the Central Maine Medical Center, and my husband, Mik Morrisey, who along with our (too-soon-gone) dog Sabine and her cats Jinx and Django kept me moving before, during, and after those seriously scary times. I write through tears of joy of their patience with me tending to so many beloved indoor plants, garden annuals and perennials, trees, compost, wild animal visitors, human and other animal family, friends, and neighbors, along with so many others who help make my life seem not only possible but downright well worth living.

Earlier versions of parts of this book appeared in essay collections and journals. Although all have been substantially revised since those publications, I am grateful for permission to develop them:

- "Animal Gods in Extinction Stories: *Power* and *Princess Mononoke*." In *Representing the Modern Animal in Culture*, edited by Jeanne Dubino, Ziba Rashidian, and Andrew Smyth, 205–25. New York: Palgrave Macmillan, 2014. Reproduced with permission of Palgrave Macmillan.
- "Cross-pollinating: Indigenous Knowledges of Extinction and Genocide in Honeybee Fictions." In *Indigenous Creatures, Native Knowledges, and the Arts: Animal Studies in Modern Worlds*, edited by Wendy Woodward and Susan McHugh, 249–70. London: Palgrave Macmillan, 2017. Reproduced with permission of Palgrave Macmillan.

- "'A Flash Point in Inuit Memories': Endangered Knowledges in the Mountie Sled Dog Massacre." In "The Global Animal," edited by Karyn Ball and Lisa Haynes, special issue of *ESC: English Studies in Canada* 39.1 (2013): 149–75.
- "Loving Camels, Sacrificing Sheep, Slaughtering Gazelles: Human-Animal Relations in Contemporary Desert Fiction." In *Humans, Animals and Biopolitics*, edited by Kristin Asdal, Tone Druglitrø, and Steve Hinchcliffe, 171–88. New York: Routledge, 2017. Copyright © 2017.
- "Shoring: Contemporary Fictions of Indigenous Cetacean Killing." In *Animal Places: Lively Cartographies of Human-Animal Relations*, edited by Jacob Bull, Tora Holmberg, and Cecelia Åsberg, 248–68. New York: Routledge, 2018. Copyright © 2018.

Introduction

When Species Meet on Killing Fields

In 2012, biologists and linguists collaborated to correlate the first global maps demonstrating significant overlaps of biological and linguistic diversity. Noting that the highest rates of convergence occur in areas that are not only biodiversity hot spots but also often Indigenous communities in close proximity to protected wilderness zones, they conclude that great losses to nature and culture alike are coming unless the cultural systems that enable biological diversity to persist are identified and conserved.[1] Scientific faith in conservation follows an obvious route toward the few remaining success stories. Yet a more complete picture of endangerment and resistance to it is emerging from different quarters through current creative efforts to narrate lost histories involving genocides, extinctions, and other less easily separated instances of large-scale death across species lines. Affect takes shape in the cross hairs, for at the crux of these stories is the potential for love shared between humans and other animals.

Love in a Time of Slaughters: Human-Animal Stories Against Genocide and Extinction brings together several contemporary narratives that address the histories of little-known human cultural atrocities to ask how they intersect with anthropogenic extinctions and more deliberate acts of animal slaughter, locating stories of cross-species platonic affection within them as a vibrant form of resistance to the forces of destruction. Set at the outer peripheries of urban-industrial centers, contemporary tales from across the globe—including those of Inuit with semiferal working dogs in the Arctic, Maghrebi tribespeople herding various species of domestic ungulates in the deepest Sahara, and Native Pacific peoples and sea creatures in temperate and tropical zones—revisit scenes of state-sanctioned sufferings on massive scales, presenting them not as ends in themselves but as entry points into lifeways centered on intimate linkages between particular kinds of animals and peoples. Adding creative dimensions to a growing sense that multispecies contexts justify integrated approaches to social and environmental theory,[2] these depictions of profound ruptures to shared relations between species concern more than losses exclusive to either cultural or biological lifeways.

Such storytelling gains urgency amid the recognition of our era as witnessing the sixth global mass-extinction event, the first to be propelled by human activity. Taking loss as a starting point rather than the usual end point, this book follows the spirit of the stories themselves by locating how they articulate histories of dynamic opposition to the settler colonialist forces that prove responsible for so much of the damage. Often by staging deep, holistic transformations to approximate ancient and highly localized knowledges of being in the world, they offer a timely focal point as well for the development of current efforts to map the crossroads of Indigenous, literary, ecocritical, and human-animal studies.[3]

While literatures of all cultures and times include representations of nonhuman life, literary animal studies has taken shape as a subfield only in recent decades, a closely overlapping time frame with the period in which so-called animist traditions have undergone intense revaluation in academics and during which the stories at the center of this book have emerged. Much can be learned from past mistakes by mapping links across these developments. While human-animal studies across the disciplines remains dominated by an emphasis on Anglophone texts and Eurowestern perspectives from the colonial period through the present, some literary scholars have studied animals in ways that have pioneered models based on an ever-growing array of stories for decolonizing representations of particular human-animal relations on their own terms. Their work provides an essential critical context for what follows.

So much depends on how animals come to matter within academic disciplines. The studied avoidance of animals in literary studies except to decode them as human symbols or other literary devices became impossible to sustain from the 1980s onward with the applications of poststructuralist theory to twentieth-century literature. Jacques Derrida's deconstructive theory has proven particularly influential in accounting for the impossibility of representing human animality, at least, within the hierarchical and dualistic terms dominating Eurowestern traditions.[4] But Derrida's last set of lectures is proving still more significant as a direct call to address the dire consequences of self-proclaimed rationalist philosophical discourse for nonhuman life. Most often cited is the standalone moment, so to speak, in which Derrida longs for a countertradition of what he characterizes as a poetic discourse—surely, according to him, to be "found among those signatories who are first and foremost poets and prophets"—that would account for a sudden sense of exchanging gazes with his cat.[5]

Wendy Woodward identifies Derrida's cat story as inadvertently inspirational to her book *The Animal Gaze: Animal Subjectivities in Southern African Narratives* (2008), one of the first book-length studies of animals in postcolonial literatures. For Woodward, "the Derridean provocative (playful?) claim that he knows of no such poets or prophets, implicitly suggesting that they cannot exist, is a spurious one," in part because none of his many references are to literary writers or philosophers who range beyond the Eurowestern discourse that he purports to be moving away from.[6] Describing the problem of "the" animal as a generic other that "the" human requires to maintain power differentials even within our own species, Derrida nonetheless takes a narrow view of where its solution might be found, a move that becomes understandable in light of the biblical-exegetical context of his final lectures. Yet its ongoing invocation among literary scholars proves harder to justify.

Whether they are also acknowledged as poets and prophets, those who are most clearly advancing nonanthropocentric—or, to phrase it more positively, animal-centric—discourses are storytellers. In the context of graphic novels, Marion Copeland defines animal-centric stories as those that offer insight into the relations of consciousness and experience when they feature nonhuman animal protagonists that are presented with realistic motives and concerns that arise from living among their own and other kinds of beings, not least when cast in anthropogenically altered environs.[7] Copeland's work is exceptionally noteworthy for identifying such stories in all kinds of undervalued genres. Among the driving concerns of this book are that her initial explorations in the 1980s of animal-centered narrative focused on Indigenous literatures[8] and that they were not subsequently engaged by scholars like novelist and literary critic Gerald Vizenor (Anishinaabe) despite his subsequently arriving at similar conclusions.[9]

The missed connections provide an important context for identifying the problems for decolonizing literary animal studies. Graham Huggan and Helen Tiffin note that alignments of extinct and severely endangered animal species with vanishing and lost human cultures risk further exploitation via reduction to a literary figure: "Above all, perhaps, the metaphorisation and deployment of 'animal' as a derogatory term in genocidal and marginalizing discourses . . . make it difficult even to discuss animals without generating a profound unease, even a rancorous antagonism, in many postcolonial contexts today."[10] Labeling groups of people with animalizing terms remains a powerful tool of oppression, one that is challenged by a growing awareness of how animal practices are enmeshed in the social constitution of human identities.[11] While the potential for perpetuating harm is real, grounding analyses of literary figures in lived, embodied relations between species can help move discussions forward.

Fear of cultural misappropriation may be a good reason early efforts at culturally attentive literary animal studies gravitated toward modern and contemporary fiction. Jopi Nyman makes the case for the value of animal stories in decolonizing the Anglophone imagination in *Postcolonial Animal Tale from Kipling to Coetzee* (2003), although his conclusions are far from hopeful, perhaps because traditional knowledges remain in the background.[12] Tracing a wider historical pattern across the literatures of settler colonialism, Philip Armstrong's *What Animals Mean in the Fiction of Modernity* (2008) identifies literary evidence of how the anthropomorphic notion of human agency—rather, what philosopher Giorgio Agamben calls its "anthropophorous" (or man-making) function—emerges under the constant threat of what he terms "anthropoluotic" textual operations, whereby nonhumans "demolish, unfasten, annul, delegitimize, or subvert" the human as a concept, at times even in the flesh.[13] Animal forms once dismissed as incoherent or confusing by literary critics thus can be seen to inscribe alternate social forms and capacities in human, animal, and human-animal relations—and with important implications for both postcolonial and human-animal studies of literature.

Attending to the persistence of highly localized human-animal relationships provides another pathway for writing and restorying literary histories as something other than colonial impositions. As Armstrong argues elsewhere, "The production of sharp, politicized, culturally sensitive, and up-to-the-minute local histories of the roles that animals and their representations have played—or been made to play—in colonial and postcolonial transactions [requires] . . . respect for local differences, suspicion of theories and values that claim absolute authority, and commitment to ongoing dialogue with formerly repressed cultural knowledge."[14] Complementing the inroads staked by Derridean deconstruction in literary animal studies, research in this vein identifies possibilities for animal stories to transform the very terms of justice, upholding related claims of feminist historians,[15] philosophers,[16] and others across the disciplines in human-animal studies, which hold that discourse and embodied experience are difficult to separate.

Less well developed to date are accounts that track how representations of animals in literature reflect interfaces of traditional and modern-industrial world views. Notable among more recent titles is Ann-Sofie Lönngren's *Following the Animal: Power, Agency, and Human-Animal Transformations in Modern, Northern-European Literature* (2015), which makes a compelling case for the relevance of literary animal studies beyond Anglophone traditions.[17] With the long twentieth century as its time frame and Bakhtinian structuralist analysis as its primary method, Lönngren's book identifies a distinctly Nordic model of cross-species shape-shifting that is informed by ancient local folk traditions and continues in contemporary fiction. Her work inspired me to look in contemporary narratives that revisit old ways of life for knowledges of human-animal relations in developments of characters, scenes, and stories that range well beyond ratio-centric principles.

More recently studying how, in the transformation from regional folklore to literary fiction, narratives of reindeer have come to signify the Sápmi region in place of the Sámi people, Lönngren shows how literary intertextuality can be enlisted against histories of erasure.[18] Rupturing anthropocentrism in service of a decolonial project in this case involves recovery of what anthropologist Elina Helander-Renvall (Sámi) clarifies as the traditional reindeer herders' metaphysical sense of intersubjectivity with their animals as of a piece with their land.[19] Shifting perceptions of places as just plain empty to having become historically emptied spaces is critical. That the sustaining human-animal intimacy central to reindeer herding becomes reasserted at once formally and ontologically only when reframed in their remote, sparsely populated homelands suggests further possibilities for queering the urban-industrial orientation (or "metronormativity") of literary animal studies.[20] In addition to being hot spots for cultural and biological diversity, for many marginalized communities, their own traditionally rural areas locate where and why transformations of old animal stories are made more compelling today.

In the persistence of various traditional African knowledges of human-animal kinship, shape-shifting, magic, and other realities in southern African novels of recent decades, Woodward also identifies how modern stories can yet defy the logics of anthropocentrism, human-animal duality, and other ideals ordinarily assumed to be the hallmarks of modernity.[21] Read in relation to broader developments in the study of animal narrative, her findings warrant further investigations into the desires and creative resistances that become articulable through discourses shaped by modern alongside traditional knowledges of human-animal relations.[22] Although there is much more to say about how "culturally specific, nonrealist elements" are proving surprisingly useful for women and writers of color in literary studies more generally,[23] Woodward's and Lönngren's studies together suggest that more widespread potentials for decolonial social justice are emerging through the integration of such elements in stories that explore how human-animal relations fare in environments profoundly altered by the legacies of settler colonialism. As a hedge against flattening various peoples, animals, histories, and literatures from several regions of the world, I follow their lead by attempting to attend to the ontological, epistemological, and spiritual particularities that are embodied in these relations. My point in doing so is to foster a farther-ranging, ongoing investigation of the politics of interspecies intersectionalities, studying how writers, filmmakers, and activists attune themselves and others to what exactly is lost in stories of lives that were long shared across species lines and ultimately learning from productive frictions within and across current assemblages of social and ecological justice.[24]

A related goal of *Love in a Time of Slaughters* is to promote a global sensibility of human-animal studies as itself having an ongoing history of having emerged across disciplines and in a time increasingly marked by mass killings on scales never before witnessed on our planet. From a handful of groundbreaking books published in the 1980s, it has become a field that at its best holds open a welcoming space for exchanging different viewpoints, which is partly what explains why it has grown so rapidly in recent decades. The initial obstacle appeared to be a pervasive prejudice in academic professions to the effect that, outside the natural sciences, animals are bad object-choices, in the old psychoanalytic sense. As nonhumans become increasingly acceptable subjects within the humanities and social sciences, what proves a more persistent concern for human-animal studies practitioners is, as Tobias Linné and Helena Pedersen phrase it, "how to create a space and a language in academia . . . to speak about, and work to change, the situation and experiences of animals in human society."[25] While there are urgent reasons to want to change the experiences of everybody disproportionately experiencing the negative aspects of these situations, there can be no preset agenda if such work is to be successful. Taking up the challenge means resisting the moral solace of limiting ourselves to any one of the ways of doing animal studies more generally that seem possible now and, in turn, allowing for the possibility of better ways yet to come.

Quite apart from visions of animal studies as a one-, two-, or "three-pronged" pursuit—in various articulations prioritizing ethical, theoretical, or practical dimensions[26]—I offer the perspective that it largely has been and needs to remain an open-ended academic project. For some, moral philosopher Peter Singer's *Animal Liberation* (1975) signaled a watershed moment, perhaps because it extends rather than questions a tradition of analytical philosophy that remains deeply invested in a notion of rights grounded in human subjectivity and that most everyone else agrees comes to a crisis by the end of the twentieth century. For activists and academics skeptical of the hierarchical dualisms reinforced by philosophical ideals and political exercises of rights, however, much of the research responsible for changing institutional and intellectual climates today pursues the wildly different potentials opened up by poststructuralist thinkers, particularly those informed by feminist, queer, antiracist, and decolonial perspectives, which posit a far more significant liberation of all from the foundational units of humanist thought.

Although not necessarily conceived as such, a major significance of the posthumanist turn made possible by these critiques is that it enables discussions of animals as agents who are not just humanlike subjects or thinglike objects but actors inextricable from human life. To pursue this point, I have chosen throughout to emphasize narratives that hinge on highly visible, culturally significant human-animal bonds—as opposed to animacies,[27] animalities,[28] or other concepts of species as primarily theoretical optics[29]—situating my claims amid the political tensions and embodied lives that anchor human-animal studies.[30] The cultural complexities of human-animal relationships make them particularly good sites for picking apart how processes of domination become interwoven and, therefore, for advancing conversations about the difficult realities of massive deaths of humans alongside other species, conditions that confound metaphorical and other controversial comparisons.

A lot is at stake in the hyphen of the term "human-animal studies." When relationships between species seem pushed beyond breaking points, stories of human-animal intimacies can reveal how these relations become consequential in and of themselves rather than as means to other ends. Seeing breakage requires cultivating an appreciation for a prior sense of continuity, an ordinary togetherness, and more: feelings for shared organismal life follow from the way in which the science of ethology shifts the epistemological grounds under laboratory-scientific ideals of objectivity, in part because it reveals how humans and other animals are always "becoming with" each other, in philosopher of science Vinciane Despret's phrasing.[31] Thinking about animals as inseparable from human lives constitutes the key break from "animal studies" as initially and precisely defined by the natural sciences: laboratory-animal experimentation on the basis of which human medical experiments are justified. Legitimizing field studies as equally important to enhancing knowledges of nonhuman lives has opened the floodgates, allowing for a radical leveling of all disciplinary perspectives. Attending to these momentous changes, historians, narratologists, and creative writers alike affirm that the master narratives of ethology itself have become contested within stories that leverage entirely different configurations of knowledges from those based on the assumption that there is a rational, objective, or really any way to transcend everyone's very basic condition of cross-species entanglements.[32]

Taking compromise as a starting point is the only way to develop the particular configurations of imaginations and materialities that converge in any given cross-species encounter. By refusing any claims of special access to understanding animals, human-animal studies scholars are empowered to learn from those who make extreme commitments to living with members of other species. Working out how to represent them in a way that is growing responsive to their histories is as important for people and animals as it is for communities and ecosystems, policymakers and advocates, not to mention academics attempting empirically to ground and ethically to guide their own work. Throughout her career, Donna Haraway has clarified how such an approach alters perceptions of even the oldest and most ordinarily recognizable companion-species relations, like those experienced by people with dogs, even if it does not change their conditions as fragile, complex, and ongoing choreographies in everyday life.[33] But it is time to take these investigations to the next level. That people live with dogs today is not in question so much as how traditionally people have done and no longer do so in defiance of the encroachments of settler colonialism. This book attempts to elucidate why such changes are intimately caught up with other significant meetings and partings of peoples and species.

Settler perspectives need unsettling. Bringing together emerging stories of radical diminishments to the lives of companion species in the pages that follow, I make the case that such narratives open critical interventions into the ways in which Eurowestern studies of Indigenous metaphysics have been warped by racism and xenophobia. Reduced to mere beliefs, some of the oldest and most complex knowledges of people living in close proximity with other animals are conveniently dismissed as stand-ins for relations among humans. As anthropologist Kim TallBear (Sisseton-Wahpeton Oyate) notes, something akin to the "new" relational theories has long been articulated by colonized peoples, warranting more inclusive as well as self-critical approaches to contemporary narratives that instead assert a sense of Indigenous continuity.[34] Echoing literary scholar Harry Garuba's argument for an irreducibly animist-materialist practice,[35] TallBear articulates a new role for animism in the social sciences that foregrounds how different notions of realities hinge on adequate articulations of what can be known through signs,[36] world views,[37] and perhaps most importantly, gifts of self-sacrifice[38] as shared between species. Stories of total human domination, so essential to Eurowestern subjectivity,[39] come undone in these ambiguous, playful, transformational counternarratives of being that are so often represented by non/human-animal relationships in Indigenous oral traditions and so powerfully redeployed in contemporary fiction.[40]

Which brings me to the question of love. When species meet on killing fields, it becomes easy to lose sight of loving in lieu of hating or even lacking feelings at the heart of the matter. Love bridges the intimate and the social, individuals and multiplicities; it concerns having histories along with creating transformations. Marxist literary theorist Michael Hardt identifies in it a rare potential to expand human powers of attachment to each other that are otherwise alienated under the rule of property.[41] But how does love concern capacities of and for nonhuman attachments beyond the obligations of ownership? Against the easy vegan-abolitionist answer—it doesn't[42]—I make the case here for stories of multispecies affective bonding as an effective means to secure shared futures.

Starting from the premise that humans and other animals are always becoming with each other, it follows that intimacies shared across species lines are inextricable from both knowledges and experiences of being alive, if mortal, critters. Love is certainly not all that (nor even predominantly what) we feel or think about in our relations, and even when it seems so, it is not evenly valued by others. Haraway rightly calls out the misogyny and ageism that cant toward ridicule in philosophers Gilles Deleuze and Félix Guattari's choice of an older woman and her fondness for "my dog, my cat" as the exemplar of Oedipal love.[43] Even as they contribute to a pattern in which human-dog love is derided to denigrate especially postmenopausal women across millennia of Eurowestern history, they call attention to it as a familiar source of social affirmation secured by and for persecuted people that extends across species lines.[44]

Recent repurposings of the same figure by feminist dog writers, including Haraway, indicate how cross-species platonic love makes all the difference for individuals enduring persecution,[45] if also strangely serving as an affective trigger within Deleuze and Guattari's anti-Oedipal model, which is founded in desire and the social. Keeping in mind their notorious contempt for all forms of power makes it difficult to read their woman-with-pet-dog-or-cat simply as an image of ridicule, for such a figure remains integral to a rhetorical strategy that is calculated to call attention to the complicities of those who might take offense.

Far from the ordinary rhetorical "trap" of seduction, Michel Foucault explains how this kind of offensive strategy unfolds in Deleuze and Guattari's work with "so many invitations to let oneself be put out, to take one's leave of the text and slam the door shut" that it "often leads one to believe that it is all fun and games, when something essential is taking place, something of extreme seriousness: the tracking down of all varieties of fascism, from the enormous ones that surround us and crush us to the petty ones that constitute the tyrannical bitterness of our everyday lives."[46] Elaborating such innovative approaches amid Deleuze's more sustained efforts "to undo the straight-jacket of phallocentrism," philosopher Rosi Braidotti argues that feminist theory stands to benefit from such "risks" with previously unexplored possibilities in theoretical positionings vis-à-vis forms of power.[47] Eschewing bitterness strikes me as central to her project of a "non-rapacious ethics of sustainable becoming: for the hell of it and for the love of the world."[48]

Continuing this vein in literary animal studies, literary scholar Alice Kuzniar adds that the point is not to defend or reject the stereotype so much as to unsettle a "false sense of groundedness in one's (for Deleuze and Guattari, bourgeois and oedipalized) subjectivity," an investment in being an individual that obstructs the development of more open-ended becomings shared between at least two.[49] Like Haraway and Kuzniar reflecting on their own experiences with pet dogs, gender and sexuality studies scholar Kathy Rudy likewise concludes "that in deep connection, we all—humans and animals alike—become something different. The very contours of stable identities shift under the revolutionary power of love" and are the hallmarks of "convincing love stories between humans and animals [that] . . . show us a world transformed by human-animal love."[50] That personal experience is coupled with literary examples in so many of these scholars' discussions and more suggests further how affective responses are highly contingent.

Thinking of how affective ideals relate necessarily to other modes of relating—not just "the ambitions and capacities of love," literary and cultural theorist Lauren Berlant elaborates, but also "proximity, solidarity, collegiality, friendship, the light touch and the intermittent ones, and then the hatreds, aversions, and not caring"[51]—helps explain why love matters at all in stories of extinctions and genocides, as well as how storytelling is gaining a sense of urgency in accounting for fatal attractions when species meet. As Berlant persuades, the important social work of attachment requires movement beyond narcissism toward a love equal to "thatness"—in other words, toward loving whatever that may be that is not just a reflection of myself—in a way that allows for interests to be overdetermined and plural; such a love works not to conflate or erase but rather to affirm differences between desires and ethics, appetites and virtues.[52] My concluding chapter develops the implications for human-animal stories of desire's relation to love and its loss, plus resurgences of feelings to defy losses. For now, it may suffice to point to Berlant's attending to how "love [becomes] deemed always an outcome of fantasy,"[53] particularly when its objects are made to "bear the burden of exemplifying and failing what drives our attachments to them."[54]

Attending to the fabulist dimensions of love serves as a powerful strategy of resistance to representing dying and dead critters in terms of mere matter, whether as embodiments of incipient meat or inhuman otherness. As such, it has become a bellwether of the shift from humanistic to posthumanistic analysis of animals in human cultures. From Robert Darnton's 1984 comparative historical study *The Great Cat Massacre: And Other Episodes in French History*, to Akira Lippit's 2000 comparative film and literary study *Electric Animal*, to the Animal Studies Group's 2006 collection *Killing Animals*, to Nicole Shukin's 2008 cultural study *Animal Capital*, to Jay Johnston and Fiona Probyn-Rapsey's 2013 collection *Animal Death*, to Margo DeMello's 2016 collection *Mourning Animals*, to Hilda Kean's 2017 historical case study *The Great Cat and Dog Massacre: The Real Story of World War II's Unknown Tragedy*, human-animal studies increasingly complicates the reduction of nonhumans made to shed their mortal coils to pure spectacle or bearers of strictly human meanings. The bookends of this brief list alone are revealing. Questioning why we should care about the suffering of long-dead cats who were gleefully dispatched by their human killers as one among many briefly outlined limiting cases of historical objectivity, Darnton's book now reads like an outlier. In contrast, Kean's meticulous archival investigation—elucidating how ordinary UK people voluntarily came to surrender their beloved pets to be destroyed in droves as part of the war effort—models how to value as emotionally charged the otherwise cold, dead facts of massacres involving members of other species.

The course of love's self-sustainment clearly doesn't always bring sustenance to others. That its self-destructiveness sometimes compels the destruction of others is one of the major insights of queer theory and explains its ever-growing relevance in tandem with human-animal studies to revolutionizing thought itself. Staying within human politics, anthropologist Elizabeth Povinelli points to love's instrumentality to the spread of European imperialism. In the form of the "intimate couple" lies a crucial point of transfer between the imaginaries and exercises of power, such that "love in settler colonies" becomes the "hege-monic home of liberal logics and aspirations."[55] Comparing modes of intimacy specific to a queer US and an Indigenous Australian community, she shows how love is not just "about desire, pleasure, or sex . . . but [also] about things like geography, history, culpability, and obligation; the extraction of wealth and the distribution of life and death; hope and despair."[56] Such ideals become part and parcel of the ways in which colonial, postcolonial, and neocolonial histories are sedimented in bodies through the affective relations made, broken, and missed between them.

Framing decolonial inquiry, Povinelli's conclusions invite comparison with Berlant's along with gender and sexuality studies scholar bell hooks's earlier diagnoses of the idealization of cisheteronormative reproductive coupling as particularly dangerous for women, queers, and people of color, for whom senses of community and belonging powerfully mitigate histories of domina-tion and consequent felt helplessness.[57] A practice of "love-politics," as Jennifer Nash further argues in the context of black feminist theory, disrupts ahistorical visions with "a collectivity marked by 'communal affect,' a utopian, vision-ary, future-oriented community held together" by forging alliances through "public feeling," a practice that has long grounded alternative narratives to those of the permanently disempowered "wounded subject."[58] Making these connec-tions is not the same as reducing them to any common condition. Declaring allegiances with the struggles of others offers no simple solutions, for as affect theorist Sarah Ahmad shows, the political conditions of alliance with some as against others—"standing alongside some others and against other others"—often strategically conceals animus, leading to violence in the name of love.[59]

In an era also marked by "lovecidal" spectacle—which, in filmmaker and gender and sexuality studies scholar Trinh T. Minh-ha's account of Tibetan self-immolation as political protest, amounts to "love suicided"[60]—the destruction of those who range beyond the fold of personally loved ones becomes all the more shocking when it provokes self-destruction among loving ones, who see the very possibility of the social as thereby imperiled. From her personal perspective as having been a child Vietnam War refugee, Trinh both honors a sense of indebtedness to the consciousness-raising efforts of the suicides of strangers on behalf of herself and so many others as well as recognizes their place in violent, ongoing legacies of decolonial movements. It is a difficult line to walk these impulses across species lines, and I am not confident that the lovecidal moments that flash up in the stories that I analyze are always so carefully handled. But the risk of fumbling seems small in comparison to repeating the colonial failure of not mapping the range of loving connections within and between species and how these relate to the dying, the dead, the gods, and the others who have always been and continue to be animating so many different non-Eurowestern cosmologies.

Academics generally and deeply are implicated in colonialist histories of identifying peoples' engagements in traditional animal practices as evidence of moral and intellectual inferiority, a disturbing history that again is calling forth new assessments of human-animal relations, especially in what anthropologists used to denigrate as animist societies. In Haraway's terms, the challenge is not lamenting or transcending so much as "staying with the trouble."[61] With good reasons, she maintains a troubled relationship with the term "post-humanism,"[62] but I invoke it here as a signal phrase for experimental theories that account for a kind of persistence in modern transformations of stories of some of the oldest human-animal relations.

Although often invoking unlovable animal qualities, literary animal studies scholars engaged with posthumanist theory serve as guides for analyzing stories of proximities that prove deadly for some humans and other animals not perceived as persons in the Eurowestern juridical sense. In *Thinking Animals: Why Animal Studies Now?* (2012), literary scholar Kari Weil shows how modern and contemporary texts trouble ethical positioning in response to questions of animal life by revealing the qualities of *bêtise* (asininity). Whereas Derrida invokes this term for "animal stupidity" to elaborate the homogenizing problem of "the" animal—arguably also compounding it in the same move by making his cat the homogenous other to *logos*[63]—Weil restores it to a wider poststructuralist interrogation of human-animal borderlands by linking it to what Deleuze notoriously diagnosed in terms of *bêtise en bêtise*, or "cruelty in cruelty," as "the origin of the melancholy that weighs down on the finest human figures."[64] Anticipating only to reject the productivity of play in the Deleuzian model that Brian Massumi maps across species lines,[65] Weil uses close readings of largely Eurowestern literary examples to explore the Deleuzian-Derridean tension in order to make sense of how scenes of caring about animal deaths complicate human melancholy.

Still more studies connect eruptions of "the bestial" directly to the human-identity questions not only of gender and sex but also of race—more specifically, the fraught racial histories shared by African and Caucasian (but curiously not Asian, Native, Pacific Islander, Latinx, and more)—Americans in modern and contemporary narratives.[66] Such developments might be understood from literary scholar Cary Wolfe's posthumanist perspective as evidence of the fundamental repression of humanism's speciesist limits.[67] But it is also possible that these very ways of conceiving of the human, conditioned so heavily by hierarchies and dualisms, are not preparing us to engage with the persistence of multiple alternative perspectives that are grounded in traditions with different metaphysical assumptions. Recent work in biopolitical theory clarifies how more purposefully destructive aggregates of "isms" require sharper analytical tools and provoke my own thinking deeper into the relations of the significances of super/natural plus un/dead relations to humans and other animals in contemporary storytelling, particularly the stories that resist relegation to colonialism's margins.

A touchstone for much of the current discussion, Foucault's separation of biopower from sovereign and disciplinary powers concerns the increasingly apparent effects of taking life and letting live when it comes to masses of bodies, correlated to a distinctive force "applied not to man-as-body but to the living man, to man-as-living-being; ultimately if you'd like man-as-species." And why "ultimately" to the human as a species? In Shukin's reading of philosophers Michael Hardt and Antonio Negri's conceptual reworking of the biopolitical in relation to economic production as a feature of present-day neoliberalism, the answer would seem to be to gloss over material contingencies and continuities shared between species. Shukin's own *Animal Capital: Rendering Life in Biopolitical Times* (2009) addresses the problem through zoopolitical critique, which is more deliberately oriented around questions of nonhuman lives and deaths.[68] More recently, she turns to literary fictions at the uneasy edges of settler colonialism to explore "how the politics of (human-)animal love bears upon the politics of reconciliation and forgiveness" through stories of animals depicted as affective agents ushering in the postcolonial era.[69]

Shukin's work overall traces an alternate trajectory to philosophical discussions that frame biopolitics more restrictively as a way of addressing the crisis of the human. The degradation of people's lives that is distilled in histories of genocide and exacerbated in neo/colonialist contexts informs a proliferation of complementary concepts, such as Achille Mbembe's necropolitics[70] and Roberto Esposito's thanatopolitics,[71] which underscore how the management of life for some invariably involves how the suffering and deaths of others become categorically excluded from the human fold. Echoing Shukin, Wolfe shows how the focus on recent histories of human-on-human violence, especially genocide, that follows largely from Agamben's interpretation of Foucault risks reinforcing precisely by separating binary divisions like non/white and in/human. After Foucault, notes Wolfe, "you can't talk about race without talking about species, simply because both categories . . . are so notoriously pliable and unstable, constantly bleeding into and out of each other," which is why biopolitics cannot sustain ontological differences between humans and other species.[72] Less clearly than the novels chosen by Shukin, Wolfe's hypothetical examples—a feedlot cow, sunflowers—indicate how human-animal studies can offer a more comprehensive account of what Foucault initially conceived through agricultural history as the calculated management of multispecies life and death on massive scales. That said, for a hedge against biopolitical thinking's potential slippage into what Berlant terms a "moral science,"[73] I turn to stories of lived relations to fill in a more complete picture of the varied ways in which everybody becomes drawn into uneven relations of power by the ratcheting up of capacities for killing through the past century.

Amid growing social and scientific acceptance of the immanent porosity of organismal life, the metaphorical associations of concentration camps and industrial slaughterhouses that offend humanist sensibilities give way to historically grounded narratives that align modern institutions of biopower over the lives and deaths of human together with nonhuman populations, a point I pursued in my previous book, *Animal Stories: Narrating Across Species Lines* (2011). Tracing how twentieth-century developments in the aesthetics of animal representation inform the mutation of utopian models from the autonomous individual toward a dynamic centered on human-animal intersubjectivity, I identified urban transformations of the intercorporeal conditions of animal breeding and meat making as key sites of attraction for industrial-scale control and, consequently, narrative interventions. Turning attention toward what gets lost along the way—that is, the remote, Indigenous, elusive, endurance-testing conditions on which these forms of modern living with animals encroach—*Love in a Time of Slaughters* advances a more radical model of human-animal studies as informed by socially and biologically inclusive approaches to posthumanism.

Focusing more narrowly on contemporary novels, films, art installations, and even a truth commission, I track the emergence since the 1990s of a narrative pattern in which instances of mass killing are revisited not simply to reveal historical erasures of whole populations but, more important, to relearn knowledges of lifeways as premised on loving relations of cross-species interdependence. By showing how capacities to imagine and articulate shared human-animal lives outside Eurowestern discursive norms concern cultural along with biological survival, I also refute claims that human-animal studies is limited from the outset by racist, speciesist, neocolonialist, or environmentally shortsighted prejudices.[74] Wolfe's work is the questionable common thread across criticism on all these fronts, which, to be fair, is mainly launched by scholars in attempts to distance their own projects from human-animal and literary animal studies. Whether the goal is to scapegoat one scholar or to avoid the rigors of scholarship itself, the outcome remains the same: a failure to recognize let alone account for the diversity of voices in literary- and human-animal studies scholarship, so much of which is necessary, at the very least, for an adequate account of the kinds of stories that have compelled me to write this book. In the chapters that follow, such claims are tested through narratives selected to highlight how often tribal—intriguingly often also nonwhite, gynocentric, as well as seminomadic—peoples pushed to the brink are being told and retold in ways that validate attachments specific to shared conditions with nonhuman animals, including complex mutual dependencies on other animals and plants unique to particular places.

Elaborating why current literary debates frame animal gods as risky narrative elements, chapter 1, "Dying Animal Gods: Metaphysical Potentials," considers how mythical critters come to be depicted as dying in such popularly and critically successful examples as Hayao Miyazaki's 1997 animated film *Princess Mononoke* and Linda Hogan (Chickasaw)'s 1998 novel *Power*. Partly historical fictions, these narratives address two different systematic eradications of Indigenous peoples—that of the Emishi (possibly also the Utari) of northwestern Japan and the Seminole (possibly also the Chickasaw) of the southeastern United States—that paved the way for settler states. Exploring in part the gains and limits of a Derridean "hauntology" for deconstructive and material analysis,[75] I track the complicated ways in which fictional super-natural beings in iconic endangered-animal forms like wolves and panthers are doomed to embody dying cultures and at the same time voice ideological challenges that extend far beyond these fictions into contemporaneous landmark court decisions regarding Utari and Seminole peoples' rights regarding animals and ecology. As creatures of the imagination crafted to speak out against the eradication at once of human cultures and biological populations, the precarious lives of gods in animal forms become interlinked with the loves shared between animal and human characters in ways that prompt further questioning about the role of fiction in sustaining Indigenous metaphysics amid ongoing conditions of endangerment.

Chapter 2, "Taxidermy Remains: On the Vitality of Lifeless Bodies," turns to the fragmentary dead bodies of taxidermy in fiction in order to consider how respectful conservation concerns more concrete relations between the living and the dead. Panned by critics as misconceived, even offensive, Yann Martel's *Beatrice and Virgil* (2010) is a fiction about a fiction of the Nazi Holocaust from a bizarre perspective: the taxidermy specimens of a howler monkey and a wild ass, possibly an endangered New World and an extinct Old World species. Like other contemporary repurposings of taxidermy, these characters discom-fortingly evoke racist legacies even as they pinpoint biological ruptures that remain deeply marked by a sense of human longing. In a period marked by what Berlant calls a "cruel optimism" or a perverse desire for the obstacles to flourishing,[76] other contemporary narratives use creative repurposings of taxidermy collections to different ends. So I analyze in detail how two novels, Lydia Millet's *Magnificence* (2012) and Henrietta Rose-Innes's *The Green Lion* (2015), elaborate to what vital effects representations that incorporate material fragments of lost lives can be used to craft effective cultural and biological interventions, which according to one of Millet's characters includes but is not limited to "lov[ing] the gone ones."[77]

Other contemporary novels incorporate a range of im/mortal characters more purposefully to confront conditions marked by the peculiar "double death"[78] of one who is representative of both a species going extinct and interdependent multispecies communities that no longer sustain traditional Indigenous lifeways. Chapter 3, "Pacific Currents: Becoming Usefully Dead," centers on two examples: Robert Barclay's *Meḷaḷ: A Novel of the Pacific* (2002), about Marshallese Islanders, and another by Hogan, *People of the Whale: A*

Novel (2009), about a fictional Pacific Northwestern American Indian tribe, both of which integrate beliefs in multinatural beings in order to explain the fragile persistence of tribal peoples and animals on and in the Pacific Ocean. Central to these stories are scenes in which Indigenous men botch a traditional and controversial execution of a cetacean. Ancient, local knowledges of species interdependence are also explicitly imperiled in these killing scenes and secured only through their affective ties to Indigenous peoples' gods as seen through the flickering perspectives of their deceased relatives. Immaterial specters and the stuff of history—things with a distinctly disembodied presence—the reappearance of ancestors in these stories works as what Despret identifies in terms of the "useful dead"[79] to people a category of thinginess that is distinct from all other things by nature of the love and other feelings they inspire among the living. Sustaining a sense of continuity beyond the ordinary limits of life, the range of their figurations within each of these novels calls attention to the possibilities for fiction itself to form the response that is the thing that makes the dead useful to sustaining social life among and across endangered groups in severely depleted land- and seascapes.

Building from the previous discussions, chapter 4, "Saharan Nonexistence: Edging near Death Camps," more explicitly examines how literary narratives model human-animal alignments as central to the lives—and deaths—of nomadic populations in North Africa. Two novels published in 1990 by Tuareg writer Ibrahim al-Koni, who is the most widely translated living Arabic novelist, figure extreme relations of interdependence among desert species. *Gold Dust* tells the story of a loving but doomed relationship of interspecies intersubjectivity shared between a Tuareg tribesman and a camel, and *The Bleeding of the Stone* uses encounters between Tuareg people—along with sheep, goats, camels, and gazelles—to underscore a shared sense of love's obligations. The backdrop of both stories is a genocide that remains largely unacknowledged: the Italian colonial authorities' 1929–33 confinement of more than a hundred thousand nomadic North African tribal peoples, who starved to death alongside their herds in barbed-wire enclosures. To establish how and why these histories emerge obliquely, the chapter begins with a discussion of al-Koni's much more recent novel *Anubis* (2002, translated in 2005 as *Anubis: A Desert Novel*). Local oral storytelling traditions that provided much of the documentation of the atrocities are invoked only to introduce animist gods as metamorphosing into and living uneasily with humans and animals. The blending of traditional and modern, formal and ontological elements across these texts anchors my

reconceptualization of biopolitics as perhaps more critical to parities specific to nomadic life—and not settled agricultural forms, as Foucault initially
theorized—competing for conceptual no less than biological survival.

To underscore some practical applications for political activism of the
aesthetic explorations of prior chapters, chapter 5, "Arctic Nomadology:
Inuit Stories of the Mountie Sled Dog Massacre," accounts for the success
of a community-produced archive in documenting the Mountie Sled Dog
Massacre. An innovative, Indigenous-led social justice project, the reports of
the Qikiqtani Truth Commission (QTC) synthesize testimonies that together
show how mass killings of Inuit sled dogs—whose numbers fell from tens
of thousands to a few hundred from the 1950s to the '70s—severed the relationships of many Inuit with their traditionally semiferal working animals. Along
with the dogs went the peoples' only means of escape to traditionally seminomadic life on the land and from permanent, prison-like communities erected
around the North American Aerospace Defense Command (NORAD) stations,
and so much more. The QTC's documentation of intimately related instances
of cultural genocide bleeds into the nationwide Truth and Reconciliation
Commission of Canada yet stands apart from that project in its commitment
to multispecies justice. Akin to al-Koni's fictions, the QTC's stories of death
and other losses detail an understanding of life with animals before and beyond
market forces that grows from a spiritually and physically sustaining love that is
not easily grasped by outsiders. Showing how the unique human-canine history
becomes haltingly visualized in the related film project, *Qimmit: A Clash of Two
Truths* (2010), the chapter concludes with an exploration of the narrative strategies through which the QTC offers a visioning of human-animal relationships
and their representation together as generative of a sense of community that is
empowered by human-animal love and persists beyond the slaughter.

What I am attempting to build throughout the project is a way of both
seeing pervasive losses as shared through more than immediate acts of suffering
and grasping biopower as ranging far beyond human control. Once euphe-
misms for sexual knowledge, the birds and the bees are largely perceived today
as disappearing in population free falls. With many species serving as pollinators of most crop plants and nearly all wild plants, their demise spells doom
for much of species life, a growing consciousness of which I track through
changing stories especially of bees in chapter 6, "The Birds and the Bees, or Life
After Sex." The best-known insects worldwide, European honeybees came to
claim that fame through histories in which colonial experiences and indigenous

frictions extend far beyond human communities. Moving away from racialized fears of "killer bees" and toward a sympathetic response to the growing crisis in honeybee health in recent decades, a broad range of contemporary novelists explore the multispecies dimensions of their colonial experience in converging contexts of extinction and genocide. Through fictions by Louise Erdrich (Anishinaabe), Douglas Coupland, and others, this chapter outlines a pattern in which the convergence of native knowledges and histories of mass killings spurs productive interventions in contemporary honeybee fictions. Through disparate theories of political scientists, biologists, and media theorists that warm to the conceptual swarm, I identify emergent ways of knowing collective life through human-animal bonds, drawing out the implications for a new politics of community rooted in multinatural knowledges of life as requiring love shared across species lines.

The concluding chapter attempts to answer a question that hovers over all my work: What is so special about using story forms to address questions of lives and deaths shared across species lines? What do narratives do for—even in lieu of—lived human-animal relations? "And," as literary scholar Saidiya Hartman asks in the context of imagining African slavery, "what do stories afford anyway? A way of living in the world in the aftermath of catastrophe and devastation?"[80] Inspired by her method of critical fabulation, I tell something of my own imbrication in human-animal love through comparison of recent theories of Indigenous and more-than-human stories, drawing heavily from literary scholars Daniel Heath Justice (Cherokee)'s *Why Indigenous Literatures Matter* (2018) and David Herman's *Narratology Beyond the Human: Storytelling and Animal Life* (2018). In this way, I try to model how writing and reading animal stories is a dialectical and world-forming process, one that reveals even as it creates connections that sustain communities.

The main challenge taken up by the writers, filmmakers, and artists gathered here is to document incredibly complex losses of life along with whole ways of living that are so remote as to seem inaccessible to Eurowestern, modern-industrial minds and to present them as perceptible as such precisely when actively interrupting the forces of erasure that continue long after the killings end. Developing a contemporary aesthetic, whereby disruptions to recording or observation provoke more deliberate thinking about animals,[81] I align their creative breakdowns of symbolism and other techniques reliant on analogical reasoning with current reconceptualizations of Indigenous metaphysics[82] as well as with emerging theories of literary nonhumans to be what Roland

Borgards terms "material metaphors" that resist compartmentalization into the material/real or semiotic/representational.[83] Admittedly, the preponderance of encounters of real-world creatures with dead as well as supernatural beings troubles deconstructive impasses regarding the immanence of animal gods, among others. But I make the case that such figures become important outside their stories not only because they are rendered plausibly material within the logics of their narration but also because they effectively infuse an ascendant animal-centric narrative aesthetic that favors concrete, vulnerable, exposed, and responsive "creaturely life,"[84] which in turn anchors the growing political force of narrating human-animal relationships.

Highlighting these and many other strategies of engagement with lots more kinds of life, even paradoxically those that persist beyond the living, the book as a whole aims to relocate human-animal bonds and their dissolutions as central points of concern for academics and activists concerned with species and cultural conservation. No longer cast as long-lost points of vulnerability in the global histories of empire but rather as lively local figures of resistance to contemporary forces of globalization, the stories at the center of the chapters that follow forge loving relations extended across species as links that chain what's been done to what yet may come.

Dying Animal Gods
Metaphysical Potentials

Once viewed as signs of persistence in the oldest human cultures, animal gods are being depicted in contemporary fictions as dying along with their peoples. By directly referencing iconic endangered species, their stories become intimately tied also to concerns about extinction, asserting interlinkages with decimations of human populations. One prominent example is the generically Native American buffalo-man from *American Gods*: from buffalo-headed divinity in otherwise human form in Neil Gaiman's 2001 novel, he becomes a fire-eyed but otherwise photorealistic American bison (*Bison bison*) in the TV series first aired in 2017, but all along, his presence is meant primarily to signal the converging lines of Native American and divine ancestry in the constantly threatened protagonist Shadow Moon.[1] Are animal gods doomed along with the cultural and biological systems that they were once imagined as protecting? *American Gods*, along with Gaiman's follow-up novel, *Anansi Boys* (2005), and so many other contemporary narratives, seems less concerned with offering definitive answers than with articulating shared human-animal experiences of endangerment through stories centered on dying animal gods.

By calling attention to painful cultural histories underpinning biological erasures, such figures become still more curious for the ways in which they enable thinking about themselves as something other than "fundamentally compromised by the human, often Western, deployment of animals and the animalistic to destroy or marginalize other human societies," the bleak situation into which Graham Huggan and Helen Tiffin see animal representations more generally as troubling postcolonial ecocriticism.[2] Haunting, obstructing, even violently resisting the advance of settler-colonialist societies, the spectral beings in animal form examined in this chapter take a different view or rather anchor other perspectives from which ecocide—the deliberate and irrevocable destruction of ecosystems—becomes entangled with cultural extinctions or erasures of languages, traditions, knowledges, and viewpoints distinct to particular communities. Most intriguing to me are the stories in which animal gods are angry about losses of lives and, along with them, of lifeways long rooted in love shared across species lines.

A close comparison of two popular and critically successful speculative fantasy stories reveals how representations of animal gods can connect underrepresented acts of genocide to species extinctions while at the same time articulating alternative trajectories through human-animal relationships. Partly historical fictions, both Hayao Miyazaki's 1997 animated film *Mononoke Hime*—released in a 1999 English-dubbed version as *Princess Mononoke*[3]—and Linda Hogan's 1998 novel *Power* address the systematic eradications of Indigenous peoples. Miyazaki's film is framed through the perspective of the Emishi (and possibly also the Utari) of northwestern Japan, and Hogan's novel shadows the history of the Seminole (and possibly also the Chickasaw) of the southeastern United States. Through the fate of these cultures' animal gods, the stories also explicitly show how genocides of tribal peoples connect with decimations of native species along with them to pave the way for settler-colonial states. Because both texts were released close to decisive court cases involving national-level legal decisions regarding Indigenous rights, including fishing and hunting endangered animal species, the stories complicate shared human-animal histories by bringing them to bear on present-day concerns.

Challenging the characterization of Native peoples as passively melting away into a bygone landscape along with extinct flora and fauna, the attachments of nonhuman and supernatural beings to the Emishi and Seminole provide platforms for ideological critiques that extend far beyond these fictions. That not all readers and viewers interpret these texts in this way indicates how reading animal gods on their own terms presents its own set of profound challenges as well. Taking them seriously is risky, for as Wendy Woodward observes, fictions in which the fluidity of characters' bodily shapes move beyond not just species boundaries but also Western-rationalist limits all too often provoke radio silence among literary critics.[4] Accounting for the narrative potentials of angry animal gods to change that story is one of my main goals in this chapter.

What makes *Princess Mononoke* and *Power* so powerful is that a key characteristic of these figures is their vengefulness toward humans and how that becomes mitigated through different human-animal relationships. Translated literally, the *mononoke* in Miyazaki's title and in Japanese folklore more generally indicates a spirit who comes to curse,[5] and it is in a form of outrage at the destructiveness of modern-industrial humans that the film's animal gods are introduced. In Hogan's novel, the panther god Sisa enters amid the scenery of industrial ruin only to damn all of humanity, including members of the novel's central native tribe. In both texts, anger about the conditions of individuals numbering among the last of their kind, those who are cast into the position of what ecologists term *the living dead*, adds menace to the gods' appearances, especially in the forms of giant wolves and big cats. In a doubled move against victimization, they curse Indigenous alongside settler communities—and in the form of the very kinds of apex predators whose decimations worldwide in the past century flipped their popular images from fairy-tale villains to the poster children of extinction.

Around both texts, the stories of their real-life referents introduce a little more hope through uncertainty. Of the two wolf species native to Japan, the largeness of the variously named Sakhalin, Ezo, or Hokkaido wolf (*Canis lupus hattai*) fits the profile of Miyazaki's central wolf characters better than the extant and comparatively diminutive Japanese or Honshu wolf (*Canis lupus hodophilax*), even if the range of the latter is closer to the film's scouting locations, and while both are listed as extinct, some believe the former could persist in Japan's remote northern islands. Although debates continued as to whether the Florida panther constituted a distinct subspecies (*Puma concolor coryi*) at the time Hogan was writing, it was designated in 2017 to be an endangered population of a much wider-ranging one (*Puma concolor cougar*). The uncertainties of species status and identity make room for animal-god characters to distinguish themselves instead relationally, by their attitudes toward historical and kinship ties to communities.

The delineations in both texts of the animal gods' relationships with their sisters, nieces, and daughters within gynocentric human societies invite elaborations of what Donna Haraway terms "the simultaneity of love and rage" in meaningful feminist critique.[6] Family ties across living and dying members of different species, moreover, introduce ways of fostering sympathetic engagement with past tragedies and imagining Indigenous resurgence as necessarily both a social and an ecological project, for one of the most important tasks undertaken by the doomed animal gods is to articulate the material and psychological situations through which their primary reference points become beings out of time—by which I mean both literally, when their numbers slip below the critical mass required to perpetuate their own kind, as well as figuratively, as they enter into the metaphysical limbo of those who are not considered historical subjects.

Deconstruction and Animal Gods

As Haraway's recent work suggests, looking outside the Euro-American canon fosters a growing sense of uneasiness with Derridean-deconstructive approaches to animal narrative forms across fiction and film. Pioneering this line of inquiry, Akira Lippit models a novel approach to deconstruction through the powerful conceptual alignment of literary language, narrative form, and representations of nonhuman death as buttressed by a philosophical consensus that animals' exclusion from language renders them incapable of death. Lippit's point is not to deny the fact that animals (and, for that matter, people) are being slaughtered through the past century and into this one but rather to provide a more precise account of why it is that animals do not simply disappear from human lives despite the increasingly systematic nature of their killing. His argument extends John Berger's famous observation that animals in modernity appear to be perpetually "disappearing" (the gerund form is key), paradoxically becoming ever more present as a fading presence in inverse proportion to the material erasure of embodied animals from everyday human lives. Perceptions of the animal who has "disappeared" or that is otherwise "rendered marginal" in modern industrial contexts reify a dynamic wherein animals continue "becoming synonymous" with humans, "fading away" in an indefinitely eroding or receding process.[7] Often characterized as nostalgic, Berger's sense of the continuing problem of representing animals gains theoretical nuance through Lippit's deconstructive approach.

Central to this process are the migrations of images of animals and other traces to the representational forms—above all, Lippit says, cinema—in which they are now perpetually caught in loops that "mourn" their passing: "the narrative of the disappearance of animals and that of the rise of the technical media intersect in cinema," which is "thus haunted by the animal figure."[8] This process entails profoundly ambivalent conclusions for political as well as aesthetic representation of human as much as any other species' lives; as Lippit argues, it "leads [both] to the threshold of literary language and [to] its possible extinction."[9] In a strangely serendipitous way, the use of "extinction" here helps illuminate the ways in which animal gods have suddenly and disruptively entered into these spectral deaths, becoming exemplary literary and filmic forms that mark the limits of human representational histories.

Such deconstructive formulations also have come under fire as being symptomatic of the ways in which deconstructive analysis idealizes animal presence beyond death. Nicole Shukin scrutinizes Lippit's theory as a disaggregation that enables figurative to be privileged over material rendering, which, as she notes, is particularly problematic in the history of photographic technologies because animal-derived gelatin is part of early techniques of film processing. In a remarkable reading that links Derrida's deconstruction of animal metaphors to his own notion of "hauntology," leading back to Berger as well as forward to Lippit, Shukin outlines a materialist critique of the theoretical conditions within which animal life more generally is seen as coming into being under erasure: "That the animal specter may itself covertly function as a fetish within deconstruction (a site where the transcendent foundations that deconstruction challenges are reconstituted in the immanent form of *animal-gods*) is matter for concern, given that the articulations of animality and spectrality can, on the one hand, lend figures of deconstruction a character of compulsive inevitability and, on the other, drain animals of their historical specificity and substance."[10]

Although I do not wish to reduce Shukin's dense and compelling argument to this lone comment, I think the key concept she attributes to (but stops short of locating exactly within) these arguments—namely, the "animal-gods"—requires elaboration, particularly in light of how they are depicted as resisting their own erasure on multiple fronts. Her perspective seems particularly helpful for understanding how the love that perpetuates the animal gods cannot be separated from rage at the shambles made of their material conditions. While ensuing chapters develop how lifeless, butchered, and metamorphosing bodies anchor life in death, here I focus on details shared across Miyazaki's and Hogan's narratives to indicate how Shukin's objections—if not a greater rift between deconstructive and materialist approaches to literary animal studies—might be addressed through these texts' infusions of dying animal gods with current events in the context of academic and aesthetic invocations of Indigenous metaphysics.

Mononoke, Animals, and Their People

Hugely influential in the mainstreaming of animated feature films, Miyazaki has himself been characterized as the god of the anime genre for his work in

creating blockbusters such as *Princess Mononoke*. Upon its theatrical release, the
film broke all box-office records for Japanese cinema. Five months later, one in
ten Japanese people had seen it and, within three weeks of its video release
in Japan, two million copies were sold.[11] An English-dubbed version featuring
the voices of established Hollywood actors and distributed by a subsidiary of the
Walt Disney Company quickly brought the film and its director to the attention
of global audiences as well. Yet the film's story constitutes a major departure
from the princess formula favored by Disney at the time because it features multiple female leads, including women who work and form friendships together.[12]
Largely due to her role as mediator between forest and settler communities,
the title character is one of Miyazaki's most beloved "beautiful fighting girl"
characters,[13] and the narrative is consequently one of his most complex because
she has to navigate deep divisions within and across both groups.

The departure from Disney's legacy might be seen as inevitable, given
Miyazaki's prominent role as a labor organizer throughout his rise to the top of
the animation industry, but concern with workmanship is more literally written
into Miyazaki's signature aesthetic, which ties the cutting edge of the form to
labor-intensive artistic processes. In a field that is rapidly moving toward total
digitization, Miyazaki's elaborate storyboards favor the expensive but high-
quality process of hand-drawing characters and backgrounds in animation
cells, famously from his own plein air sketches that, in the case of *Mononoke*,
required visits to Japan's few remaining primeval forests. His complexly hybrid
production aesthetics provide one way of beginning to understand why animal
gods are so compellingly presented as actively manipulating and manipulated
by historically specific technologies in his films more generally, an approach
that many see as the key to their popularity. So, for instance, in his 1988 feature
Tonari no Totoro (translated as *My Neighbor Totoro*) the hybrid cat-bus with
glowing headlight-eyes ordinarily runs like a feline but at times glides atop
power lines. Far from being seen as alienating or anachronistic among the
film's fans, the cat-bus rivals the phenomenal popularity of the titular ancient
tree-dwelling spirit and helps explain how Miyazaki prepared them to accept
his insertions of modern elements in fantastic stories featuring historically
ancient and Indigenous figures.

"Harshly denounced by critics in Japan" but not the United States—where
an inverse trajectory of critical but not box-office success prompts one film
historian to speculate whether Miyazaki might be the new Akira Kurosawa[14]—
initial reviewers were quick to note that *Princess Mononoke*'s greatest potential

Dying Animal Gods

problem was not in terms of the plausibility of animal gods but rather in its treatment of form, history, and genre. Far from narrating a progression from feudal to capitalist society, *Mononoke* presents different kinds of people alongside animals and gods as all together engaged in struggles that concern differences of class, gender, sex, race, ability, age, and species. The point is to offer what its director sees as "a far richer, more diverse history than is generally accepted."[15] The historical setting of *Mononoke* is clearly the Muromachi period (1336–1573), when burgeoning iron production led to widespread clearing of primeval forests in Japan, a time of ecological crisis exacerbated by chronic wars that in turn proved fatal for many of Japan's Indigenous peoples and cleared the way for the eradication of many native species. Although in these ways it remains rooted in a particular place and time, as one critic bluntly states, "*Mononoke* is certainly not a conventional history film."[16] Rather, it uses animation to mutate the Japanese genre of *jidaigeki*, inverting the typical focus of this "premodern historical genre," the stereotypically charismatic authority figures, in favor of the nameless others who usually enter these dramas only to be immediately eliminated or ignored.[17]

Playing still more directly to twenty-first-century sensibilities, the film displaces the conventional period-piece heroes of Japanese film, "the samurai, peasants, and feudal lords," foregrounding instead what Miyazaki characterizes as "people and wild gods (*kamigami*) who usually do not appear on the stage of history."[18] Aligned with the deities of this film, who are all directly associated with nature's forces in ancient Japanese folklore, these ghosts of history include the wild-child title character, whose clothing and accessories are styled to evoke the pottery figures of Japan's ancient Jōmon people, as well as Emishi tribespeople, whose genocides are understood likewise to predate the period depicted in *Princess Mononoke*. The self-characterization of central players like Prince Ashitaka as Emishi is an intriguing choice, given that this term, literally meaning "barbarians," was used by their conquerors to designate a "diverse grouping" of peoples who were the presumed descendants of the Jōmon people, who in turn "vanished" centuries earlier.[19] More clearly still, the narrative reframes the tenuous ties across human cultures through fraught connections to the animal gods, constructing different ideas of historical and social agency that hinge on relations in and between species. Encouraging "activism in the present for the future" rather than a sense of escapism to lost times,[20] in subtle but persistent ways the film's patterns of connection among human, animal, and theriomorphic-god characters work to reframe past within present struggles.

Love in a Time of Slaughters

The film's pivotal representation of Emishi is enabled in part by the fact that little is known about these peoples, who are assumed to have been wiped out centuries before the film is set, as one character pointedly observes. Circumstantial evidence suggests that they are missing ethnographic links between the Jōmon and the Ainu—or, as they prefer to be called, the Utari—who are the remaining Indigenous people of Japan. So it is in a halting way that *Mononoke* introduces the Emishi in the desperate situation of a people resisting assimilation against the odds. Restricted to one self-isolating community within the film, they represent a tiny and severely persecuted minority that is continuing to live only in hiding from the Yamato, who historically laid claim to their destruction with advanced weaponry.

Against historical accounts of Japan's natives as "savages" overcome by the more technologically savvy Yamato, the film relates their disappearances directly to the rise of imperial forces and the consequent degradation of the Emishi's harmonious relations with their local environment, which includes their animal gods. Because they are nothing if not conquered people, the visual cues that link the Emishi to Shinto—problematically still termed by some the "natural religion" of Japan in order to legitimate modern imperial ideology— are more productively troubled here than in Miyazaki's other stories.[21] Aligning Shinto with the peoples that they conquered constitutes a radical inversion of the traditional spiritual justifications of "the Yamato imperial line and the Japanese people themselves."[22] Admittedly, Miyazaki's "total rejection" of the term "Shinto" in public talks and prose writing creates a tension with his constant visual referencing of Shinto iconography here and elsewhere, making his position uncertain in relation to the overt racists and xenophobes who continue to defend the co-optation of native folk traditions in the ideological service of State (as opposed to religious) Shinto by the Empire of Japan (1868–1947), justifying widespread abuses of its colonized peoples.[23] What seems less ambivalent is how the film more directly cultivates sympathy by depicting the Emishi as caught between the ravages of colonization and its backlash from their animal gods.

Princess Mononoke's opening sequence features an Emishi boy, Prince Ashitaka, doing the unthinkable: killing the *inoshisigami* (boar god) after the latter has been rendered a *tatarigami* (demon spirit). Cursed by a human gunshot, the film's first animal-god character enters the picture after having been transformed into a raging mass, smashing around the countryside in a grotesque form that resembles a ball of worms or leeches propelled by giant spiderlike legs.[24] Only with his death does he regain the shape of a giant boar, rapidly rotting down to scant remains. Although Ashitaka regrets having to kill the enormous beast, using his expert skills with bow and arrow in order to save his own village, the demonized boar proves to be one of the film's several *mononoke* (gods who come to curse). With his last breath, he damns the young prince with the wormlike infection that thenceforth disfigures his arm and causes periodic, painful fits of rage. With his dying breath, *inoshisigami* curses all people, "You filthy humans. Know my pain and hatred."[25] Aligned with the god as a victim of historical circumstance, the boy becomes the unwitting target of the animal god's anger, which was sparked by a system that also targets the boy and his tribespeople. The cast-iron musket ball that the village shaman finds in the dead god's body is the source of pain and hatred because it represents the destruction of ancient forest habitat in order to extract and forge iron ore in support of the Yamato's war machine.[26] Compounding the starkly demonic associations conventionally attributed to animal multiplicity and extending them across animal and human bodies as the story unfolds,[27] still more animal gods burst onto the scene as avatars of the physical and social deformation that follows from environmental destruction for industry.

But the film also complicates the structures of settler colonialism by depicting hierarchies within it. Amid the Emishi's precarious seclusion, Ashitaka's infection means that his villagers, though grateful for his self-sacrifice on their behalf, must follow the orders of the old woman who is their shaman and banish him from their tribe. With no other options, he cuts off his topknot in a traditional Japanese sign of social death and sets off on a dubious quest for healing by the deer god, or *shishigami*, a term which was translated more ambiguously in the English version as "forest spirit," perhaps because of his hybrid human-bird-deer bodily features. Ashitaka eventually arrives in Iron Town, a combined ore-extraction and forge operation, which proves the source of the bullet that caused his curse. He sympathizes with the complexities of this community, whose profits are used to buy the freedom of prostitutes and to provide care for lepers and whose production facilities are designed to provide desirable jobs to members of these otherwise outcast groups. But it is through his love and her hatred for the titular character that the boy gets caught up in the struggle of their leader, Lady Eboshi, to make the town independent of both their Yamato overlords as well as animal gods, who menace their operations as revenge for their systematic devastation of the forest.

The boy's precarious positioning between warring peoples and incensed animal gods, who respectively proclaim and protest the inevitability of environmental degradation, supports a deeply ambivalent vision of Iron Age technologies as both endangering and helping different populations, one that pointedly contradicts the view that the production of metal unambiguously lifts humans into civilization. Along with the wormlike lesions around his arm and the waves of anger that inflame them—by which again he incorporates the tortured, multispecies morphing of the animal god disintegrating, or rather corporeally decomposing, even before death—Ashitaka mediates other hybrid relations that involve his animal companion and trusty mount, Yakkuru, and his newfound love interest, San, the self-dubbed "Princess Mononoke." At multiple levels, the film connects human, animal, and supernatural agents to create potentials for imagining cultural continuities.

References to the nonhierarchical, hunter-gatherer Jōmon culture, dated 14,000–1000 BCE, gain significance in light of recent research. Their mortuary practices indicate that their dead "were not detached from the society but kept at its core, as a materialized reference of kin networks."[28] San's personal history complicates these connections. Despite sporting a Jōmon-styled mask, jewelry, and weapons, San declares herself from the start to be at war with humans.

Raised as the daughter of the wolf goddess Moro after her own human parents abandoned her as an infant, San wears a white fur cloak and trimmings to her mask that blend into the fur of Moro and her wolf children, who are San's constant companions and sometime mounts. Wavering between human and animal, associating almost exclusively with animal gods, and remaining all the while "a raging mix of anger and aggression," this "wolf-girl" herself seems like a specter of the systemic obligations that were once acknowledged between species, at least through Ashitaka's people's time.[29] Not surprisingly in a film working to "subvert all the clichés," Ashitaka in the end "does not get the girl," for she instead joins the collective of animal gods in a final, failed battle to protect their forest from human destruction. Their losses only confirm San's hatred of Iron Town and all that it represents. Despite her growing attachment to Ashitaka, San does not want to see herself as human and absolutely refuses to return to life with humans after a final battle that results in their beheading of the shishigami and destruction of their ancient forest.

For some viewers, the forest god's human facial features make it so that his later beheading—brought about because Eboshi schemes to leverage a truce with the emperor of the Yamato only to find herself double-crossed by a confidence man—lends itself to interpretation as a symbolic commentary on this kind of mutilation within the modern Japanese state. Arguably, this aspect of the film resonates with the changing national concern following the conclusion of the Second World War: from the question "What is a divine emperor who can declare his humanity?" (the declaration required to overthrow State Shinto) to the problematic of modern industrialism, "What is a god who can die?"[30] But because it also potentially unleashes total destruction on the world within the film, the beheading of the most powerful of gods suggests that even more is at stake. Just as Eboshi declares that there can be no dealings with the animal gods, her similarly matriarchal counterpart Moro, the wolf god, in turn despairs of all dealings with humans, acidly observing that in the infant San's case, people cannot be trusted even to look after their own. The oft-repeated proclamations of irreconcilable differences between the self-appointed defenders of the downtrodden on both sides contrast strangely with the silences of others, chief of all the forest spirit, who in all his morphs says nothing throughout the film. In part, this silence heightens tensions about whether his supporters or self-styled destroyers win in the end and, ultimately, about whether the reattachment of his head through the coordinated efforts of San and Ashitaka really does bring him back to life.[31] Reticence also aligns the shishigami with the film's companion animals, notably Yakkuru, who, along with the forest god, quietly insists on better ways of relating than those articulated by the film's human characters.

Drawn to resemble a bongo (*Tragelaphus eurycerus*), Yakkuru is consistently referred to as a red elk, referencing the extinct giant Irish elk (*Megaloceros giganteus*), a species that once ranged across Eurasia, as far as Japan. Like the Emishi boy, Yakkuru constantly draws attention from others outside the film's Emishi community for his rarity, rhetorically linking the two through the impending exterminations of their kinds. Although it lacks in historical precedent, Ashitaka's relationship with the elk fancifully develops another dimension of cross-species relating. Like San and the wolves, Yakkuru and the boy are shown as constantly caring for each other, in pointed contrast, for instance, to Eboshi's attitude toward her oxen, who are treated as expendable along with the men of Iron Town when attacked alongside them. But boy and elk are more literally drawn together here as well.

Akin to the details triangulating San with the wolf gods and Jōmon figures as well as those of the *detarabochi* (the shishigami's Night Walker morph) to the markings on forest gods and the tattoos as well as textile prints of the Utari, visual cues link Yakkuru to the shishigami and the Emishi. An early sequence catches the pair in a downpour, in which the elk's wet, buff-colored ruff visually echoes the texture of the boy's traditional straw hat and cloak. More obviously, throughout the film, his long horns mirror the curves of the boy's ever-ready (if anachronistic) Emishi bow, not to mention the elaborate antlers of the forest god. Limping from a wound sustained while trying to take them to safety but otherwise persevering at the end, Yakkuru and the boy also both become violently wounded characters who elect to care for each other, sharing and enduring suffering even before the forest dies along with its god.

At the end, the sudden rebirth of the forest signals hope, as does Ashitaka's love for San and her acceptance of it, despite her declaring that she can "never forgive humans for what they did" to the forest and the gods. They are destined to live apart, he in Iron Town and she in the forest, only he chips in cheerily at the end, "Yakkuru and I will visit you whenever we can, all right?" Thus the unspoken love between human and animal frames the bond between boy and wolf-girl, a fate articulated much earlier by the animal god Moro. But a more profound love shared across species lines permeates the picture: the elk's lack of speech remains a point of profound difference from the boy, one that still more powerfully aligns Yakkuru with not only all of the other mortal animals but also the forest god as well as the countless *kodama* (tree spirits) that signal his presence. Although the question of whether the forest god actually dies fits Lippit's bill by leaving viewers with a sense that he is perpetually dying, something of what Shukin terms animals' specificity and substance inheres in what remains unsaid—or unsayable.

Silently witnessing the disintegration of animal gods and deformations of human subjects, Yakkuru subtly and consistently mediates between the worlds that San spans, only without choosing between them. Wherever he goes, the elk is universally recognized as smart, wary yet not easily spooked, carefully earning and granting the trust that seems so profoundly lost between and among humans and animal gods. Aligned perhaps most plainly with the forest god in cervid form and with the beasts of burden in silent suffering, Yakkuru nonetheless communicates a sense that cross-species alliances, constantly built and never taken for granted, provide another source of social power. Ashitaka's unlikely mount and friend thereby holds out hope for a shared sense of agency based in human-animal cultivations of coexistence, mutating the conceptual respect for gods into mundane realities of shared lives. In this sense, the relations of humans, animals, and animal gods seem critical to Miyazaki's explicit effort in the film to trouble "the weak sense of life of this age [*seimeikan no kihaku na jidai*]"[32] and to offer instead a powerfully shared sense of human-animal lives and loves as traces of an alternate historical trajectory. How this might be related to a tribal-feminist perspective becomes more obvious in comparison with Hogan's *Power*.

Sisa, Sisters, and Their Animals

The fact that *Princess Mononoke* was released in 1997, the same year that the Japanese judiciary decided a landmark case that for the first time in Japan recognized Indigenous peoples—namely, the Utari—as a legal category, begs further speculation about how these aspects of Miyazaki's long-awaited film might be read as responsive to still more immediate cultural debates, particularly in comparison with Linda Hogan's novel *Power*. Published a year after *Mononoke*'s release, *Power* addresses the genocide of the Seminole and other Native American tribes from the Southeastern United States initiated by European colonization more explicitly through the lenses of ancient and contemporary justice systems. Like Miyazaki, Hogan imagines animal gods despairing of humanity amid their own demise but from an even more deliberately postcolonial perspective.

Hogan's fiction focuses on a Native American woman accused of killing an extremely endangered Florida panther (a severely diminished population of the species *Puma concolor*), and it is loosely based on a 1983 incident in which a Seminole man named James Billie was tried in US federal court for having killed one of these rare big cats. Although Billie's leadership role as sometime Seminole tribal chairman proved crucial to his defense, Billie himself was also "an alligator wrestler, songwriter, and Vietnam veteran"[33]—as Hogan says elsewhere, "a very complex man."[34] After four years, the trial concluded with Billie's acquittal on the grounds that the killing represented his exercise of religious freedom. The acquittal was largely seen as a victory for tribal sovereignty over federal environmental regulation. The news media, however, reduced the story to even more simplistic terms and cast it as a case of Native rights trumping animal rights. Like Miyazaki, Hogan crafts a fictional version of events that allows for far richer and more diverse histories to emerge from the living legacies of extinction and genocide.

Power explores what Hogan terms "the gray area between laws that affect sovereign nations and indigenous, religious freedom and the [US national] Endangered Species Act."[35] For Hogan, whose historical fictions relentlessly interrogate the histories of First Nations peoples, the patronizing implication of the outcome of Billie's trial problematically asserts that Indigenous cultural practices are permitted within the national rights of people or, to put it more starkly, that genocides not only trump treaties between peoples but also sever all historical ties between particular cultures and animal species. Pursuing this point, the novel *Power* imagines how different judgments proceed from the various governing forces of Florida's panthers and peoples, which in this story include those of animal gods. While it is possible to read the novel in human terms as counterbalancing the rhetorics of imperialism with those of sovereignty,[36] I think that option underestimates the ways in which the novel's visioning of human, animal, and human-animal relationships through the perspective of an animal god concerns profound reconceptualizations of power itself.

While echoing Billie's story in many other ways, Hogan's novel transforms the killer into a female member of the Taiga, an imaginary and gynocentric native Floridian tribe in which the panther is revered as a sacred family member. Like Miyazaki's vision of the Emishi, the Taiga hover at the edges of history and existence. Hogan casts this imaginary tribe not as a comparable or rival people to historical Florida Indians but rather as forgotten ancestors who, along with the animal gods, maintain fragile connections to the precontact past. So "fallen" that "no one has heard of us," that even other tribes like the "Seminole and Mikosukkes" who remain in the Florida region "do not remember us now," says narrator Omishto, the Taiga people likewise embrace cross-species heritages: "Like them, we are related to the panther, Sisa, one of the first people here."[37] But the people along with the animals are becoming deformed by the turn of the twenty-first century—the animals literally through the inevitable inbreeding of a shrinking, isolated gene pool—and together cling to life on the edge of suburban sprawl, in the vestiges of the wooded swamplands where they once flourished.

Despite these highly localized details, akin to Miyazaki's detailed drawings of the few remaining Japanese primeval forests that are incorporated into the shishigami's home, Hogan is clear that her story is a fiction. By moving away from straightforward representations of North American Indian cultures, the novelist avoids the charge of appropriating other tribes' stories that has been levied against her earlier historical fictions of the Osage in *Mean Spirit* (1990) and Canadian First Nations in *Solar Storms* (1995).[38] Although important to acknowledge, authorial identity politics again may underestimate the challenges of the text, particularly its imaginary elements, for certain dimensions of Hogan's fictional Taiga tribe also can be seen to serve a more complex agenda.

Taiga is a blanket term for the coniferous forests that span North America, Europe, and Asia, and by using this wide-ranging habitat name to designate an imaginary, marginalized people fading away in modern-day Florida, Hogan subtly and broadly aligns historical erasures across several groups, including her own.[39] It therefore follows a similar logic to the designation of Yakkuru as a red elk, signaling similarly broad-sweeping ties across northern lands, their peoples, and their nonhuman denizens. Moreover, Hogan herself is a member of the Chickasaw tribe, who like the Seminole ancestrally resided in parts of Florida and were divided if not entirely conquered by US national resettlement policies that forced many out of the region. The representation of the marginal situation of the Taiga tribe highlights the ways in which geographic dispersal and subsequent fragmentation have been keys to undermining the treaties that honored different cultural beliefs about human-animal relationships and led, hand in glove, to destroying wild habitats by draining the swamps for farmland and housing developments.

Again like Miyazaki, staging the underrepresented past to resonate immediately in the present historical moment, Hogan's story of a fictional tribe's "relationship with other people, with animals, with the land"[40] spells out the ways in which this wider-ranging world view complicates questions of what is relative. Here it is crystallized through a case centered on the killing of a sacred and endangered animal who is also kin to them, their "older sister."[41] Moving questions of power more directly in alignment with systems of justice, Hogan fictionalizes details from recent history as well so that the cat-killer's crime here is judged not only by her nation's courts but also by the elders of her tribe as well as by the killer's own panther god.[42] Like Billie, the fictional character Ama is found not guilty by the official justice system and to the outrage of environmental activists who, her informally adoptive teenaged niece Omishto reflects, protest the killing of animals but not the genocidal history informing this particular species's endangerment.

Albeit more dreamily, the presence of ancestors challenges tribal peoples within the text too and allows all of its readers to recognize their part in past injustices. Throughout the story, Omishto remains haunted by visions of ancient women whom she recognizes as members of another tribe and simultaneously assumes to be her ancestors who instituted the familial obligations between panthers and people. Seeking refuge in her aunt's swamp-side shack from increasing persecution from white peers at school and the looming threat of molestation by her creepy evangelical stepfather at home, she remains aware but never afraid of the far more tangible if unseen presence of the wild panthers.

If anything, it becomes a matter of course that she becomes an amanuensis for
the thoughts of animal gods in big-cat form. Taiga, ghostly ancestors, Florida
panthers, and their gods—in her mind, all are united by "an old story," albeit
in Florida's "world of new people" where "no one much believes in stories any-
more."[43] The converging perspectives of girl and panther god also set in motion
the narrative mechanism whereby the relevant questions of power inform different constructs of justice.

Following the first trial's conclusion, the elders of Ama's tribe conduct a
separate trial in which, as a member of the Panther Clan, the killer must be
punished with banishment for sororicide—that is, for killing her sister, Sisa
the Panther. "Ama loves the panther," Omishto recognizes early in the story,
yet feels compelled to kill her in order to end her suffering.[44] But Sisa is also an
animal god, who returns via Omishto at the end of the novel to offer a final and
most severe judgment. Sisa sees the blame as more broadly distributed, shared
because "humans have broken their covenant with the animals, their original
word, their own sacred law," and thereby dooms everyone.[45]

Like *Princess Mononoke*, there are no clear answers in the end. The novel
brackets off the question of whether the panther was "sacrificed" as in the old
tribal creation story—from which act followed the renewal of cross-species relations and environs alike—or just killed as the consummate act of degradation
in the new story.[46] Instead, the central query becomes, What is Ama's crime
of killing her sister compared with the crimes that condemn all to extinction?

Where humans can only assign or absolve one from blame, the animal god
sees these female relatives—killer, witness, and victim—as "all, all three of them,
the sacrifice" to modern industry.[47] Recalling *Mononoke*'s wolf-god matriarch,
Moro, and her similar despair of a future that includes humans (a sentiment
spoken to and eventually voiced again through young female San), much more
could be said about how apocalyptic ecofeminism gives way to a more localized intersectional critique of human and human-animal relationships in both
stories. Moreover, the animal god's vision stakes out a crucial narrative strategy
of staging erasure, at once shared by and distanced from the girl who is her relative. Through this maneuver, both stories insist on the historicity of any ethical
system and the necessity of moving beyond the limiting terms of human subjectivity in order to take up shared conditions and responsibilities of relatedness.

Because the future of their culture beyond the current generation remains
unclear, like *Mononoke*'s presentation of the Emishi, Hogan's fiction of the Taiga
refuses the colonial fantasy of finitude in its converging stories of genocide and

extinction. Intricately enmeshing Indigenous stories with those of the Florida panther brought to the brink of extinction,[48] Hogan clarifies that Sisa, though once beautiful and all-powerful, is now sick, starving, and suffering from parasites as well as genetic disorders. The encroachment of invasives is presented as another part of their problem. In the novel's vision, all sorts of indigenous creatures are not simply displaced by Spanish moss, horses, and Euro-Americans. Echoing the industrial buildings and fumes of Iron Town, the scene here indicates how transplant and native alike are losing ground to building and chemical contamination. Sisa says that she can recall the sweetness, beauty, even immensity of a shared past in which "panther people" protected not just the Taiga but also all humans. In this context, the god's vision of "all, all three of them, the sacrifice" condemns more than just Ama, Omishto, and Sisa but even conceivably all the people, animals, and animal gods "in this place that has grown small with rusty nails and oil drums in the shadow of buildings."[49] Such an interpretation begins to explain why what she grimly "believes and remembers" is that "she, the cat, Sisa, is doomed."[50] But hers is not the final word.

Again like *Mononoke*'s Moro, whose dying act is to use her own severed head to bite off her nemesis Eboshi's arm, the final dying animal god raging against the machine, so to speak, here manifests a narrative form that refuses the comforts of closure and symmetry. Hogan's novel ends with Ama accepting banishment and Omishto electing to live deep in the swamp with the remaining Taiga elders, closer to her non/human kin. Reinforcing the blurriness of human-animal relations, the girl in one last encounter with a panther proves unable finally to identify whether it is the literal mate of the dead one—the panther god Sisa—or, still another possibility, her own spiritual twin: as she says, "the one that was born alongside me at my beginning."[51] With their triangulated and ultimately uncertain visions of severely damaged and endangered humans, animals, and animal gods, the novel and film together stake out how the theoretical problems of agency that form both within and between species at the center of human-animal studies research enmesh the historical together with urgent problems of cultural as well as species diversity.

Animal Gods, Indigenous Metaphysics, and Cross-Species Intimacies

What remains to be seen is why, in contemporary narratives, animal gods assert themselves and rally others to their defense and how their deaths prove no simple vanishing points. Linking the passing of these figures of legend and story to more literal displacements of humans and animals in otherwise strikingly different contexts, Miyazaki and Hogan marshal animal gods as figures who reject a transcendent vision of cross-species harmony as tautological fantasy, a sort of nostalgia for nostalgia that Marxist literary critic Fredric Jameson a few years earlier had marked as more broadly symptomatic of "the disappearance of a sense of history" from contemporary consumer society.[52] Rather than simply inhabiting a rustic or archaic past, their visions of animal spirits become central to *Princess Mononoke* and *Power* precisely because they signal the endurance of earlier social forms and traditions that are all but wiped out to make room for the postindustrial landscapes in which they now appear. That the fading of animal gods matters most to female-centered Indigenous communities—again the significance of tribal human sisters, nieces, and daughters to humans, animals, and animal gods, gaining force in numbers—begs further discussions of how literary techniques like metaphor imply and preclude a range of metaphysical potentials that the ensuing chapters attempt to elaborate.

While the convergence of literary and interdisciplinary animal studies has opened up space for discussions of the historical contexts alongside the animal qualities of animal-god characters, as Shukin suggests, their significance as supernatural beings has been conspicuous largely for critics' silence about it. For instance, discussions of *Power* in literary studies foreground its narration of "ethnic representation and empowerment" in human terms,[53] thereby aligning it with other Native American novels of the late twentieth century. Following ecocritic Lawrence Buell's influential reading in which he argues that environmental justice, nonanthropocentric ethics, and narrative form converge in the modeling of what he terms the "environmental unconscious" in Hogan's novel,[54] literary scholars more recently laud it for giving voice to animal and human subjects, more specifically, "articulat[ing] the subjectivity of both the Native American . . . and the endangered Florida panther."[55] Arguing that Hogan "turns the trope to her own ends," Indigenous literature scholar Catherine Rainwater points to the equations of people and animals in the novel as significant to its critique of settler colonialism—that is, as "a measure of Eurocentric, tragic estrangement from the natural—not a measure of Western, heroic transcendence of it."[56] While indicative of the growing influence of literary animal studies, the tendency to privilege material relations between species comes at the expense of exploring why *Power* introduces the converging politics of ecocide and genocide through the representation of peculiar character

40 forms—namely, extinct and endangered animals depicted as enraged natural-
istic and supernatural entities.

The checkered past of Eurowestern scholarly treatments of animism looms
large in this context. Early cultural anthropologist E. B. Tylor's notoriously
patronizing characterization of animism as the most rudimentary or primitive
form of religion empowered settler-colonialist disparagement of Indigenous
knowledges seemingly ever since, creating a problematic legacy for later generations of academics seeking to distance themselves from racism and xenophobia.
Citing recent attempts by social anthropologists and religious scholars to
intervene in this history, literary critic Dan Wylie outlines how a recent "revital-
ization" of animism has required epistemological critique, "a respect-oriented
recognition of an animistic heterogeneity, in which successive historical periods and developments, geographically distinctive bioregions, cultural beliefs,
human-animal representations, and various poetic forms coexist, in simultane-
ous tension and reinforcement, within an entirely novel 'assemblage.'"[57] While
Wylie's analysis is suggestive of how translations of anthropological interviews
and their subsequent publication as poetry challenge assumptions about literary form and its limits, I invoke it here more simply to identify aesthetic
conditions in which figurative representations concern not just physical but
also metaphysical relations.

At once referencing biological and cultural endangerments, the dying
animal gods of *Princess Mononoke* and *Power* also resist the hierarchical pairing
of the literal and the metaphorical that has long implicated literary studies in the
diminishment of animist perspectives. Expanding political scientist and activist
Vine Deloria Jr.'s influential concept of an "American Indian metaphysic" as a
relational way of knowing,[58] anthropologist Kim TallBear "include[s] an interspecies community or networked set of social-biological relations [to] living
beings that are material and immaterial," frustrating separation of the natural
from the supernatural, the living from the dead, and more to her point, remaining inseparable from "a Lakota/Dakota (or 'Sioux,' as you may know us) ethic."[59]
TallBear's point is to draw attention to articulations of what might be more
expansively termed Indigenous metaphysics. Reframing beliefs as ontologies
enables anthropologists to represent Indigenous human-animal relations apart
from terms in which metaphor is only ever opposed to reality[60]—only, I would
add, with important implications for literary animal studies. When all sorts of
others—the nonhuman, the dead, and the supernatural—are seen as animate
and interrelated with living human beings, ignoring why authors and artists

Love in a Time of Slaughters

need them to appear together in these very precise ways risks perpetuating histories in which such perspectives become discounted as naïve or primitive.

Contemporary animal-god stories provide a useful pivot to the discussion because so often they concern the fragile material presences of other species. While "real" animals are tricky at best to locate in film and fiction,[61] the increasingly intense concern with the mortality of the animal gods calls attention to how the problems that Wylie, TallBear, and others see with metaphor also might explain the sudden and widespread appeal of animal god characters for authors and artists calling attention to the imbrications of postcolonial politics and current ecological crises. Approached as never simply human or animal, metaphor or referent, the dying animal god opens a perspective through which narratives that revisit mass killings of the past can begin to make critical interventions in the present, even change course toward sustainable futures. Just as the debates about deconstructive analysis help elaborate why it is important that such characters are never simply killed off but staged in ongoing states of demise, these discussions concern what their presence makes possible far beyond the fictions themselves.

While *Princess Mononoke*'s and *Power*'s nonhuman deities rage against the dying of the light, quieter cross-species intimacies persist, staking out a final frontier against ongoing wipeouts of cultures and species. Their creatures of story, broadly writ, are not trivial psychological projections, mere fetishes, but quite necessary features of sufficiently complex representations of how affective bonds between species mediate what otherwise seem to be competing claims to histories, lands, lives, and livelihoods. As rhetorical devices developed to intervene in conditions of representational crisis, the dying animal gods provide a framework for shifting perspectives beyond the conventionally human identity forms and into shared imaginative spaces in the chapters that follow.

Pursuing the point "that nature too has a history," environmental theorist Alexander Wilson outlines the immediate implications of not thinking of humans and other denizens of nature as coconstructed: "Ignoring this fact obscures the one way out of the current environmental crisis—a living within and alongside of nature without dominating it."[62] More suggestively still in light of the present discussion, Wilson posits that the story of animals and humans as "proximate" or "interrelated yet autonomous" can emerge powerfully through narrative reversals of perspective—more specifically, when humans are viewed from animals' perspectives.[63] Writing in the early 1990s, Wilson anticipates many of the most significant elements that come to characterize contemporary extinction fictions, except how the presence of animal gods moves the dynamic from a simple reversal of hierarchy to a cutting across of power relations that also concern histories of genocide, for creative stories such as *Princess Mononoke* and *Power* explore further the formal mechanisms that leverage productive breaks from earlier eradication narrative traditions, which otherwise reinforce a sense of division between historical humans and mythical animals.[64]

Although these particular texts address specific traditions, their uses of nonhuman deities as characters also model some ways in which contemporary animal narratives work through the limits of representation, whether aphasia, diaspora, or extinction. Figuring humans together with animist gods who articulate their own myths alongside animals who are significantly silent, these texts posit fiction and film as forms that are capable of contesting expulsion from history, of being "out of time" in the broadest sense. Such stories not only force reconceptualizations of people as something other than simply archetypal saviors or destroyers of nature but also locate human subjectivity along a spectrum that includes familial, intersubjective, and nonhuman social forms all as fictions of relating. Through triangulated human-animal-god alignments—like those of Ashitaka, Yakkuru, and the shishigami/detarabochi alongside those of Omishto, her panther "twin," and Sisa—the stories negotiate shifting perspectives on old and new terms.

Seen together from the perspective of the dying theriomorphic gods, the histories of animals and people disappearing en masse become more than just pathetic. Importantly, in these texts the gods remain active forces, dying but not dead yet. Ranged alongside peoples and species all but lost to history, the animal gods' angry protests make narrative representation as an act of erasure all the more visible. By sketching how the dying animal gods of contemporary extinction fictions illuminate their own and others' unmaking as historical subjects, and from perspectives that yet assert their viability, my point is to prompt further questioning about the ideological as well as physical conditions of ecological alongside cultural sustainability—and possibly even renewal. Guided by Haraway's assertion that the "hope" of cross-species "stories" lies in the fact that they "are much bigger than ideologies,"[65] my own hope in pursuing this line of inquiry is to demonstrate the ways in which narratives that engage Indigenous metaphysics can be adapted as tools of intervention in dying acts of not just repudiation and hatred but also their inspiration in love shared by humans and other animals.

2.

Taxidermy Remains
On the Vitality of Lifeless Bodies

The follow-up to Yann Martel's Man Booker Prize–winning novel *The Life of Pi* (2001), *Beatrice and Virgil* (2010) is a fiction that focuses on writing fictions about the Nazi Holocaust, the most prominent of which is told from a bizarre perspective: animal taxidermies. Panned by critics as "disappointing," "perverse," "misconceived," and even "offensive,"[1] the novel as a whole proves hard for many readers to separate from the aborted creative efforts that it recounts— namely, a flip-book by an established novelist and a play by a taxidermist that both try "representing the Holocaust differently" from the usual formula of a lone survivor's story.[2] Only the play is developed in any detail, presented in fragments of dialog between the monkey Virgil and the donkey Beatrice, who are characters modeled after a tableau also made by the taxidermist, in which a monkey is mounted on a donkey. The story of these characters' violent demise in turn is recited by the taxidermist and would-be playwright, who insists that his play is about animal extinction, not human genocide.

Criticism of *Beatrice and Virgil* as anti-Semitic would seem predictable if Martel were not at such pains throughout to avoid it. "In quantity and variety, put together, two thirds of all animals have been exterminated, wiped out forever," proclaims the taxidermist. "My play is about this irreparable abomination,"[3] which he has the characters Beatrice and Virgil haltingly term "the Horrors." The novel's protagonist, Henry, rejects that interpretation with all the authority of a professional creative writer; indeed, he baits the critical charge against "using the Holocaust to speak of the extermination of animal life"[4] when he concludes that the taxidermist's play is a veiled confession of "a stinking old Nazi collaborator."[5] Henry's reading depends on slim circumstantial evidence, and it seems an especially important detail that he never makes his accusations explicit to the taxidermist. Nevertheless, reviewers were less concerned about whether the novel's conclusion, in which the taxidermist stabs the protagonist, sets fire to the shop,[6] and commits suicide, constitutes confirmation of these suspicions than whether having written the play within the novel makes Martel guilty of the same offense. Is the playwriting taxidermist just a foil for the novelist's struggle to write human trauma with animals?[7] Or is fictional taxidermy a means of breaking down speciesist limits to ethical community[8]—in the taxidermist's words, of "see[ing] if something could be saved once the irreparable had been done"?[9]

From the opening pages, the protagonist's linkage of narrative, taxidermy, and human exceptionalism would seem to rule out the latter option: "Stories— individual stories, family stories, national stories—are what stitch together the disparate elements of human experience into a coherent whole. We are story animals."[10] Introduced as the best-selling author of a fiction that, like *The Life of Pi*, prominently includes wild animals as metaphors—according to Henry's reasoning, animals can only be useful to writers "for reasons of craft rather than sentiment"[11]—the protagonist invites direct comparison with Martel, yet he is even more overtly troubled in his animal politics. Henry likes zoos, proves a fatally negligent pet owner, treasures a monkey skull that the taxidermist gave him, and in the end, "regret[s] not having saved Beatrice and Virgil" from the burning shop.[12] He is the one who aspires to write the Holocaust flip-book, and his obsession with the failure of that project is a plausible pretext for his reading of that genocide into the tortures, humiliations, and terrors endured by the play's Beatrice and Virgil. But reading them simply as perversions of his normative model of story animals profoundly underestimates what they are and what they can do as taxidermy.

Comparison with contested interpretations of taxidermy's repurposing in contemporary art history proves instructive. Steve Baker initially described the titular figure of *The Postmodern Animal* (2000) as manifesting an aesthetic of "botched taxidermy." Citing many fine-art examples, including actual taxidermies subjected to intentionally botched restoration and "displayed deliberately out of place," Baker's point was that they invite viewers "to rethink human relations with animal others"[13] and, at the same time, "what it is to be a human now."[14] But the normative implications of "botchedness" or "gone-wrongness" become reductive when applied to works including actual taxidermy, according to Giovanni Aloi, whose *Speculative Taxidermy* (2018) attends instead to the ways in which the materiality of the medium more radically reframes the human within multispecies communities.

Aloi's attention to "the actual manipulation of animal skins (manual as well as mediatic)" gestures toward ineluctable entanglements with "the discourses and practices that reciprocally shape humans, animals, and environments" via taxidermy. So he argues that the material and indexical dimensions both complicate historical recovery of the relations that taxidermy represents as well as demand that taxidermy art develop its own tools for open-ended interrogations of how people perceive, render, and consume nonhuman animals.[15] Adding a more obvious layer of mediation, fictional taxidermy more pointedly invites speculative methods that engage social and cultural histories of violence toward human and nonhuman animals.

While Aloi's speculative taxidermy is uniquely self-reflexive of its own representation, literary taxidermy calls attention to how it might be conditioned as such, inspiring reflection on the wide range of human-animal relations in social, ethical, environmental, and political problems writ large: "In contrast to artistic forms displayed (or not) in art museums, galleries, and private collections, literary taxidermic fictions regularly circulate among popular audiences, and are copied and proliferated on the wider scales of bestselling novels and blockbuster films. Perhaps most conspicuously, they pick up surpluses of meaning as they mimetically mirror and/or explode socio-historical narrative structures, for taxidermy, like stories, may be made by humans, but in the convergences of these forms, it becomes plain to see how more-than-human stories are always at stake."[16] In this chapter, I drill down further into the more specific figure of the taxidermy collection in fiction in order to elaborate how it becomes enlisted in nonreductive narratives of genocide and extinction.

In one obvious way, the titular figures of *Beatrice and Virgil* illustrate the erasure of animal discourses. Stuffed in multiple senses, Martel empties them of a key scientific detail: they are not identified as members of particular species. They are identified only as specimens of a howler monkey (*Alouatta*) and a wild ass (*Equus africanus*), possibly representatives of endangered New World and extinct Old World species. If the purpose were to distinguish clearly genocide from anthropogenic extinction, then they could have easily been designated as members of species listed as endangered or extinct—say, as a Mexican howler monkey (*Alouatta palliate Mexicana*) and a Nubian wild ass (*Equus africanus africanus*). Absent the details—or indeed, any aspect of their lives as animals—it becomes easy for the characters Beatrice and Virgil to illustrate Henry's belief that writing is only ever about "being human and what it means."[17]

Yet as taxidermies, they introduce the material presence of manipulated remains of the dead. Henry's desire to pluck them from the ashes in lieu of his fellow man reflects how taxidermy elicits strong affective responses at the intersections of not just species' lives but also life and death. Whether readers can identify exactly what they are, the tableau of Beatrice and Virgil, like all taxidermy, would be sourced from individuals of particular species by individuals of another, who in turn might have incorporated wax, shellac, and other materials sourced from still more critters in the process of preserving them as objects to be contemplated, consumed, and conserved by even more others. *Beatrice and Virgil* may downplay these elements to assuage Henry's (or Martel's) fears of "story animals," but they are enlisted to much different effect in other contemporary taxidermy fictions.

Several novels of the past decade incorporate taxidermy in order to explore the discomforting ability of dead, fragmentary animals to anchor stories of extinction not as substitutes for human suffering but, more compellingly, to address atrocities marked by human, together with animal, death on massive scales. Avoiding Martel's allegorical trap by showing how taxidermy remains deeply enmeshed in the discourses and practices of settler colonialism, they link biological with cultural catastrophes, and all as deeply marked by a sense of human longing. Two fictions in particular—Lydia Millet's *Magnificence* (2012) and Henrietta Rose-Innes's *The Green Lion* (2015)—stage various repurposings of taxidermy collections as acts of mourning that loft fragile alternatives to the melancholia, narcissism, and depression that predominate in responses to histories of mass killings. Emerging at the turn of the twenty-first century, a period marked by what affect theorist Lauren Berlant terms "cruel optimism" or a perverse desire for the obstacles to flourishing, these stories frame larger questions concerning to what vital effects uses of lifeless bodies frustrate recovery efforts in our time.

Metaphor has only ever been part of the problem with taxidermy stories. Through North American examples that show how whole peoples become subjected to a metaphorical taxidermy in practices like ethnographic filmmaking, Indigenous-literature scholar Pauline Wakeham identifies the "matrix of racial and species discourses, narratives of disappearance and extinction, and tropes of aboriginality that have been crucial to the maintenance of colonial power . . . from the beginning of the twentieth century to the present."[18] Elaborating on anticolonial theorist Frantz Fanon's description of a "corporeal" that gives way to "racial epidermal schemas," Wakeham's reading of taxidermy "tackle[s] notions of the human as it interfaces with gender, coloniality, slavery, racialization, and political violence without mapping these questions onto a mutually exclusive struggle between either the free-flowing terra nullis of the universally applicable or the terra cognitus of the ethnographically detained."[19] Wakeham's theory—that taxidermy "as both biological tissue and discursive schema overdetermined by colonialism's obsession with racial and species categorization"[20] configures strategic separations as well as convergences of human and nonhuman bodies—provides a framework for my analysis of the multispecies ethical entanglements of taxidermy collections with animal and human histories in literary fiction.

In different ways, Millet's and Rose-Innes's novels link the histories of colonized tribal peoples to collections of animal taxidermy that are literally unwanted inheritances. Yet the collections in both stories eventually inspire creative interventions into their initial curation. Cumulatively, they reveal how a creature made into a realistically lifelike form by people preserving and assembling parts of the dead may be made to conceal its own function as a site of contested narratives. Along the way, the two novels map contrasting views of taxidermy as either an object of individual melancholy or an inspiration for mourning lost populations, provoking me at the end of the chapter to explore what related consequences taxidermy stories have for vulnerable living bodies across species lines.

Historians of the form note how the "bio" of taxidermy often confuses biology and biography, as it concerns relations among people and species plus relations with other representational objects.[21] Prevailing natural history aesthetics cloak these relations in an idealized past material presence that is brought through preservation into a sort of life after death. Narrative proves indispensable to the process, for it is "through the stories that we tell about them . . . [that taxidermies] spring into an afterlife."[22] Collecting them therefore involves careful choreographies of human/animal proximities that in the past all too often mapped directly onto those of colonial centers/margins. Their arrangement in institutional spaces designed to foster a sense of neutrality in objects is one of the most powerful ways in which natural history was made to be enlisted in what Michel Foucault terms the power/knowledge that proceeds through the regimes of the visual from the Eurowestern Enlightenment onward.[23]

While the earliest taxidermy collections date back to the 1500s, the practice of mounting skins in pursuit of a lifelike aesthetic gained momentum much later, in the 1700s, with the intensification of European colonization around the world. Although collecting mania gave way to desires to protect, save, or conserve increasingly rare creatures by the twentieth century, the preservation logic of taxidermy became so deeply entrenched in colonial histories of extermination that hunting for endangered animals to preserve bits of them remains seriously debated as a hedge against their extinction. The heroic narratives of specimen procurements that figure large in the provenance of individual taxidermies cast a long shadow over the involvements of and impacts on local peoples together with the other denizens of their original environments whose lives and livelihoods became compromised in such processes.

Repurposing and even recovering them requires a different approach to narration, one that recognizes the unevenly felt horrors that taxidermy also represents, which is captured in sociologist Anna Samuelsson's neologism "zoombie." A mashup of "zoology" and "zombie" that resonates with the zoom-in/out optics of natural history specimens, zoombie designates a "border creature balanced on the dualisms between nature/culture, life/death, science/art," and others, restoring a sense of how dead bodies actively shape how museums and other "theaters of science" organize knowledges of the living.[24] And it helps explain how taxidermy, as in zombie fictions more generally, is gaining a sense of collective force in decolonial critique.

From this perspective, the disproportionately large spectacle of humans rendered into taxidermy in fiction as opposed to fact—almost all black, African, tribal people—provides an important background to Millet's and Rose-Innes's novels.[25] Reduced to skin and mounted for display alongside similarly prepared animals, humans turned into such specimens are brutal reminders of colonialism's skin fetish[26]—and more. Gutted of life stories, human zoombies witness a deadly discursive conflation of animality and aboriginality through which some bodies are rendered to be revered as primitive, wild, and above all, lost objects. In lieu of providing a more complete account of their literary biographies,[27] my aim here is to situate increasing discomfort with taxidermy's signification of human along with animal populations, ultimately by linking Millet's fictional alignments of the remains of those subjected to biological and cultural extinctions with similar moves in Brett Bailey's *Exhibit B* (2010–), a controversial traveling art installation that, among many other things, uses live humans alongside animal mounts to invite viewers to decolonize their own gazes. Quite apart from the Indigenous metaphysics outlined in the previous chapter, these texts rely on the relentless materiality of taxidermy as an "animal-thing"—one that is "no longer quite an animal" yet hardly "mistaken for anything other than an animal"[28]—to unpick the sutures that hold traces of humans and other animals within the singular taxidermy mount's illusion of commemorating a life in solitude.

Some will say that it is counterintuitive to look to literary writing to reveal the operations of taxidermy, which is a predominantly visual display. After all, doesn't the vexed reception history of *Beatrice and Virgil* prove that literature only ever represents people's thoughts about tangible stuff? In contrast, vibrant materials—the real fur, the actual feathers, the true scales—are said to be the defining quality of a taxidermy,[29] perhaps because the European history of taxidermy as a strictly secular form requires that its enchantments remain reducible to mere matter.[30] Contemporary artists who engage with the form counter that taxidermy's command of the visual story of the life that it is meant to resemble is never absolute. Aloi's discussions of Mark Dion, Snæbjörnsdóttir/Wilson, Nandipha Mntambo, and others show how the spell it casts—of pure nature or scientific objectivity—is readily broken by representing taxidermy through other visual forms, like installation art and photography. Akin to photography's spectral remediation of what presents itself in taxidermy as the material fact of death,[31] literary representations can separate the matter at hand from the stories that guide perceptions of it, potentially opening up a critical distance from which other narratives can take shape.

Most surprising of all, the literary fictions that I examine here show how taxidermy can foster a sense of respect, obligation, and rarest of all, love for the lost. Part of the difficulty of mapping such potentials is that, unlike the photos and artworks along with the mounted animals themselves, fictional taxidermies are hard to find. In sharp contrast to the millions and more taxidermy specimens stored and displayed worldwide, scarcity has been the rule for their literary counterparts—that is, until recent decades, when writers moved beyond the horror aspects of this exceptionally storied stuff. Turning away from villainizing stories of taxidermists—commonly known as "stuffers"—and toward tales of taxidermy itself, contemporary fiction writers like Millet and Rose-Innes are realizing this potential most spectacularly by tapping into the changing histories of taxidermy collections. Central to these developments is an understanding of taxidermy as a site of convergence for multiple lives and deaths and of longing for the kinds of "visceral knowledge" that only comes through contact with animals.[32] To get there, it may help first to sample what is the matter with, of, and in taxidermy's literary histories.

Beatrice and Virgil's staging of the taxidermist as a murdering psychopath has its own storied history in literature, one that contemporary fictions increasingly contest. A coming-of-age novel focused on the dramas of identity in 1970s Hawai'i, *Heads by Harry* (1999) presents Native Hawai'ian (Kānaka Maoli) characters as racially unmarked, while Asian Americans and European Americans are constantly labeled as such, and its progressive racial politics are informed by its complex representations of human-animal relations. Author Lois-Ann Yamanaka's nonwhite central characters express support for de-extinction projects yet harbor deep ambivalence about *haole* (Eurowesterners) management of *pua'a*, or feral pigs (*Sus scrofa*), which are descended of the ones brought by Polynesian settlers nearly a millennium ago. The pigs are both reviled for their destructiveness to the fragile forest ecologies and embraced as living links to the culture of Hawai'i,[33] laying bare key tensions through which de-extinction projects and decolonial projects alike would gain ground there in the decades to follow. While some characters wonder whether they themselves might be the cultural equivalent of biological invasives to the islands, others just want the freedom to hunt the pigs. Why they take such intense interest in wildlife may be the most revolutionary aspect of all, for the novel's title is also the name of a Japanese American man's taxidermy shop, the future of which depends on the owner's training his daughter, plus the brothers who are her two Portuguese Chinese–American baby daddies, to replace him as the resident taxidermists. The daring premise of Yamanaka's novel is that practitioners of taxidermy are all kinds of ordinary people caught up in mundane dramas of family and work, a radical departure from the typical treatment of taxidermists in fiction.

Characters who engage in the practice usually fall into ill repute. Téa Obreht's 2011 best-seller, *The Tiger's Wife*, begins ordinarily enough, describing the character Dariša, who hunts in order to indulge his true passion—namely, "the preparation of pelts" for taxidermy display: "He indulged the occupation he was known for so that he could earn the occupation that gave him pleasure."[34] Hearkening back to a fragile peacetime in the Balkans before the Second World War and recounted within a frame story set during the Bosnian genocide— significantly, both the frame and main stories also feature zoo animals who are members of endangered species—Dariša's narrative, like those of so many other literary taxidermists, nonetheless devolves to isolation and murder.

Might such stories be read as voicing a sense of nostalgia for a time when taxidermists were not damned for what they do? "Generally not highly esteemed" in real life, as the practice fell from scientific craft to rustic hobby by the mid-twentieth century,[35] the fictional makers of taxidermy devolve in the same period from seedy to downright criminal, eventually becoming seen as appropriate targets of backlash for horrors inflicted on humanity. *Psycho's* Norman Bates is the poster child for the postwar emergence of the taxidermist-murderer trope that scripts the fate of taxidermists in *The Tiger's Wife* and still more precisely *Beatrice and Virgil,* even as it marks them as dated. A dead giveaway of a dying trope, Martel's would-be victim departs significantly from the usual profile of the villainous taxidermist's prey chiefly because he is male and seems to be the one exercising the power to let live or die.

Fictional taxidermists more often than not map the underside of the "teddy bear patriarchy" that Donna Haraway identifies as reflected in and encouraged by the shifting aesthetics of museum taxidermy dioramas toward modeling what would later be termed nuclear families as early as the turn of the last century.[36] Queering the connection of capitalism and heteronormativity through violence, taxidermist characters subsequently have become targets of feminist backlash in recent novels and film. So powerful have these associations become that female characters who fight off taxidermist-murderers in popular films, including Stretch in *The Texas Chainsaw Massacre 2* (1986) and Clarice in *The Silence of the Lambs* (1991), are seen as heroes rather than victims, momentarily slipping the patriarchal ordering of taxidermy if not quite taking out the sexist along with racist and colonialist systems that lend it such significance.[37]

Exploring the gaps between the film version of *The Silence of the Lambs* and its source novel raises further concern about whether the sex, gender, and orientation of serial killer Buffalo Bill trouble his unmarked white heterosexual masculinity.[38] The plot reveals the skins that he collects from his victims to be not mere trophies but rather raw materials for a transformative object, the "woman suit" that he makes for himself to wear. In the same way that his poodle, Precious, becomes perversely humanized for him through the same containment strategies whereby he animalizes his human captive,[39] skin's symbolic value becomes confused; small wonder that the film visualizes his victims as all white. More troubling still to the argument at hand, Buffalo Bill is trained as a tailor, not a true taxidermist, a plot hole regarding the acquisition of flaying and hide-tanning skills that, far from queering the serial killer as many have argued, naturalizes taxidermy as an intuitive extension of white patriarchal power.

Literary fictions by women writers more effectively pivot taxidermy's toxic masculinity by introducing female taxidermists as avengers. Through flashbacks to the immediate postwar years, Alice Munro's 1993 short story "Vandals" presents main character Ladner as not a murdering but a child-molesting taxidermist, largely through the perspective of his girl victim Liza. Groomed in part by serving as his apprentice, she eventually takes revenge by trashing his house full of prized specimens. As a vigilante, Liza can no longer be seen as an innocent victim by the end of the story. But because her actions also appear driven by a desire to redress the untimely death of her brother, who himself had been trained in taxidermy en route to being molested by Ladner, as well as to punish Ladner's wife, who witnessed the crimes but did nothing, Liza's destructiveness becomes understandable, even sympathetic.

More recently, Kate Mosse's 2014 novel *The Taxidermist's Daughter* similarly features a sexually assaulted female taxidermist-turned-avenger. Set at the turn of the twentieth century, when "taxidermy was not considered a suitable job for a woman" but women and girls also often contributed in significant ways to family-run shops,[40] the story mitigates her demands for justice. In her final tableau, she reveals the mounted specimens of all but one of her violators especially to terrorize the remaining one, who was their ringleader. Yet in the end, her death dovetails with the restoration to good social standing of the white patriarch who trained her, limiting the potential for feminist critique.

A portrait of a sexually and otherwise traumatized taxidermizing girl as an instrument of broader social revenge emerges through Alissa York's novel *Effigy* (2007). Dorrie is polygamist Hammer's unwitting child bride and, unbeknownst to him, a survivor of a historic US massacre in which he and his Mormon compatriots slaughtered her birth family in a settler-on-settler ambush. With her extraordinary talent and dedication to making taxidermy dioramas, the otherwise unremarkable Dorrie not only attracts her molester's attention but also wins the love of the farmhand with whom she escapes at the end. That their escape depends on being aided and abetted by a Paiute man known only as the Tracker, who up to that point is depicted as a refugee on his own ancestral lands, builds in a far more complex vision than Martel's of the conditions of taxidermy as proceeding from genocide—in this case, the American Indian Wars.

Just as in *Heads by Harry*, the material practice of taxidermy is portrayed in *Effigy* as drawing people into a tangled postcolonial politics of familial, environmental, and racial justice, only in this case, taxidermy spurs humans and animals into action. Following the aesthetic dictated by Hammer, Dorrie's final tableau depicts a mated pair of animals, for which Tracker has slaughtered a pack of gray wolves (*Canis lupus*). Yet he substitutes a yearling for the adult male, a deceit that initially "was a comfort to him, keeping something from the white man, holding a piece of the story for his own."[41] The actual wolf mate who trails his dead family's remains to Dorrie's workshop initially inspires the sympathies of the Tracker, who similarly is haunted by the spirit of his dead wife, but then seals the Tracker's fate by exposing his deception. When Hammer determines to kill the remaining wolf, the Tracker needs to leave but concludes that like all the Indigenous peoples and animals around him, he has nowhere to go: "into the barren hills. . . . the People follow the rabbits and deer or, worse, stay and cling like children to the skirts of towns," only to delay their inevitable "starving" or assimilation.[42] In the end, he knocks Hammer down and sets fire to Dorrie's workshop, and readers are left to assume that together the men will be consumed in flames along with Hammer's beloved collection, which burns "beast after beast."[43]

Prefiguring the blazing taxidermy shop in *Beatrice and Virgil*, *Effigy* more clearly follows "Vandals" with this ultimate scene of a collection that means so much to an abusive white man and that is deliberately destroyed by a victim of his abuses of power. That female taxidermists in Yamanaka's, Munro's, Mosse's, and York's stories all eventually find love despite intense suffering in early life signals a more recent growth of taxidermy's narrative potentials for forging social connections in the relics of colonialism.

Taxidermy: From Object to Active Force

Taxidermy may inspire extreme actions in characters, but zoombies themselves remain rarely animated in fiction. One of the earliest precursors to Martel's characters Beatrice and Virgil erupts in children's fiction—more specifically, in *The Marvelous Land of Oz* (1904), L. Frank Baum's sequel to *The Wonderful Wizard of Oz* (1900). A character called the Gump features just the head of a moose-like animal (confusingly also called a gump) that had hung above a mantelpiece "in the great hall," becomes provided with a body of sorts, then becomes reanimated with magic powder.[44]

Taxidermy Remains

Baum's narrative is prescient for linking the mounted head to characters who had nothing to do with its death or severance. Manipulated in the story by people who are neither its killers nor its stuffers, the Gump gains interest as a creature reborn by becoming cobbled together with other things by still other characters. It is fleshed out, so to speak, with couches tied with clothesline to palm fronds that operate as wings and a broom as its rudder—ordinary child's play, as befits its context in children's fiction—and for much of the novel, it serves as a vehicle for physically shuttling around those who befriend it. Disassembled by the end, the Gump has proven itself as one of the few friendlies in the very scary place that is Oz. And the love is returned: at his request, his head is rehung on a wall, which makes sense, as the novel's illustrations clarify, because the Gump is a mount on a board—in other words, a hunting trophy.

Innovated as a method of preserving bits of rare or novel fauna, taxidermy in the early days focused on the fragment, not the whole animal, a history that persists through its most storied of forms, the hunting trophy.[45] "All taxidermy makes death overt," according to museologist Rachael Poliquin, but through "the nightmare of a disembodied head,"[46] hunting trophies announce that the story of someone's death involved dismemberment. In fiction as in life, hunting trophies generally remain the inanimate furniture of a hunter's life; only in the literary imagination have they been enlisted as signs of monstrous villainy. A classic example, Richard Connell's short story "The Most Dangerous Game" (1924) introduces the shared hunting passions of the host Count Zaroff and his would-be human prey through Zaroff's dining-hall display of "mounted heads of many animals—lions, tigers, elephants, moose, bears"—all "large" and "perfect specimens," in accordance with the guiding aesthetic of the hunting trophy.[47]

Connell's trophies set the human target on a continuum with animals, although not quite in the same way that some of Martel's readers find offensive, and like the Gump gain interest for appearing with no reference to any taxidermist. Yet unlike the Gump, who converses like every other extraordinary character in the Land of Oz, they are realistically silent, their fragmentary, cumulative presence alone delivering a message about Zaroff that the protagonist ignores at his peril. A century later, fiction writers more readily imagine the creative afterlives of taxidermy at a distance from killers and mutilators primarily through collections of multiple specimens, exploring affective negotiations of lives and deaths of populations more directly cast in engagements with the form's history.

"Scientific taxidermy loathes idiosyncracies," notes Aloi in his historical account of how human-exceptionalist ideologies extended the classifying
imagination into the institutionalization of mounted skins in natural history
museums.[48] Accumulations of taxidermy effectively train a way of seeing animals as representative species types and, in turn, a way of seeing humans as
the only animals whose individuality matters. Aloi notes how this strategy
has become powerfully disrupted through a "double distancing" or reframing of animal taxidermy in another visual medium, such as photography: "It
is in this double distancing from the live animal, first through the rendering
into taxidermy and thereafter through its transposition into another indexical
medium, that a critical approach, an undoing of human/animal past histories
and [fostering of] future potentialities for engagement, can arise."[49] It is a big
claim—and one that contemporary literary fictions of taxidermy collections
suggest expanding to include critical undoings of not just human-animal histories but also attempts to restrict history itself to a purely human endeavor.

Among many significant uses of taxidermy in Marcel Beyer's *Kaltenburg*
(2008), the extensive taxidermy collections of Dresden's State Museum of Zoology
set the stage for the critique of the institutionalization of biological knowledges
and its implication in genocide. The novel overall attempts to think through the
mixed legacy of fictional famed zoologist Ludwig Kaltenburg, whose passion for
jackdaws, enlistment in unethical medical experiments, and other biographical
details parallel that of real-life Nobel Prize–winning ethologist and Nazi Party
member Konrad Lorenz,[50] but with the significant differences that Kaltenburg
moves to the German Democratic Republic and has no human significant others.
Narrated by Hermann Funk, a wartime orphan and Kaltenburg acolyte who uses
present and future-perfect but never past tenses, the novel's structure attunes readers to its invention of history and a particular perspective on it that is distinct in
contemporary fiction.[51] Far from providing "escape into the apolitical, fascinating
world of birds," the constant use of tormented and slaughtered avian bodies to
symbolize human victimization—such as the flaming birds Hermann sees falling
from the sky during the firebombing of Dresden, in the absence of any other
mention of burned bodies, and the flocks he remembers in lieu of people traveling along the train tracks toward concentration camps—indicate "Hermann's
inability to talk about the Holocaust directly."[52] Moreover, his lifelong fascination
with birds leads directly to apprenticing with Kaltenburg and so enables the story
plausibly to introduce taxidermy as another way of representing devastations that
follow state-sponsored terror.

After his parents' death, young Hermann studies and later curates the Dresden museum's ornithological specimen collection, initially under Kaltenburg's tutelage. His life's passion leads to his stewarding a taxonomy project, but he nonetheless values the life represented by each specimen: "You have to get to know every single bird individually in order to learn anything about the unique characteristics of its kind."[53] Thus critical of the colonialist ideological bent of scientific taxidermy, his perspective helps explain how the museum collection, in his view, comes to waver in status as a national institution, teaching tool, and final resting place of beloved animal companions. But only through a pivotal scene in which he is seen learning the skills of taxidermy does it become clear how it serves as an affective conversion point in his boyhood love for Kaltenburg.

Through stagy flashbacks, Hermann struggles throughout to make sense of his own wartime and Cold War traumas that include mounting evidence of his mentor's participation in the Nazi genocide. In a scene in which young Hermann is being coached through skinning and mounting a bird, the man who is always to him "Professor" Kaltenburg gazes out the window and notes how a government-sponsored cull of any potentially rabid creature is devolving into a free-for-all—"a regular slaughter"[54]—in the Great Garden around them. In lieu of filing an official complaint, Kaltenburg ostensibly turns the lesson to personal history. He recounts the story of the spectacular backfire of his initial conservation attempts to protect vulnerable populations of bird species by attaching rings to the legs of individuals so their fates could be more easily tracked for research purposes. He explains that his well-intentioned animal experiment led instead to hunters killing "massive numbers in the hopes of bagging one" of "Kaltenburg's birds," which they perversely valued above all others.[55]

Lest readers miss the looming question of whether science is good for animals or people, the novel clarifies that the hand-reared wild birds that ordinarily teacher and pupil would be out studying are undoubtedly among the dead, made prime targets again by virtue of being marked as animals of the professor's interest. What is more, as part of the requisite logging of what gets bagged, these two, who knew those birds in life most intimately, are tasked with either preparing as skins or simply recording as numbers the remains of the wild birds they cared for, including his free-ranging pet jackdaws. The novel's alignments of biological research, behavioral theory, and storytelling practice at one level explain how Hermann becomes disenchanted with Kaltenburg and how the ultimately antihumanist Kaltenburg becomes alienated from even his animal companions. But the implied moral of the story—a narrow passion for science fuels the violent destruction of whole populations—says so much more about why a lesson in taxidermy here propels rather than conflicts with a novelist's meditation on genocide and extinction.

One of many suggestive moments in a profoundly allusive novel, Kaltenburg's self-implication in the mass killing of endangered birds is the closest that he comes to owning that his celebrated career led to his participation in the endangerments and exterminations of any populations. Just as in Martel's novel, the suspect never confesses to being a Nazi, but his resignation to taxidermy as a tool—like so many others, meant to serve science at all costs—makes it so that he doesn't have to. While Beyer's bringing together of the pursuits of natural history and state-sponsored mass killings contributes to a far more profoundly melancholic effect, one of the crucial means by which it does so is by enabling separations of taxidermy's metaphorical and material values.[56] In still more recent fictions in which the taxidermy collection becomes both a measure of irrevocable biological and cultural destructions as well as a means of intervening in these processes, the intersections of human, animal, and human-animal histories pursue these critical potentials far afield of old European colonial centers and through more overtly creative interventions into the histories of slaughter that continue to affect vulnerable populations.

Taxidermy Collections: Sadness to Love

Among "the saddest objects in the world," according to Poliquin, is a particular kind of taxidermy mount, "not a souvenir of personal remembrance but rather of biological commemoration: the extinct species."[57] After inheriting what might be construed along these lines as the saddest collection in the world, Susan, the protagonist of Millet's *Magnificence*, eventually comes to identify sadness as a problematic response to being confronted with the preserved material remains of vanished populations. At the end of the novel, Susan enters an underground bunker on her late, estranged uncle's southern Californian estate. Unexpectedly finding herself the sole heir of a rich hunting enthusiast by this point in the story, she has already sorted out his Pasadena mansion, which was left crammed full of eclectically arranged taxidermy in need of restoration. But an anomaly in the architectural plan leads Susan to discover an otherwise invisible basement enclosure that is filled with a carefully preserved, orderly collection of the remains of all sorts of creatures, even the incredibly rare skeleton of a dodo.

Searching for the principle organizing the secreted cache, she at last finds a building plan for the space, labeled with a sort of explanation: "At the top of the plan were the black words, in old-fashioned type, GLOBAL HOLOCENE EXTINCTIONS @ 1800–2000. At the bottom, THE LEGACY COLLECTION. A PRODUCT OF HUNTERS CLUB INTERNATIONAL."[58] Thus Susan learns that her inheritance includes a comprehensive monument to anthropogenic extermination, which instantly raises in her mind concerns for "how the skins were acquired . . . the question of whether they were murdered for the sake of their own history, murdered in order to become mementos of themselves."[59]

A decommissioned, recycled, repurposed, or vintage taxidermy—one that, in any event, is decidedly "not killed by the current owner"[60]—ordinarily brackets off questions of ethical obligation, except that Susan's story up to this point shows her coming to care for her uncle's animal-things. Following the impulses of a curator rather than a zookeeper, Susan finds, through the process of having the household taxidermies restored and rearranged to her taste, that she enjoys what she sees as "the happy captivity of precious things."[61] Her satisfaction with sorting out the house displays toys with colonialist visions of worldwide dominion: "When the project was finished the home had a globe-like aspect in its sectioning off, its variety of scenes, its separation by palette. It was multi-colored like a globe, and also like a globe it represented reality only partly, with the failure of all maps but also the same neatness, the same quiet satisfaction."[62] When confronted with the enormity that is the Legacy Collection, however, it calls forth a more complicated emotional response in her.

The development of Susan's responsiveness follows the trajectory of taxidermy's literary histories away from killers and toward the objects, which gain gravitas in numbers. Appearing as "a version of the dead that had, in the end, almost nothing to do with who or what the animals had been,"[63] the Legacy Collection at first blush strikes her as haunted exclusively by "the invisible presence of those who had hunted them, those who had dug them up or even stolen them. The unknown or the dead people—no, their desire, that was the presence that hovered there, their deep wanting, part of the sacred air."[64] Alongside the ghosts of animals crowded out by "the phantasms of men's desire,"[65] she contemplates a deeply ambiguous vision of the purpose of preserving taxidermy as providing access to immortality. In Susan's expansive curatorial vision, determining who "live[s] on forever in a glorious museum" follows from the recognition that the collection contains "both God and molecules, even our passion for ourselves that brought smallpox to baby Indians."[66] In other words, she gets that extinction and genocide meet at least conceptually in the taxidermy collection, only that does little to prepare her for then finding herself in possession of material evidence.

Susan's inherited monument to extinction extends beyond animal-things when she looks into an unfinished section of the Legacy Collection only to find meticulously labeled human remains. They are not taxidermy or skins but mummies and skeletons whose labels clarify that they represent "members of vanished tribes," Indigenous peoples whose lifeways are gone. While Susan might reasonably be expected to respond with revulsion or horror, she instantly expresses instead a more personal sense of the Legacy Collection as representing no longer the lost uncle's "celebration of killing" but instead something more "plain, sad."[67] In this dramatic unfolding, sadness emerges not as an inherent property of the animal-thing but as a highly contingent affective response shaped through proximities and perceptions of different kinds of bodies and objects.[68] Far from becoming "overwhelmed and horrified"[69] by the discovery of dead people stored in her backyard, Susan indicates no plans to contact police, funeral directors, or any of the ordinary authorities to address the human remains as a separate, more pressing concern than those of the extinct animals (though, to be fair, Susan is drunk throughout this final sequence). Instead of seeking justice for past wrongs, she concerns herself with their future.

Lumped together across species lines as subjected to "Holocene extinctions" on the archive map, the peoples and animals are initially framed by the uncle squarely within what Wakeham would identify as a colonialist discursive matrix. Passing into Susan's purview, however, their remains expose a sadness that signals the start of an alternative set of imaginings of the inevitability of colonialism's destructions. While some read *Magnificence*'s conclusion as indicating Susan's resignation to being accountable for the exterminations that the human and animal remains together represent,[70] many details across the trilogy concluded by this novel ground a more complicated potential.

Susan's profound sense of grief and guilt for her husband's murder at the hands of a random stranger—the culminating act of *Ghost Lights* (2011), the second novel in the series, which haunts the entire story of *Magnificence*—appears to give way finally to a positive and plural sense of the imperative to move beyond just being sad in order to "love the gone ones," not despite but because they will "never come back again."[71] This response to discovering the Legacy Collection signals the crucial difference famously identified by Sigmund Freud between the psychological morass that is melancholy and the productive work of mourning in staving it off. While ecocritic Ursula Heise laments as missing from the novel any sense of "multispecies justice" to bridge "differences of culture as well as species,"[72] I read Susan's relinquishment of a self-absorbed melancholia, which occupies the majority of the novel, in favor of loving all who are lost as a sure sign that she has come to care about more than personal problems. And it is as a prelude to effective multispecies justice projects that she takes up the social work of mourning called forth by the Legacy Collection, a point that becomes sharpened through direct comparison with other characters.

Prefaced by Susan's growing feelings for taxidermy, her final embrace of the Legacy Collection on these terms posits taxidermy as a conversion point for the feeling of cruel optimism regarding efforts to save doomed species that takes shape through other narrative threads across the trilogy. A far from perfect solution, Susan's affection for all "gone ones," human and animal alike, nevertheless offers an alternative to the neocolonialist project of salvation that emerges through another character's confrontations with personal and species loss in the series' first novel, *How the Dead Dream* (2007), and that Rose-Innes, in *The Green Lion*, positions as an even more directly self-destructive and otherwise counterproductive response to anthropogenic extinction.

Broadly exploring the politics of affect, each volume of Millet's trilogy centers on a single character dealing with a profound sense of loss in stories that realign the relational networks of all three. The first centers on Susan's employer, Thomas, who goes by "T." and is a self-made rich white guy whose obsessions with money give way to passions for being with critically endangered animal species. Fueled by several personal traumas—including his girlfriend's sudden death, his mother's dementia (triggered when his father comes out as gay and abandons the family), and pivotally, his own accidental killing of a coyote with his car—T. develops a melancholic fixation on "animals in the middle of dying, not one at a time but in sweeps and categories,"[73] in other words, the "final animals"[74] or members of species doomed to extinction. At night, he breaks into zoos and captive-breeding facilities in order to make himself vulnerable to these rare animals, explicitly not to look at them but to enable them to notice him feeling the loss of their kind. It remains unclear what that does for the animals.[75]

For T., engaging in these practices spells the end of life as he has known it. Through these encounters, he comes to care more about how his business ventures contribute to anthropogenic extinction. In the end of the first novel, he travels to what would have been his next big real estate development, promptly getting lost in Belize's backcountry. The sequel, *Ghost Lights*, centers on Susan's husband, Hal, who, in an act of drunken bravado that follows directly from his discovery of Susan's many infidelities, volunteers to travel there to find T. In Belize, Hal has a fling with a married woman but intends to return home to Susan after having found T. Only T. makes it back to California, however, because at the end of the second novel, Hal is stabbed to death while being mugged. Alignments of deaths and failed or failing love affairs bring the larger story of anthropogenic extinction in different ways to histories of genocide. After his own near-death experience, T. returns in *Magnificence* to deliver Hal's remains and to announce his plan to liquidate his real-estate development business in order to reinvest his substantial fortune instead in species conservation efforts. As his plans take shape, he marries Casey, Susan and Hal's paraplegic daughter, who with sharp, crass humor invigorates all the novels (she's my vote for the most sympathetic character of the entire cast). In the last book, she introduces in real time critical perspectives on T.'s miraculous transformations.

After a brief romance in *How the Dead Dream*, Casey drops all contact with T., having sensed in his growing feelings for her a basic condescension regarding her paralysis. Accounting for her equally abrupt change of heart in *Magnificence*, Casey explains to her mother, "He's less of an asshole now."[76] After they marry, Casey and T. leave their US home for Borneo to, as Casey says, pursue his desire to help "poor people" maintain a forest home for the "Sumatran rhino that's practically gone. Also orangutans and pygmy elephants. He loves those little fuckers."[77] Once there, Casey learns that the "poor people" are Dayak, the Indigenous peoples of Borneo who are so persecuted by both police and logging companies that their future is as uncertain as that of the many endangered species who share their ancestral lands. Just as Casey herself initially appears to disparage interest in endangered species, T. exhibits no particular interest in Indigenous peoples' impending genocide—yet she at least is beginning to learn to appreciate that human and animal stories are not so easily separated.

Set in 1995, the situation outlined within the novel has only grown more dire for Borneo's Indigenous peoples and animals alike—as would be well-known to Millet, who worked for the Natural Resources Defense Council as well as the Center for Biological Diversity—and all of which raises grave questions about what it means that T. "loves those little fuckers." Will T.'s plans effectively counter colonial control? Or are they a more masterfully executed form of it, of a design that is all too familiar, featuring a rich, white Eurowesterner using his money to pursue his own ideas about who or what will be saved, protected, or conserved?[78] Whereas Susan's mourning—"loving the gone ones"—recasts the remains of those who have already vanished into a response that ruptures the pattern of colonial history, T.'s melancholic love risks fixing others in the process of becoming lost ones, a course that leads in other stories to more immediate and violent erasures.

Like T., *The Green Lion*'s central character, Mark, experiences multiple traumatic losses that fuel his own obsession with final animals, beginning with the death of his sister Lizzie, mysteriously killed as a child, and then that of his father, "who never really recovered" from Lizzie's death.[79] Mark volunteers as a zookeeper in order to gain access to the last remnants of the lushly black-maned or Cape lion (*Panthera leo melanochaitus*), an extinct local subspecies of Transvaal lion (*Panthera leo krugeri*), which, like all lion species today, is in rapid decline due to disease and habitat loss. As the zoo's director explains, colonialism complicates the definitive disappearance of this particular subspecies: "There were Cape lions all over Europe, even after they were shot out here. In zoos, circuses."[80] Referencing real-life breeding-back programs for animals "like the quagga"—thought to be an extinct species until genetic testing of taxidermy remains redefined it as the southernmost subspecies of plains zebra (*Equus quagga quagga*)[81]—the zoo director clarifies that two lions exhibiting "ancestral features" like huge, dark manes were acquired from Europe in order to achieve the zoo's mission of bringing the Cape lion "back from extinction."[82]

Unluckier than T., Mark's similarly illegal after-hours visits to the animals' enclosures—he reasons, "Because there are so few wild creatures left now, we have to find different ways of getting in contact"[83]—result in his being severely mauled by one of the lions, who, according to zoo policy, then must be executed. Abruptly transformed by the lion into a speech-impaired amputee, Mark's melancholia not only proves self-destructive but also accelerates the doom of a final animal. What seems especially intriguing in light of Millet's fictions is how taxidermy introduces into this novel as well an alternative approach that allows for different possible endings.[84] While the initial assessment of Mark's sometime friend Con metaphorically links Mark's battered body to taxidermy—"Skin removed and stitched back on. The stuffing coming out. Bits left off, bits gone missing"[85]—the lion who is killed also offers a rare glimpse in fiction of a corpse en route to become a taxidermy mount, one that eventually becomes the crown jewel of a repurposed collection of animal mounts at the story's conclusion.

Set mostly in Cape Town, South Africa, Mark's story emerges at a distance, through the perspective of Con. The novel begins when Con, despite not having been in contact with Mark for years, reluctantly consents to the request of Mark's mother, Margaret, that he visit the zoo in order to retrieve her son's effects. Con is surprised to learn from zoo staff that the executed lion is being prepared as a taxidermy. The explanation—"He's special. There's only a few specimens in the world. None in South Africa"[86]—clarifies how taxidermy marks not just the loss of a life but a convergence of many stories of loss and recovery at the colonial margins.

A white South African like Mark, Con expresses subtle antipathy toward the black, female zoo director's enthusiasm for the planned taxidermy, and it is a sentiment that seems to cross species lines when he takes a meandering route home after their initial conversation about lions at the zoo. He ruefully reflects that nowadays the "only animals tolerated were indigenous"[87] as he walks home past the Rhodes Memorial, a monument to the nineteenth-century politician and philanthropist Cecil Rhodes, which is famously flanked by eight giant bronze lion statues. While no characters in the novel espouse or embrace racism, given the novel's 2015 publication date—the same year in which the memorial was vandalized at the height of the Rhodes Must Fall student protest movement, which renewed global criticism of Rhodes as architect and symbol of the racial, economic, and educational inequality that persists in the postapartheid state—in this particular place, the politics of indigeneity become charged with human histories too. Just as in Millet's *Magnificence*, flagging the convergence proves not enough. *The Green Lion* also then turns to a collection of taxidermy to outline a way of moving forward.

When Con delivers Mark's things to his old family mansion, the novel introduces a taxidermy collection that once again becomes the site of affective conversions. Akin to the house taxidermies in Millet's *Magnificence*, the "historic family trophies"[88] and full mounts inherited by Mark's late father have become dusty and damaged over the years, but the sympathies of his mother, Margaret, toward them track an inverse trajectory to Susan's. She says that she "used to feel sorry for the poor dumb animals" but over time "started to loathe" them.[89] When Con visits Mark's bedroom, where the two had found a special love together as children, he discovers his own strong feelings along

64 with another dimension to his childhood friend's adult obsession in the form of a particular piece of taxidermy. A "small, dusty lion" has been separated from the rest and subjected to "terrible indignities" such as being smeared with green paint.[90] Discovered at the epicenter of the boys' long-lost intimacy, the defaced taxidermy initially appalls Con, who recalls a young Mark being slapped down by his father for once climbing on the same mount and pulling out its glass eye. Con is left to wonder, Has Mark been turning his grief against the long-dead lion? Or is his weird treatment of it connected to his deadly desire to commune with the zoo lion?[91]

Upon hearing about the collection, Con's girlfriend, Elyse, a performer specializing in the intersections of art and natural history, expresses interest in repurposing the collection—"[My troupe] could even use something like that [in a performance with] . . . dancers interacting with the trophies"—a prospect that Con immediately dismisses as "morbid, crazy shit."[92] As he begins to piece together the story of how Mark ended up in the lion's cage, however, Con starts to recognize how what he sees as the defacement of the one lion taxidermy dovetails with Mark's attempt at a more far-reaching aesthetic response to the living dead. An iteration of an ancient alchemical symbol on the cover of a pamphlet included among Mark's few things left behind at the zoo, the figure of a green lion appears to have served as an artistic model for an educational poster of sorts that Mark made for the zoo. Con learns that it also serves as the emblem of the underground Green Lion Club, whose members' desire for wild-animal contact informs a kind of mystical faith in the inherent goodness of such contact. And so taxidermy provides a clue to solving the mystery of Mark's fatally flawed decision to enter the enclosure of the lion who maims him.

As one of many representational interventions into conventional visions of lions, Mark's creative manipulation of taxidermy offers a foretaste of Elyse's and her friends' more public and hopeful vision at the story's conclusion. Elyse arranges the donation of Mark's family's unwanted heirloom taxidermy collection to her own theater group, who use it to bring life back to the zoo. Following the escape of the last remaining lion, the zoo had been forced to close, but it reopens as the site of weekly family-friendly performances by Elyse's theater troupe. They use "needles and thread, paint and latex, and knocked [the] stuffy old trophies into some more appealing, kid-friendly shape. And why not? [The zoo] is, after all, a Centre for Arts and Science now, and taxidermied animals are its perfect emblems. Never particularly rigorous scientific documents, these ones are now almost wholly imaginary creations."[93] Featuring actors dressed as animals and working with animal puppets, the performances act out animal allegories in the former lion enclosure, around which the patched-up heirloom taxidermy collection has been regrouped in tableaux that encourage visitors of all ages to touch them. Whereas realistic aesthetics mask the death of an animal, the "fundamentally theatrical" power of taxidermy[94] is redeployed by the actors to tell stories of the lives of animals.

The whole scene is crowned by the intact mount of the lion who mauled Mark, now relocated as a showpiece at the park's entrance. Utterly transformed and in public view, the taxidermy collection elicits a swell of positive feeling—reflected in the crowds of people who had given up on the old zoo but suddenly return, bringing children to the performances—that runs counter to Mark's doomed melancholia. Like Millet's Susan, Elyse imagines into being a productive engagement with mourning processes through the repurposed and here creatively manipulated remains of the dead. In this light, it becomes easier to imagine how Susan's "love for the gone ones" in the Legacy Collection grounds a plausible alternative to the predominant narratives of settler colonialism—how the incorporation of taxidermy into the human performance of animal stories more generally reenchants the zoo and instills a much-needed sense of sympathy in Con for his beloved childhood friend.

In a way intimated but not quite realized by Millet, Rose-Innes's reusage of vintage taxidermy arrives also as an opportunity to enact large-scale affective conversions in our behavior toward endangered species and, less clearly, toward endangered cultures. *The Green Lion's* section epigraphs include citations of the San (Bushman) anthropological informant //Kabbo that in turn share Indigenous knowledges of how humans once lived among wild lions and further suggest how fictional zoombies can foster a sense of how more is lost than individuals with the death of populations. What remains to be seen is how human remains press these questions of taxidermy's legacies to reckonings with the social and environmental injustices of settler colonialism.

The questions hovering over Millet's Legacy Collection regarding the degree to which the preserved remains of humans as well as animals might provoke productive responses are pursued in greater detail in *Exhibit B*, a highly controversial installation artwork by South African artist and playwright Brett Bailey. Staged in several European cities beginning in 2010 and instantly faced with angry protests, "*Exhibit B* takes the form of live actors playing the roles of objectified historical (and contemporary) people,"[95] all of whom self-identify as black Africans, unlike Bailey, who is a white South African. Settings are crafted to reference "people shows" and other ethnographic displays of Indigenous Africans once popular in Europe and the United States alongside re-creations of more recent crime scenes, all in order to call attention to "current dehumanizing policies toward immigrants in various parts of the world."[96] Perceptions of Bailey as extending racist and colonialist power over the actors inspired protests and even riots that threatened the work's future and were empowered by the large role given to audience participation in the artwork itself.

Listed as one of the artwork's materials alongside historical details on the signage for each tableau, spectators are conceived as an integral part of *Exhibit B*. Actors, all locally recruited black people, are trained to remain silent and motionless except to make uncomfortable eye contact with viewers. Immobile human bodies illustrate the power of the colonial gaze that the living actors' intensely moving eyes powerfully unsettle from within the tableaux. Actors and viewers alike attest to experiencing profound revelations regarding visceral feelings of racism and colonialism as part of the aesthetic experience.[97] Several of the tableaux include nonhuman taxidermy, whether as the furnishings of a room in which a woman is shackled to a colonial officer's bed or as the décor of museum-like spaces featuring people scantily clad in stereotypic "tribal" garb. Only one tableau directly references human taxidermy.

In the scene titled "The Age of Enlightenment," a figure arranged to resemble an embalmed corpse on display is dressed in the tailored clothes and turban nearly identical to those worn in portraits of Angelo Soliman, who was born into the Kanuri people of western Africa, then stolen as a child and sold to Europeans. A slave who later became a freeman, Soliman was a "court Moor," whose career eventually flourished in the eighteenth-century Vienna of emperors Joseph II, Leopold VII, and Francis II, where he became a pioneering freemason, expert chess player, Christian, tutor, and scholar. Yet upon Soliman's death and against his daughter's repeated and insistent protests, Francis ordered his corpse skinned, mounted, clothed only in stereotypically "native" beads and feathers, and exhibited "in a fine glass case" in the imperial cabinet as part of a collection that included several animal and a couple of anonymized human taxidermies—until all was destroyed in a fire decades later. Many contemporary writers and artists struggle to represent Soliman's story.[98]

In Bailey's words, his own very unique staging in *Exhibit B* is meant instead to initiate a process of public mourning, to create "a way of honoring Soliman with the tomb he never had."[99] In the tableau, a taxidermy bird mount overlooks the figure, who, like the body of Soliman, also has a museum catalog–like numbered tag prominently attached. Proximity to the animal's prominently displayed skin in the tableau offers a creative solution to the difficulties of re-creating human taxidermy with live actors, not because the one is a stand-in for the other but rather because together they activate taxidermy's special nar-rative condition: never simply a record of one life, a taxidermy represents how proximities of different bodies serve relations of power. Embodied skin and taxidermy can never be viewed the same—one is affected, the other only elicits affect—yet the depiction of Soliman in *Exhibit B* indicates how creative integra-tions of their representation loft powerful counternarratives to conceiving race and species as entirely reducible to skins or limited to discourse.

As its preoccupation shifts from twisted characters to the inheritances of wounded people, it may be too much to ask of fictional taxidermy that it not only represent but also become a tool of affective conversion in the histories of people's exploitation of other species and each other. Charting movement toward this goal, *Exhibit B* attempts a live-action version of something like the novel *The Green Lion*'s relocation of a private taxidermy collection to a public space for self-reflexive theater, where people and animal-things but not (or no longer) members of other species perform the act of mourning (and maybe loving) all the lost ones. Incorporating material fragments of lost lives and in ways that destabilize the stories that surround them, taxidermies in these ways and more locate the materials for shifting a stagnated human longing for lost ones into productive concerns about how affect matters and for whom.

In light of the previous chapter, the finitude or material fact of death in taxi-dermy could suggest a point of contrast to the processual dying of the animal gods. Yet the similar ways in which they enter into contemporary stories to thwart sentimentality or a nostalgic form of love and instead anchor a sense of love as a call to action, shaping sustainable lives between species, strikes me as far more momentous. Through stories combining these elements—humans and animals, living and dead, plus less readily identifiable spirits—the next chapters explore still more complex ways of dislodging the finitude of exterminationist history from within the framework of fiction, dislodging what Braidotti terms "an affective political economy of loss and melancholia" in order to make room for "an ethics of transformation" in contexts marked by mass killings.[100]

Thinking further about the importance of dead relatives to all these stories—Mark's sister and father, Susan's uncle, Ashitaka in social death sep-arated from his sister and village, and above all Omishto's fleeting vision of her long-gone female ancestors—opens another potential for love in a time of slaughters. If, as Braidotti insists, mourning is part of a "double necessity"—that is, it is an action that must be grounded in responsibility for social sustainability in the future[101]—then it would seem to be a concern of far more than just the living, as the next chapters elaborate through stories of affective bonds that cross non/human as well as super/natural boundaries.

Pacific Currents

Becoming Usefully Dead

At a pivotal moment in Amitav Ghosh's novel *The Hungry Tide* (2004), Piya, a cetologist born in the United States to Bengali-immigrant parents, tells a story to explain her obsession with saving the Irrawaddy dolphin (*Orcaella brevirostris*), a vulnerable species of river dolphin persisting today only in small groups across Southeast Asia. As a student member of a research team in Cambodia, she was assigned to monitor one after he became stranded in the Mekong delta, a remnant of a population that had been decimated alongside Cambodia's peoples, first by US carpet-bombing and then Khmer Rouge slaughter (dolphins became a cheap fuel-oil source for the regime). Piya kept him alive for days by buying fish to feed him and named him Mr. Sloane in recognition of her sense that he "returned her gaze," so to speak. Then one night, he disappeared by truck, likely sold on the black market to a commercial aquarium, leaving Piya "haunted by a nightmare in which Mr. Sloane was driven into a corner of his tank by a line of hunters armed with fishnets."[1] Nameless and faceless, local fishermen are villains in the field scientist's primal scene.

Relayed late in a novel about the tensions between conservation biology and human economic migration in India's Sundarbans region, which is home to many more iconic endangered and extinct species as well as three million extremely impoverished and otherwise vulnerable people, Piya's career-origin story marks how far she has come throughout the novel. In her work with Fokir, the poor illiterate fisherman, she does not share a language, yet she comes to depend on Fokir in order to locate Irrawaddy dolphins and consequently improve scientific conservation of them. It also reveals an absolute difference in their perspectives, for Fokir in turn explains that he became involved with Piya's pursuit only after a dream encounter with his dead mother, Kusum, who in life taught him reverence for the dolphins as messengers of a local forest goddess. "Haunted" by a dolphin hunted with "fishnets," the affluent scientist returns to the land of her family's roots in order to save his species, only to find the conditions for their sustainability maintained by a fisherman who is guided by gods through the dead, and with whom she falls in love.[2]

What is more, the novel comes to reveal that Kusum was one of many displaced people murdered nearby at the massacre of Morichjhãpi (1978–79), orphaning young Fokir. Detailing the incident makes the novel the first extended treatment in English of events in which hundreds of people initially dislocated by the Partition of British Colonial India were killed and many more dispersed by authorities for attempting to found a Dalit (untouchable caste) nation on rare conservation land for severely endangered Bengal tigers (*Panthera tigris tigris*). Ghosh's commingling of the living and the dead in scenes that concern both environmental and cultural justice—in Ursula Heise's terms, his searching for "multispecies justice"[3]—is a strategy that other writers also use to reframe discussions of conflicting human and animal interests to foster shared commitments in such scenes. Mr. Sloane and Kusum reflect how the dead provide complex points of convergence for the presence of ancestral spirits and the material fact of the deaths of populations in stories that concern shared human and animal futures.

Whereas the previous chapters focused on the spirituality and materiality of death as separate dimensions, their simultaneity in contemporary fiction provides further opportunities for exploring alternatives to the enlistment of death as the ultimate human "other." Pointing to the iconic image of walls made of Rwandan genocide victims' bones, Achille Mbembe identifies the flip side to biopolitical exertions of control over the maintenance of neo/colonial life: the "necropolitics" that extend far beyond the murdered victims of mass killings to include even "'survivors,' [who] after a horrific exodus, are confined to camps and zones of exception."[4] The assumption that necropolitics, and biopolitics before it, can be restricted to interactions among humans is something that the cases at the center of this chapter and the next ones aim to unsettle, as Fokir's situation suggests.

In Ghosh's novel, the fates of slaughtered peoples (Cambodians, Dalits) and wild animal species (dolphins, tigers) seem to follow this pattern in the aggregate, yet individuals resist. Fokir's having once survived a mass killing and eking out a meager, illegal living on conservation land would seem to relegate him to necropolitical victim. However, his choices—to use traditional if less efficient fishing nets, to join in the illegal revenge killing of a man-eating tiger, to teach his son to fish with faith in his own dead mother and their gods, and to risk and then lose his own life to help Piya in her dolphin-conservation work—script a far more complex set of necropolitical-as-enmeshed-with-biopolitical potentials across species lines. Ghosh's is one of several contemporary fictions in which characters like Kusum are introduced as dead but whose memories as well as world views nonetheless continue to shape the world of their descendants. Their presence complicates clean lines between not simply the material and the spiritual but more importantly survivors and victims of mass killings, which may be why so often writers hold them at a distance at their peril.

More so than that of mortality or vulnerability, the language of survival becomes ethically problematic when death is reframed biopolitically as a condition or precondition of existence. It is in this sense that Braidotti claims "death is overrated,"[5] and in the special power of "*Thanatos*," which she locates in "the dead body, the corpse, or spectral other,"[6] emerges a way of accounting for the peculiar narrative agency of figures as diverse, say, as the fisherman's dead mother and his catch. But what about their relationships with the gods of the traditional fisherman and, through him, to each other? Ghosh's more recent musing that the nonhuman is primarily an "uncanny/improbable" fictional element[7]—at best a reminder that "most people never acculturated to Cartesian dualism," at worst a throwback to tradition at the peril of "serious fiction"[8]—might help explain his underdevelopment of these elements in *The Hungry Tide*. After all, Fokir's speech remains entirely translated by other characters, his mother present only through their memories, their cosmology thus effectively bracketed off from readers along with that of all animals, including the only named nonhuman character, Mr. Sloane, who is presented only through Piya's distant memories.

Thinking instead of Braidotti's vision of the dead on a continuum with spectral others in pursuit of an explicitly vitalist and nomadic feminism adds significance to Fokir's status as both survivor and migrant, with no legal and little heritage claims to the lands and waters from which he makes his living. A transformative global ethic of environmental and social sustainability for future generations requires the reframing of how survival relates mortality and vulnerability through sharing stories of sufferings as a hedge against the extreme isolation in abstraction that is Mbembe's states of exception. While Ghosh's novel offers a glib conclusion—featuring the establishment of a multinationally funded, locally administered fishing-friendly dolphin-conservation project to commemorate Fokir—other contemporary fictions posit less clean outcomes.

They also include more violent encounters of the dead, dying, and spectral with living creatures whose survival at the fringes of marginalized human communities hinges on shared human-animal, place-based cultural knowledges that in turn have been shaped by histories of genocide and extinction.

Central to two novels about peoples and animals on and in the Pacific Ocean are scenes in which Indigenous men botch a traditional and controversial execution of a cetacean. In both stories, minor characters raise objections because whales and dolphins are "metaphysical" creatures in need of saving, voicing the predominant Eurowestern-industrial vision newly produced by "holistic popular ecology, quasi-mystical and highly speculative neuroscience, and popular culture."[9] Ancient, local knowledges of species interdependence are also explicitly imperiled in these killing scenes and secured only through their tentative contacts with animist gods as seen through the flickering perspectives of the Indigenous peoples' deceased relatives. As both immaterial specters and the stuff of history—things with a distinctly disembodied presence—the long-gone ancestors become uniquely useful to the narratives by nature of the responses they inspire among the living. Sustaining a sense of continuity beyond the ordinary limits of life, the range of their figurations calls attention to the possibilities for fiction itself to form the response that is the thing that makes the dead useful to sustaining social life among endangered groups in severely depleted land- and seascapes.

In Linda Hogan's *People of the Whale: A Novel* (2008), a Native American teenager named Marco tries to stop a neotraditional shore whale hunt when their quarry, a young whale, communicates with him. His failure costs both of their lives, to the horror of spectators, natural and supernatural alike. Elements of this deeply disturbing scene echo another in Robert Barclay's *Meḷaḷ: A Novel of the Pacific* (2002), in which the Indigenous Marshallese father of two young boys kills a dolphin, only here the otherworldly creatures around them take a more active role to protect the boys' lives. In both, people and sea creatures come to some shared understandings across super/natural lines in places where they and their kind share histories that include enduring colonial exploitation. Facing what anthropologist Deborah Bird Rose calls a "double death," as individual representatives of threatened populations and as interdependent members of multispecies communities,[10] their meetings conjure the powers of their belief systems through the dead, who intervene as active presences within these scenes, enabling different possible endings.

Significantly, the animals are killed through shore-based practices modeled after traditional forms of "fishery" that once centered on marine mammals. The choice of species enables further interrogations of how such practices become haunted by the twin specters of cultural and species extinction. Both stories leverage from the late twentieth-century "cetacean turn" that associates conservation of these creatures with a political platform of "non-aggression, protection of the environment, respect for indigeneity, [and] harmonious co-existence,"[11] a still more contemporary shift toward a "postcolonial cetacean turn"[12] that extends respect for certain nonhuman species to include peoples who share their ecosystems and attendant threats to their livelihoods. But that shift is also problematized in these cases by the uncertain conservation status of the animals who are killed. Both Hogan and Barclay intensify these aspects further by depicting the killings as botched, the killers as acting up against social injustice, and their life-and-death struggles as taking place on their own ancestral shores, in the presence of ancestors, and amid severely depleted fish stocks.

The killing shores in turn emerge as exceptionally storied places, in Bird Rose and Thom van Dooren's sense of the term, "in which animals, sites, and stories all shape, and are shaped by, entangled and circulating patterns of intra-action" that are relationally constituted.[13] Importantly, intra-actions are not restricted to the world of the living. Hogan and Barclay present Indigenous world views that conflate cultural, natural, and supernatural—all together, multinatural[14]—intra-actions, in order to capture the potentials of an ecology shaped by sensation, valuation, and contestation. As multinatural entities who imbue these scenes with a precontact sense of propriety and who provide justification moving forward to act in accordance with place-based Indigenous knowledges, the dead relatives might be understood through Vinciane Despret's concept of *les morts utiles*—literally, the useful dead—by which she means those who "expire then inspire" the living, whom they never simply leave behind.

Despret's concern is with not fictional but actual experiences of people perceiving the dead in their daily lives, so she rightly cautions against romanticizing representations of Indigenous people as figures of the dead. The "last one" trope is, after all, one of the most powerful representational strategies of erasure, all too often enlisted to naturalize genocides and other atrocities.[15] But what makes these stories so effective in decolonizing uses of the dead are their integrations of them within multinatural spectrums that string together lives, deaths, and ways of knowing the living together with the dead. They posit multiple kinds of immortal and magical alongside more ordinary beings as involved in the shaping of events that neither point Native peoples back to the "good old" ways nor bog them down in colonial legacies. They instead model precise adaptations of older, relational, and sometimes shared senses of non/human agency.

Killing Cetaceans

People of the Whale and *Meḻaḻ* not only imagine Indigenous people as criticized by outsiders for setting out to kill members of species that are their traditional prey but also present killing processes in ways that are botched. Thinking back to Steve Baker's argument about contemporary art aesthetics, botched-ness and other signs of imperfection in what often appear to be revoltingly messed-up images of nonhuman life and death are understood not as signs of artistic failure so much as deliberate signpostings of the limits of animal representation.[16] While the presence of actual animals and the orchestrations of their killing for art remain controversial (in some infamous examples, artists kill or direct the killing of animals), novelistic slaughter scenes that are deliberately staged as going awry create distance for contemplation and so may be more effective at inviting empathy,[17] if not also discomfort, with judging what is right or wrong. Drawing awareness to what makes these interactions so powerful in their very gone-wrongedness therefore could be seen as a subtle but effective strategy to engage larger questions about intersecting experiences of oppression across species lines. More is at stake than just the mortality and other vulnerabilities of individuals in stories that concern threatened futures of cultures and species, so a main concern of my discussion here is to what degree these stories promote decolonizing as imbricate with environmentally friendly visions—in other words, multinatural justice.

That makes it important to recognize up front that the two novels could not be any more different in their imaginings of the killing scenes. Loosely based on a historical incident—namely, the Makah tribe's controversial resumption of whaling in the US state of Washington in 1999—*People of the Whale* depicts a melee, with dozens of North American Indian tribesmen shooting and stabbing a young animal blindly at sea, in broad daylight, and at the center of a media circus. Exercising what some of them assert is their treaty right to kill whales, the hunters from the fictional A'atsika tribe are portrayed as spurred by conflicting motivations: greed for the cash surreptitiously offered to some by multinational whaling corporations; interest among others in the revival of a community impoverished by the destruction of whale, salmon, and other species that were their historical mainstays; even just desires to party with the boys. (It is a mad scene.) And they are watched by an equally broad range of detractors, some alive and some long dead.

The most traditional traditionalists, "the old women in dresses of red with woven grass earrings and hats and shells," stand onshore as their living female counterparts would have done during a traditional whale hunt.[18] Shades of a deeper past, these gals remain silent and perplexingly "unseen."[19] And they are drawn in parallel with another set of apparitions, the shadowy Mysterious Ones, described ambiguously as "old people" who live "on the other side of the water" in shell-and-whalebone houses that were long ago buried by mudslides but then revealed by storm tides in the course of the story, like the centuries-old Ozette archaeological site recorded as lost to a mudslide in Makah oral history and recently unearthed. Becoming visible exclusively to particular Native characters, the Mysterious Ones stand ashore alongside the others, offering a play-by-play narration of how the hunt goes all wrong and proving influential in other ways as well.

They have taught A'atsika teenager Marco to communicate with whales, so he recognizes that the hunters' chosen quarry is inappropriate to a traditional hunt: "Marco felt its presence first, heard the deep rumbling sound of the whale. . . . 'It's young. It's not the right one to hunt. It is friendly. It just wants to see us. We are its relatives.'"[20] Like his father, Thomas, Marco has elected to participate in the controversial resumption of whale hunting, joining his tribesmen in one of the old-fashioned cedar canoes because he believes it will catalyze a renewal of A'atsika lifeways. But because everyone else disregards the Mysterious Ones' teachings, the hunt devolves into a disorderly bloodbath in which the young whale is killed and the killing becomes a screen for the ultimate silencing of Marco. The young man may be too good to be true to some readers, and the novel hints at his status as no mere mortal but a "transformational being" or supernatural creature who is neither impersonal nor universal but eminently personal in dealings with individual humans.[21] Only within the story, his living and dead kin mourn his loss as a mortal human, a "promising young man, a new traditional."[22] The bulk of the story concerns how his parents make amends to the gods and whales through the help of their ancestors, the Mysterious Ones.

In contrast, in the cetacean-slaughter scene of *Meḷaḷ*, the killer, Rujen, acts alone, under cover of night, and in response to a deeply personal sense of political awakening to his situation as a Native and colonized Marshall Islander. The novel's most poignant absent presence is Iia, Rujen's long-dead wife and mother to their two children, who is depicted as one of thousands of Marshallese directly exposed to radioactive fallout as part of a process in which the US military contaminated, blasted, and in some places even entirely vaporized their island and marine environments.[23] It is set in 1981, near the end of US occupation, which entailed fifteen years of nuclear testing on and around the now-uninhabited Enewetak, Rongelap, and Bikini Atolls, which included the detonation of sixty-seven atomic and hydrogen thermonuclear bombs, with an estimated combined impact of seven thousand Hiroshima bombs.[24] Her untimely death from related illness has left Rujen a single father to their two young sons before the novel's start.

In an uncharacteristically rebellious moment, fully aware that he is in violation of one of the many US ordinances designed to discredit and disrupt his people's traditions, Rujen methodically kills a mature dolphin who appears to be sick or dying at the crux of the story. The act is immediately witnessed only by the animal's mate, who has likewise been dumped by their US-mainlander would-be saviors in a decrepit turtle pond on the whites-only island of Kwajalein. Confiscating the animals earlier from two other Marshallese men—who, like Rujen, recognize in the dolphins a traditional offering from the sea that can be refused only at one's peril—the white people's plan is to return the cetaceans to the open ocean, only with no thought as to why the animals have already made the laborious, dangerous effort to swim ashore. In butchering the sick one and releasing the other, Rujen prepares to share the gift of meat with his people, reasserting old local lifeways developed across millennia on their shorelines, and along the way comes to peace with his sons and his own dead father.

Again the absence of the old procedures makes for a mess. Ill-equipped to be ceremonious, Rujen does the killing surreptitiously, alone in the darkness of the park after nightfall. He is armed only with a barely adequate knife that features a novelty fish-shaped handle. To transport the meat, he uses plastic shopping bags that trail blood, which also soaks into his clothes, all details that derail any sense of the killing itself as anything but a brutal spectacle. That said, other elements of the novel clarify that through this act, Rujen renews a sense of connection and traditional obligation to his relatives, both dead and alive.

Instead of writing in supernatural beings as direct witnesses, the run-up to the killing scene here is intercut with a sequence in which Rujen's sons, Jebro and Nuke, are lost at sea, their boat sunk by white boys playing a prank, and saved only through the intervention of an *ak*, a great or lesser frigate bird (*Fregata minor* or *ariel*, the novel does not specify), whom the older boy recognizes as an *ekjab*, or ghostly manifestation, that he takes to be their dead grandfather. Unbeknownst to the increasingly desperate boys, the trickster god Etao and the magical dwarf Noniep are also watching as ravenous demons close in on the fast-weakening younger brother, Nuke, and only decide to stop because "to take his soul requires [that the demon] destroy the ekjab first, and to do so might attract others of his kin whom [the demon] prefers remain as dormant, as powerless, as they have been for such a long . . . time."[25] Their guard let down, the demons then are vanquished through the intervention of the old trickster god Etao. The scene balances a modern sense of the insignificance of individual human life with a much older sensibility of the interdependence of human with nonhuman worlds.[26]

Marshallese cosmology enters as an alternate ontological framework to necropolitical colonial legacies, one that allows the boys to perceive the ekjab as such,[27] and more. Within the world of the living, Nuke's death is explained as averted through the guilty conscience of one of the white boys responsible for sinking Rujen's boat. With no clue that the ak is an ekjab, the guilty boy spots them in the nick of time because he recognizes the frigate bird as acting highly unusually, hovering over the same spot. Although more like *The Hungry Tide* than *People of the Whale* in terms of keeping the gods invisible to live humans, the novel carefully plots a range of human non/perceptions of multinatural worlds that likewise complicate ideas about people taking cetacean life.

That the killings of marine mammals are staged as spectacularly botched, albeit in different ways, moreover underscores the impossibility of returning to the old ways, a point that is not lost on the principal players. Wondering whether his generation could relearn how to make and operate traditional seagoing fishing canoes, Jebro concedes, "Marshallese can never live like in the past,"[28] a sentiment developed more explicitly by Marco's father, Thomas, who ultimately and actively embraces anachronism. Finding a sort of redemption in following his dead son's lead in studying with the Mysterious Ones, Thomas exhorts his fellow A'atsika to join other First Nations in making and sailing old-fashioned cedar whaling canoes "to strengthen ourselves, not to kill a whale."[29] Both characters come to recognize that the same forces endangering their own cultures threaten members of other species where together they once flourished. Understanding how both novels somehow conclude with a sense of hope requires closer examination of their ways of extending story traditions that align hunters, hunted, and other creatures as native to particular shores, as well as those in which the dead become useful in securing these alignments.

Sharing Shores

The prominent signs of extreme poverty that mark the homes of Indigenous characters in these novels serve as reminders that the edges of seas are home to not only most people worldwide but also the most vulnerable people. Storms and tsunamis have always happened, but with rising sea levels becoming the most widely recognized marker of anthropogenic climate change, coastal zones have become places of endangerment as never before for the world's poor. Whereas Ghosh's concluding superstorm sequence, which costs Fokir his life, historicizes the threat in a way that is appropriate to the Sundarbans, Hogan and Barclay turn the focus from epochal weather events to slower but no less deadly processes disproportionately affecting Native seafaring peoples and the animals on whom they traditionally depended for their livelihoods.

Attempting to correct for an overwhelmingly terrestrial bias, proponents of oceanic studies are quick to note that conventional literary approaches to the sea as metaphor risk distorting the unique epistemological structures drawn from seafaring life.[30] Starting from the plural materialities of water more generally,[31] an appropriately fluid and dynamic thalassology attends to the sea as a place "continually being reconstituted" by various forces, including "the non-human and the human, the biological and the geophysical, the historic and the contemporary."[32] Such perspectives help explain the significances of Barclay's and Hogan's settings as the traditional coastal homes of Indigenous Pacific communities that, in contrast to Eurowestern views of time as the significant narrative factor, privilege spatial relations as anchoring stories.[33]

People of the Whale's main setting, the A'atsika village Dark River, appears to be located within a region known as the Cascadia Subduction Zone. The region attracted the attention of archaeologists, geologists, and others when it became established that it was an old earthquake hot spot based on a representational pattern, across every one of the tribes in the region, depicting seas overwashing homes. In their cosmologies, Whale, Thunderbird, and mountain dwarves

variously cause the earth to shift catastrophically in tales through which people
teach each other to make long cedar ropes with which to bind their canoes
to trees and stones in order to survive the tsunamis that have followed major
seismic shifts. Colonial histories maintain a fragmentary record of such folklore, but following the 2004 Indian Ocean tsunami, a similar oral tradition is
among the factors credited with keeping the Indonesian death toll to seven
on the island of Simculue, whereas two hundred thousand perished in nearby
Banda Aceh.[34] So much more than historical records, Pacific Northwestern
First Peoples' oral traditions reveal "how indigenous people make sense of the
unpredictable destructive natural forces in their landscape" and consequently
cultivate a sense of resilience amid coastal dangers through storytelling.[35] Such
an understanding hinges on the continuity of the cosmological as social presences that lends whales a particular narrative power among whaling peoples.

Hogan's fictional tribespeople likewise have learned from the old storytellers to prepare for the tsunami, drought, and deluge that come on the heels of
the botched whale hunt and cause the temporary disappearance of the salmon
that are the community's main source of income. As one of the Mysterious Ones
observes, "A wrong thing was done. Maybe more than one wrong thing"[36]—a
phrasing that quietly refuses to prioritize Marco's or the young whale's deaths,
neither animal nor cultural politics—as a consequence of which the gods must
take revenge. To make amends, Marco's mother, Ruth, follows their advice and
temporarily relinquishes her commercial salmon fishing boat to the Rain Priest,
who appears at various points in the story in human or octopus form. Weaving the
dead whale's story into human, hydrogeological, and immortal narratives,
the novel adapts old traditions to make productive engagements with the ongoing history of Indigenous shore whaling.

In *Meḷaḷ*, environmental catastrophe is the stuff of more recent memories, and resilience is promoted through even more direct adaptations of
ancient multinatural knowledges in the context of colonial histories. In the
Marshall Islands—subjected to an explosive yield equivalent to 1.5 Hiroshima
bombs detonated every day for twelve years and infamously dubbed "by far
the most contaminated place in the world"[37]—there is an even more direct line of
storytelling to account for multinatural disasters. Throughout Marshallese
mythology, the old trickster god Etao (also known as Letao) provides for people
but also causes great suffering.[38] Echoing the problems faced by Hogan's earlier
fictions, debates among literary critics about whether Barclay's invocation of
this and other figures from Marshallese mythology enables an apologetic[39] or

critical[40] view of US involvement in the island nation's history hinge on perceptions of whether and how to conceive of continuities in folklore and fiction beyond the framework of cultural appropriation. "Many in the Marshall Islands now view their US patron as a latter-day Etao"[41]—an often-told tale today casts the trickster as a consultant to the US government, incorporating while subverting empowerment of the United States through assimilation to Marshallese heritage—and these developments reveal how applying strategic know-how in order to make the most of fate remains highly valued in Marshallese culture.[42] *Meḷaḷ* might therefore be seen as extending this ongoing narrative evolution by representing Etao as becoming enamored of "a place where many mysterious things were happening at an incredibly fast pace"[43]—namely, the US mainland—and returning with atomic weapons to use against demons bent on destroying Rujen's people.

Infusing traditional practice with colonial troubles, in Barclay's novel, Etao disappears from his homeland following a typical trickster incident in which he convinces a greedy tribal chief to cook himself in place of the more typical dolphin roasted in a pit, Etao's reveal of which coincides with the arrival of "demons" in conquistadores' clothing, saying, "Espanya . . . espanya."[44] The novel thus places Etao at the primal scene of a complex colonial history in which colonial Spaniards preceded Germans, who were then replaced by Japanese and finally US nationals as militarizers of the Marshall Islands. In the novel, hundreds of years pass before Etao returns to his home shores on Rujen's fateful day—sporting US basketball star Kareem Abdul-Jabbar's jersey and flinging missiles in the sky while calling, "Skyhook!" (the sport star's signature shot)—to the terror of the otherwise menacingly powerful demons. Telling stories of practices of storytelling, these aspects of the novels show how tribal peoples remain attached to their shores while adapting to and accounting for historical changes. In other words, they engage in ongoing processes of making them multinaturally storied places, notably in resistance to the necropolitical deathworlds that preclude such capacities.

To this process, the deaths of the dolphin and whale as symbols of dying species threaten a radical rupture. Once viewed as windfalls of meat, bone, and other materials helpful to subsistence living, as well as animals to whom people owed obligations in hunter-gatherer societies,[45] cetaceans disappeared in the era of industrial-scale offshore whaling and with the implementation of modern techniques like purse-seine fishing, which in the first few years alone killed tens of thousands of dolphins as bycatch. Food insecurity also factors directly into ongoing issues with hunting and fishing regulations following the illegal postwar US expansion of its own territories into what until then had been understood to be the ocean commons.[46] Because slaughtered cetaceans have become highly politically charged representatives of a threatened class of being, if not the ultimate poster children for environmental conservation, these stories of peoples historically and culturally closest to the consequences must negotiate an ethics of killing that shores up the needs of the living with relations to the dead.

They do so in part by depicting landscapes and peoples alike as diminished by the losses of animals and lifeways shared with them. In Hogan's novel, whales no longer visit the "old rubbing beach," where they used to go ashore to "rub their backs into sand and stone, to scratch and remove the barnacles," and where people watched "with awe and laughter."[47] In Barclay's story, the old pleasures are displaced by demonic influences, according to the magical dwarf:

Ņoniep, the last of the little jungle people whose laughter once tickled the ears of Marshallese children and whose charms once seduced women who wandered the jungle alone, dreams of a legion of demons long since thick on Ebeye [the island where Rujen lives] . . . feverishly intent . . . on wringing death from life, on replacing everything pure and natural with stinking rot and ruin, a living death, life inside-out. . . . [Nonetheless, Ņoniep also] dreams of a plan, a hope, a small and unrealistic chance of stopping what looms like a monstrous wave risen to a precarious height.[48]

Such descriptions clarify that the consequences of displacements from traditional shores are material as well as aesthetic, because in them, peoples' ways of living are imbricate not just with spaces shared by other species but, more important, with their perceptions of the world. Ņoniep's death foregrounds how the lives and deaths of logical and cosmological creatures alike are at stake. His return after death, like Thomas's, enables closer and more explicit connections between super/natural entities. Ecocritic Elizabeth DeLoughrey sees the presence of ancestors especially in contemporary Maori fictions as signifying "hope that a multispecies community of the waters is not beyond human reach,"[49] and I would add that even more is at stake in Hogan's and Barclay's novels, which reframe the human as inseparable from communities that are at once both multispecies and multinatural.

Digging deeper into the similarities between the novels reveals how attachments to particular shores and their colonial legacies shape the fraught journeys of the main male protagonists toward becoming cetacean killers. Fishing practices and literatures alike notoriously concern constructions of masculinity,[50] and the absence of significant female human characters from *Meļaļ* alone makes it risk extending this dubious tradition. But intersecting oppressions offer other explanations for the absence of women.

A frontline victim of "nuclear colonization,"[51] Rujen's wife Iia's backstory clarifies that, having been evacuated from the Bikini Atoll directly into the line of fallout, she died following a series of miscarriages of grotesquely deformed fetuses, the newly normal postwar occurrence that Marshallese call "jellyfish babies."[52] Iia's personalizing her shame about these birth defects leads to the multiplied traumas crystallized in Rujen's memories of her burying her several, spontaneously aborted, deformed fetuses alone at night. Lauren Berlant's notion of "slow death," which refers to "the physical wearing out of a population and the deterioration of people in that population that is very nearly a defining condition of their experience and historical existence," helps elaborate the multilayered sufferings that converge in these characters; in their love story, the acts of ordinary "life building and the attrition of human life are indistinguishable."[53]

Also, in both texts, fishing and hunting are not imagined as restorative to a sense of wounded masculinity. While neither man claims ill will toward any animal, each becomes a cetacean killer after having grown up in impoverished Indigenous shoreline communities and becoming a young widower. Moreover, the mothers of their children die as a result of violence enacted by US military interventions that are shown also to sicken or kill still more people and other animals in their surrounding communities. The horrors that they personally endure become difficult to separate from the tribal, national, species, and environmental histories endemic to the places to which they feel the strongest sense of spiritual, familial, and communal connections.

The stories clarify how settler colonialism is present not simply through memories of past events but, more important, as a structure, perhaps most obviously through failed infrastructures. The opening sequence of *Meļaļ* introduces Rujen attempting to manage the raw sewage that is backing up into his kitchen sink, explained as a common occurrence on the island of Ebeye, which is described as "more filthy and crowded than almost any other place on earth" and so becoming the titular "Meļaļ," or "playground of demons."[54] The end sees Rujen limping home with burst blisters in borrowed boots and torn clothes that are "soaked in blood mostly not his own" as well as rancid chum, the latter from a prank pulled on him by white kids. He is attempting to return home for the

night from Kwajalein, where as a Marshallese he has long worked as a menial   83
worker at a high-functioning sewage plant yet gets ticketed for trespassing when
caught on the island after working hours. From beginning to end, Rujen's sufferings paint a vivid picture of the degradation of colonized people.

As the only one of them with a job on the whites-only island, Rujen is the
sole supporter of his extended family following the passing of his wife and,
along with her demise, the end of a series of payouts that she received from
the US government. In need of a means of supporting their children—and in
glaring contrast to his deceased father, Ataji, an old-school islander who had
protested all the US-imposed rules—Rujen tries to play it safe for a paycheck,
turning the other cheek to everyday racism and other humiliations on the job.
At least, he does so until the day in which the novel takes place, when his dead
father's spirit appears to return again in the form of a frigate bird and other
magical creatures also appear to intervene around the sequence in which Rujen
kills the dolphin.

In *People of the Whale*, the same sense of slow violence adds a collective
dimension to the apparent post-traumatic-stress behavior of the whale's killer,
Thomas, who returns home to the A'atsika reservation long after disappearing
from military service during the Vietnam War. Deeply disillusioned during his
active duty by racist white fellow soldiers who taunt him for looking too much
like "one of them," Thomas mutinies, then "goes native," so to speak, fathering a
daughter with a local woman vaguely identified as tribal, possibly Hmong, and
living as her husband and passing as one of their tribe members. After the war,
she is killed by a leftover land mine, and Thomas is forcibly repatriated by the US
military. Alone by choice for many years afterward, having abandoned his first
wife, Ruth, and their son, Marco, at home and his daughter, Lin, abroad, the
news of his tribe's proposed resumption of whale hunting offers what he initially
sees as a chance at much-needed personal along with community restoration.[55]

Giving the lie to the traditional views of fishing as spiritually restorative,[56]
never mind the hunting-as-healing-for-veterans schemes presently proliferat-
ing in the United States, the excitement of an approaching whale only triggers a
dangerous flashback for Thomas, who defaults into soldier-survivalist mode and
repeatedly fires his automatic weapon at the animal, starting the fracas during
which Marco is killed along with the whale. Initially, Thomas thinks that joining
the hunt will enable him to reconnect with and reinvigorate his downtrodden
tribal community, only to despair afterward upon discovery that his fellow hunters refuse to apologize, sing, or pray to the dead whale—and worse: "He realized

that they didn't even believe in the lives of their ancestors, that it was as if those old ones, the ones whose presence he often felt, were only stories to them. Maybe they'd lost all feeling because they'd had to in order to survive in a place where kids shot guns, killed dogs, and died of alcohol poisoning, but he'd hoped this would be something different than just a killing, that it would mean something for them, that it would do something for them."[57] In contrast to Marco—who becomes more like Ghosh's Fokir as his story veers toward that of the "ecological Indian," the essentializing fantasy of precontact Natives living in perfect harmony with nature,[58] before culminating in his similarly violent, abrupt, and total removal from the scene (Marco's body is never even recovered)—Thomas asserts that separation and elevation of old from new ways is not an option, that lives and deaths are messily entangled in pasts and presents involving stories that bring back the dead as active presences shaping futures.

Rujen likewise is presented as compelled by larger forces to kill a ceta-cean in equally messy circumstances, again with no sense of malice toward the animal. Dolphins mean nothing to him, and he doesn't even like dolphin meat, he says on a number of occasions, but news of the pair of dolphins caught in the lagoon then confiscated by white authorities from two Marshallese men prompts him to explain to his horrified white US-mainlander coworkers that Marshallese custom dictates that a landward-bound dolphin is a gift from the sea and therefore must be killed and eaten. Later, seemingly inexplicably drawn to where the animals are being held captive in a decrepit public-park pond, Rujen recognizes what all the white people around him cannot—namely, that one dolphin is sick, likely dying, and kept going only by the other.

Confronted later in church by a white acquaintance mounting a "Save the Dolphins" campaign, Rujen comes to realize that he is now being seen not as he sees himself, as a Catholic among fellow parishioners, but as one of "the hated dolphin eaters who did not belong" by still more white US-mainlanders, all of whom, he starts to realize, always seem "to get their way."[59] Huggan and Tiffin read the scene as ambivalent: "The Americans see only animal abuse, Rujen only environmental racism, [and] . . . both are right in their own way, [because] cultural beliefs are not necessarily incompatible."[60] Yet the confron-tation spurs an affective conversion in the Marshallese man that both reflects a growing political awareness[61] and deeply connects the fates of the dolphins and his family members, both dead and alive.

Just as Hogan's Thomas suggests, losing connection to dead ancestors can be fatal. In church on Good Friday, the devoutly Catholic Rujen's recognition

of the racist hostility directed toward him is followed by a feeling of the presence of demons that the novel reveal to be closing in on his sons through an
enriched super/natural vision of reality that is more sketchy than Hogan's, one
in which the gods and the dead can see the living but the living barely, if at all,
sense the others' presence. Although Rujen, like Jebro, is one of the few living
humans who seem capable of doing so, his Catholic faith seems to cloud these
judgments. Only when he inadvertently causes the church's crucifix to come
crashing down, nearly killing himself, does Rujen imagine Jesus Christ with
Marshallese features, a vision that sends him running back to work to get the fish
knife to perform a task that will enable him "to redeem his soul and be true to
himself, his people"[62]—namely, the killing of the sick dolphin.

There is no evidence that Rujen experiences the kind of spiritual connection to the dolphin that Marco enjoys, however briefly, with the whale. Instead,
reduced to a stinking, bloody, limping mess, he has lost faith in his religion and
the respect of his religious community. What he gains is a greater sense of
appreciation for his dead father, for himself through upholding the old ways,
and for the integrity of a Marshallese sense of community that he extends
through sharing the dolphin meat with his kids and other kin.

Free at last from the sway of settler-colonialist religious doctrine, Rujen's
use of old animal practices to create new ways of overcoming the pressures
of assimilation, environmental racism, and other modern ills intersects with
similar efforts by Ṇoniep and even Etao. While Rujen, in the mortal world,
does the only thing that "make[s] sense" to him—that is, dealing with the
dolphins in accordance with the customs of his people—the ghost and soul
of Ṇoniep, who by this point has committed suicide after chanting all of his
knowledges into an ancient breadfruit tree, becomes overwhelmed while using
old magic to try to exorcise the demons polluting and tormenting the people
of Ebeye, whom he, now in spirit form, can see gathered at the dump, haunted
by the ghosts of their own lost children. Saving the day at the last minute, the
trickster god Etao vanquishes the demons, but his divine intervention makes
Ṇoniep only more committed to helping the lost souls, particularly the ghosts
of jellyfish babies, whom he takes away in his spirit canoe. While helped in
the process by whales, whose souls he pairs with human ones so that "over
time, with love, [the dead babies] might stop their squalling and maybe even
learn to sing,"[63] Ṇoniep is passed by the now-ghost dolphin, who refuses his
invitation to join them and elects instead to swim away, accompanied by
her still-living partner. Although ambivalent, the super/natural relations at

the end are bridging species divides along with ir/rational limits, following instead logics of love.

Although finding no redemption in the act of killing itself, Thomas, like Rujen, is watched and later guided into community leadership by a multinatural range of beings. Initially sent into an emotional tailspin by his son's death and fellow hunters' disregard for old conventions of the hunt, as part of his recovery, Thomas hones the traditional skills of old A'atsika whalers like his grandfather Witka, such as paddling unwieldy cedar canoes and holding his breath for long periods underwater, aided as was Marco by the shadowy old people. When he is later killed in the canoe by the same jealous war buddy who killed Marco, the Mysterious Ones receive his body from the Rain Priest and use magic to revive him. Whether this proves, as Thomas believes, that he cannot die or it transforms him into one of the Mysterious Ones is not a question to which the novel offers any clear answers. Instead, these interactions bring the story to an Indigenous-initiated movement for justice, here involving the prosecution of Thomas's sometime war buddy for the killing of Marco and for financially defrauding his tribe in profiting from the whale's meat. At the very end of the novel, Ruth and the by-then un/dead Thomas are reconciled, restoring a long-lost love that extends to Ruth's caring for Lin as kin and thus providing her an entrée to her tribal inheritance with the A'atsika.

Just as in Hogan's *Power*, in both texts, there is a sense that justice requires engagement with an alternate metaphysics that exceeds Eurowestern norms, one in which humans and nonhumans, dead and living, supernatural and culturally subjugated, cannot be separated. Liking animals—or liking to kill them—is not the issue. Killing cetaceans (and for that matter, people) is not presented as economically necessary or as environmentally viable but rather as a site of botched relations specific to coastal communities, a powerfully con-tested shoring up of traditions on specific shorelines. Getting there requires the narratives to show how the dead become useful to address past grievances and model better futures.

What the consequences will be for contemporary youngsters born of these shores is the question at the heart of the fictions. Well-schooled to fishing for all sorts of sea creatures by his grandfather Ataji, Jebro does "not doubt his elders when they boasted of Marshallese as at one time the greatest fishermen and navigators of the world,"[64] yet he is ashamed of the fact that most can no longer afford boats with which to fish and that they have fished out their few areas of onshore access. On other islands like Ailinglaplap, it remains possible to sell locally caught fish at less than a quarter of the price of imported canned tuna, and cheaper still than frozen fish sold in the supermarket, but this option no longer exists on Ebeye, where most Marshallese live.

Another powerfully absent presence, Marco's great-grandfather Witka, "the last of a line of traditional men who loved and visited the whales to ensure a good whale hunt," possessed "knowledge of the ocean so great that scientists came to question him."[65] Yet when his grandson, great-grandson, and other tribesmen attempt to resume the hunt, "no one . . . even remembers the taste of whale meat," their tribe having abandoned traditional practices when the animals were fished out generations earlier. Again, A'atsika history shadows that of the Makah, for whom, in the post-Reconstruction United States, came significant "alteration in the social structure that whaling had depended on and reinforced, as well as the steady depletion of whale populations due to European and American commercial hunting, [all of which] led the Makah to gradually cease whaling by the 1920s."[66] The precarious sense of shared human-animal pasts relies on locating continuities within and between communities, those here and those of the hereafter. So the dead come to be seen as more purposefully shadowing the living, moving along with the creatures of their belief systems. Significantly, they are not drawn as figures of the past—or rather (to paraphrase William Faulkner), they are drawn in a past that is not past yet.

A danger permeating both novels is the eclipsing of a sense of history by consumer society's perpetuation of attunement to the present. Lending greater significance to Etao's basketball jersey, a playful way in which both novels show how the otherwise otherworldly creatures are depicted as no more free from corrupting influences than the living is through references to their interactions with familiar US brand-named products. "No one sees . . . the earlier people, the Mysterious Ones . . . now except as a memory made of words" in Hogan's novel, but when Ruth visits, they serve her Girl Scout cookies, because "every single creature loves these."[67] Barclay's Noniep chants away demons, even becomes invisible to Rujen's boys visiting his island, but can't avoid being bonked on the head by a crushed Pepsi can that Nuke carelessly tosses into the forest. Funny incongruities unto themselves, such details undermine any sense that the dead or the magical are more pure, innocent, or otherwise transcending ordinary life. Instead, mutual contamination becomes a shared condition across the multinatural perspectives of non/human animals, gods, and at least some of the dead—as much a condition of their present as their futures.

So what are the fictional cetaceans killed for? A better question is this: What special value does the attempt at a traditional slaughter of members of these particular species bring to narratives that connect biological to cultural devastation? Shock value is an obvious answer whenever animals are shown dying at the hands of humans, but like so much contemporary visual art with animals,[68] the verbal distancing from actual events leveraged by the literary often bears greater scrutiny, particularly when engaged with broader representational histories and current cultural debates. Animal narratives are first and foremost crafted objects, involving lives of a different order passed through human filters, and as such often say more than their authors, audiences, and zeitgeists even know, an aspect that makes them both alluring and troubling.

The inclusion of ghosts and local gods as active presences in these stories indicates that there is something more significant than sensationalism involved in contemporary representations of whale and dolphin slaughters in fiction, something that is connected to the disruptions on a massive scale of particular kinds of humans, animals, and their shared lifeways. Teasing out further the several, subtle, interrelated similarities in Hogan's and Barclay's visions of cetacean slaughter clarifies how the dead whale and dolphin serve as more than mere spectacle.

First and foremost, the scenes are not about the killing of just any animals but explicitly about the traditional slaughter of marine mammals gone horribly awry. Marco disappears under the waves in the melee, and his father is left feeling responsible for his death. Rujen is battered, bloodied, fined, and otherwise humiliated for the trouble he takes to kill the one and release the other dolphin. The animal victims, both wild creatures who are presented and perceived as sentient within the text, suffer painful deaths, in part due to the lost knowledges and tools of local customs, albeit very different ones.

The killers are identified as members of Indigenous communities historically colonized by the United States and enduring poverty, un- or under-employment, violence, and other threats that all too often are representative of current conditions. Rujen is a Native Marshallese, while the killers of the whale are all members of the fictional A'atsika tribe. All are underdogs with complex motives, not cardboard-cutout villains.

Less clearly, the cetaceans are members of species whose statuses are in question. The gray whales (*Eschrichtius robustus*) swimming through Hogan's novel are among the few kinds of cetacean who have made a robust recovery following the moratorium on whaling imposed by the International Whaling Commission (IWC). But no one is sure if the more vulnerable coastal-dwelling populations constitute a separate or a subspecies, which is why in real life, the IWC and the US government initially allowed and have since suspended Makah whaling in the 1990s, the events upon which Hogan's novel are loosely based. Spinner dolphins (*Stenella longirostis*) and Fraser's dolphins (*Lagenodelphis hosei*), the two kinds of *Delphinidae* native to the Marshall Islands that plausibly could be the species captured in *Meḷaḷ*, are listed by the International Union for the Conservation of Nature respectively as lower risk / conservation dependent and data deficient, so it is unclear whether they too are endangered. The novels do not say any of this but leave it to readers to bring this knowledge to the stories.

What is far more obvious is that both tales are staged amid polluted landscapes and seascapes. The lingering human tolls of radiation are made evident not only in Rujen's family medical history but also in their forced relocation to an overcrowded island, Ebeye, actually the most densely crowded of all Pacific islands, with approximately fifteen thousand people living on one-tenth of a square mile[69] and an infrastructure that is realistically portrayed as spectacularly failing throughout the novel. From the raw sewage backing up into the drains at the start through the rag-clad kids playing on a garbage-encrusted beach at the end, the failure of the United States to deliver on its promises of a good life in return for destroying Marshallese culture and environments is impossible to miss.

Thomas's fragmented family—including not only Marco, raised in his absence by Ruth and her parents, but also his second child, Lin, whom he effectively orphans when he is evacuated from Cambodia—are casualties of his personal failings, yet none of this can be understood outside the longer history of US imperialism. Their lives were irrevocably diminished before he was born with the collapse of the Northwest fisheries following not only the near-extinction of whales but also the destruction of various species of salmon (*Oncorhynchus*), populations blocked from spawning migrations by the construction of the Grand Coulee Dam—another curious omission from the novel—and the devastation this caused for Native American peoples, who were consequently flooded out of their ancestral homelands and waterways. In short, the stories start with central characters in necropolitical limbo after the horrific devastation of their Indigenous communities following US colonization and its long-term, ongoing impacts on land and sea, but they do not end there. Instead, they work to situate immediate culture clashes over rights and obligations to cetaceans amid deeply interconnected histories of human, animal, and environmental devastation as well as spiritual connections to dead and immortal beings.

Read in the context of colonial histories, the killings raise larger questions about the operations of literary representation. How might the animals, people, and others read as dead in these scenes become useful—that is, how do readers come to see them as more literally and actively engaging imaginations in the world of the living? What if readings of these deaths were opened out from, say, an interpretive play with metaphorical meanings and into a more dynamic encounter with the possibilities for the dead to continue to act in and upon the living? What is more, what if that wrong or wronged-thinginiess of those rendered dead is not simply represented by the text but instead precisely what makes fiction work as a tool of intervention?

The last question is this: What makes the stories' structural turnabout away from the hunter's viewpoint—which has until recent decades been the predominant perspective across millennia of human-cetacean relations[70]—itself another innovative aspect of the depiction of deceased ancestors and gods acting together with living people and animals in Hogan's and Barclay's fictions? Their depictions of Indigenous hunters' whale and dolphin killings reveal more than just people purposefully killing the animals for food. These characters are presented in direct defiance of those who tell them in no uncertain terms that such slaughter is abhorrent, backward, and savage. Given that Hogan is not Makah nor Barclay Marshallese, it might be fair to ask whether the characters (or even novelists) demonstrate how environmental racism for some is a consequence of others' positive identifications with animals.

For a significant danger of the "cetacean turn" is that it discourages critics from examining the full range of sea life required for sustainable futures in favor of the charismatic few. As Huggan and Tiffin note, "the doe-eyed whales" at the end of Barclay's novel appear in significant and "stark contrast to the otherworldly, monstrous creatures that thrash a destructive course."[71] That they don't even mention the aloof dolphin couple suggests further that cetaceans risk their own special status when they fail to return human affective overtures. In the case of *People of the Whale*, such affinities encourage reductive interpretations of Ruth's leadership of other tribeswomen protesting the whale hunt as a reflection of Hogan's collaboration with Makah women elders to revision their tribal relationship with this kind of animal.[72] Given that in Makah traditional practice, whaling was not only strictly gender segregated but also highly codified by class—the pastime of elite men who relied on slaves to provide labor and sometimes to become ceremonial sacrifices in whaling[73]—such interpretations at best drastically underestimate the distortions that follow from ignoring the heterogeneity of multispecies histories.

Even when cetaceans are taken off the table as mainstay meats, the problem that remains is that the hopes for Indigenous people's communal futures in these stories rely entirely on fishing, on the precarious assumption that a more nebulously defined category of animals will function as a limitless resource. Anthropological records of Makah recollections state that the arrival of Eurowestern people on traditional fishing grounds coincided with a rapid decline of fish stocks[74]—a problem that continues to grow in the Marshall Islands.[75] This links Native seafaring life to dead sea creatures in a way that might become more useful for working out the implications for cultural and biological conservation. At least, I would like to try to work out how dead fish become useful in these fictions.

As both immaterial specters and the stuff of history—things with a distinctly disembodied presence—the useful dead are a category of thinginess that is distinct from all other things by nature of the response that they inspire among the living. It is well worth considering further how fiction itself participates in forming the response that is the thing that reanimates the useful dead in social life, particularly when representing hunting and fishing. Proposing the trope of "huntology" to mark the consequences of moving from subsistence to sport hunting in Eurowestern culture, literary theorist Antoine Traisnel clarifies, "For Derrida, 'hauntology' evokes and revokes in the same gesture the violence of ontology. . . . Likewise, huntology . . . should be understood as eluding the logic of philosophical language, dreaming instead of a non-hypotactic, illogical grammar that would upset certain preestablished associations concerning the animal and disturb the unyielding predation of grammatical predication [and therefore could] . . . provide the grounds for an alternative, non-nihilistic posthumanist perspective."[76] Likewise dreaming of anti-ratio-centric connections only against the current of nonconsideration of fish within critical discussions of these novels to date, I conclude by identifying how a particular dynamic of huntology disturbs the distinctions when children find the practice of fishing to be haunted by their gods, ghosts, and animal neighbors.

Ecofeminist Val Plumwood voices a tension that resonates deeply in both of these novels when she writes, "I have to say that I personally *feel* the same outrage at the mass murder and machine gunning of seal colonies and dolphin pods as I do about similar mass killings of humans. . . . On all these levels, the observational, scientific, social, moral and experiential, the exceptionalist paradigm saves mind discontinuity at the price of closing itself off from wider experiential and self-critical encounters. That this is required is a sign of its intellectual weakness rather than of its strength."[77] And it begs the question, why do we automatically, sometimes even against the evidence, want to link each and every marine mammal killing to atrocities, mass killings, even extinctions?

Why are there no comparable perceptions of fishes, for which the evidence of impending doom in dwindling fish stocks worldwide is mounting to dire degrees? And how do these representational patterns relate to the issues of food sovereignty and in turn hunting and fishing rights for Native peoples at the heart of these novels? To return to the initial concern, how does death enter into these stories in ways that foster an ethics that transcodes between discourses of social and environmental justice?

A lingering problem for both stories' uses of the dead is the distinctions that they make between two kinds of animal killing: hunting marine mammals versus fishing, well, fishes. The verbs are telling. In both texts, as in fishing literature more generally, the killings of members of mammal and fish species are not treated as equally important. Whether through the thumps of fish suffocating in coolers on the white boys' boat before Jebro and Nuke are rescued or the regularity with which Ruth bashes salmon to death on her trawler, these animals are sought only in order to be killed. Characters may identify totemically with sharks along with whales, as members of their clans, but actual fish are portrayed as actively disregarded, never as members of communities. Fish remain nascent or actual commodities. Even the settler kids pranking Rujen with the rancid chum adopt the ruse of trying to sell it to him, getting him to handle it long enough until its stink sticks. Why are fish deaths so readily disregarded? To mangle Traisnel, how to conceive of a pesco-huntology?

Studies in comparative thanatology would appear to support *Meḻaḻ*'s representation of cetaceans as caring for dead conspecifics and to identify practices that are more like those of humans than noncetacean marine mammals.[78] Yet the paucity of behavioral research on nonmammalian creatures, especially fishes, troubles such conclusions. Even research that attempts comparisons of death recognition in aquatic mammals with those in invertebrates like eusocial insects avoid consideration of fish species.[79] That the novels both introduce these considerations at all in itself is therefore noteworthy, and the way in which they do it draws interesting parallels. The notion that individual fish, let alone many species of seaborne life, are suffering and in need of saving, as much for humans' as their own and other species' well-being, enters only obliquely, through the actions of Indigenous children.

Fishing potentially flags a generational turning point, a fertile if unlikely grounds for seeds of hope. In both novels, young people's sensitivities to animal suffering are honored by elders who nevertheless themselves go fishing for food. Ruth prefers "shore fishing" for salmon not just because it is safer than going to sea but also because she can leave her son out of it: "Marco, like her, hated to kill fish."[80] Introduced to the practice much later, his half-sister, Lin, likewise expresses a profound aversion, so again Ruth takes on the hated task of smashing their heads because she says that someone "has to": for Ruth, "fish [are] . . . all [we] have to depend on to survive."[81] But the next generation holds a different view.

For Jebro, fishing more precisely provides "a way out of the hole" of dependence on wage slavery in his plans for his own future,[82] as well as a mechanism of transferring cultural knowledges that he learned from his dead grandfather to his younger brother, who is too young to remember the old man. Still, Jebro indulges Nuke's sense that the sea turtle that he teaches him to catch has in turn taught him, so therefore is entitled to be released. Although the unindividuated tuna that the boys then proceed to pursue apparently merit no such consideration, Nuke clearly values the turtle's life: "'*Yokwe*—Love to you,' [Nuke] said [to the turtle]. 'You don't have to sacrifice your life for me.'"[83] The choice of animal adds dimensions to the scene, for sea turtle biology makes them especially susceptible to long-term effects of nuclear contamination.[84] That their significance in Marshallese culture exceeds that of all other marine species and food sources[85] helps explain why he utters *yokwe*, the same traditional salutation that their father utters when he kills the one dolphin and frees the other. In both instances, the spontaneous giving freely of love across species lines seems complementary to the dwarf's expectation that the whales will give their healing love to people's jellyfish babies, but it has far more substantial cultural precedents.

Fishing to Marco, Lin, Jebro, and Nuke extends the dynamic of huntology to include consideration of less charismatic animals than cetaceans, suggesting further that fishing might provide a stronger basis than whaling for reconsideration of "transpacific and transindigenous" solidarity in these and other contemporary fictions.[86] In the end, both novels are as brutally honest in their depictions of devastated communities as in their bloody scenes of botched animal killings. The hope that remains for resilience and renewal is rooted in the peculiar assortment of multinatural beings integrated into their respective shore communities, at sites where particular histories can be made apparent and used to reroute connections by decolonizing emotional responses to cetacean deaths and, to a lesser extent, other sea creatures'. While much work remains to rethink oceanic spaces, from literary animal and postcolonial perspectives, as more than merely containers of resources, the novels model suggestive starting points through the work of shoring up the materialities of land- and waterborne life, the liminality and other meanings built into shoreline habitation, and the recognition and mobilization of the dead as useful presences for bridging contemporary Indigenous lifeways and metaphysics.

Within the narratives, not only are the hunts critiqued by Eurowestern members of the general public seeking protection for what they see as animal victims. This is also done by the hunters' own long-dead relatives as well as their cosmologies' mythical beings, who instead see ill-equipped people from tribal communities that are enduring ongoing devastation as part of colonial legacies, which includes gaps in traditional knowledges and practices of killing marine mammals. While the hunters are getting injured or killed, members of species whose futures may be likewise threatened endure bloody, painful deaths. Quite apart from assigning blame to individuals, the gods and the ghosts—human and animal alike, perceived by only some of the living characters and even then not entirely—cast the killing shores as places where cultural continuity requires children and other loved ones to recognize and respect the dead in many forms. These perspectives prove crucial, since, in the end, Eurowestern impositions of cetacean conservation agendas inspire resistance, while Indigenous children's expansive love for members of their cultures and other species emerges as a far more promising pathway for the conservation of all. The next chapter explores further this linkage of love and death across species lines through fictions of traditional companion-species relationships likewise framed in contexts of extinction and genocide.

Saharan Nonexistence
Edging near Death Camps

The most widely translated Arabic novelist today, Ibrahim al-Koni now lives in exile in Switzerland, but he was born in southeastern Libya into the nomadic, matriarchal, and pastoral Tuareg tribe.[1] Set in the landscapes of his childhood home, his novels consistently highlight the perspectives of a people who traditionally roam with livestock across their own Saharan countryside, foregrounding a desert viewpoint that places al-Koni on the leading edge of Arabic literature. Perspective is one of many ways through which these fictions challenge settler-colonialist stories of the region by negotiating "the balance between . . . indigenous and imported forces" in resistance to the historical exclusion of his own particular tribal perspective from within a form that is largely (and erroneously) assumed to have originated in European-language traditions.[2] A few of his more recent novels more specifically counter colonialist views through representing highly localized human-animal relations.

Libyan writers from the 1960s onward more generally have trended ahead of Arabic fiction by turning away from concerns of nation and instead toward those of species or rather by embracing multispecies traditions within modernity.[3] Literary scholar Charis Olzcek explains, "In literature, Libya, as a postcolonial nation-state that rapidly transformed into a dictatorship and rentier state, compels a hunt to imagine not the modern nation, but the land's imprisonment by one ideological force after another, from the Phoenicians to the Romans, Arabs, Ottomans and Italians."[4] The expediency of animal metaphor in politically dangerous situations has obvious attractions, but for Libyan writers, "imagining the human through the nonhuman, and voicing solidarity with the nonhuman, represent ways of conveying the long suffering of the land and its inhabitants, under political oppression and climactic extremes, and relating this suffering to the breadth of history."⁵ For these reasons, the growing significance of animals in al-Koni's prolific writing career, which spans more than fifty years, gains significance, for it draws specifically from the hybridity of and within cultural traditions to link the extermination of Saharan animal life with the sufferings of traditional herdsmen amid the modern genocidal history of Libya under the Italian colonial state and its aftermath.

The killing fields of Libyan tribal peoples, including al-Koni's Tuareg, remain doubly tragic for only just now gaining scholarly and worldwide recognition. They were sites of a singularly grotesque genocide in which tens of thousands of people were forced to watch as the animals they depended on for transport, food, and even companionship in this extreme environment perished of starvation first, fully aware that their own deaths were sure to follow. In one of the earliest scholarly accounts, anthropologist E. E. Evans-Pritchard described one exceptionally horrible scene of atrocity: "In this bleak country, in the summer of 1930, 80,000 men, women, and children, and 600,000 beasts were herded into the smallest camps possible. Bedouins died in a cage. Loss of livestock was also great, for the beasts had insufficient grazing near the camps on which to support life, and the herds, already decimated in the fighting, are almost wiped out by the camps."⁶ More recently, political scientist Ali Abdullatif Ahmida has been working for more than a decade to interview survivors, conduct research in remote Libyan and restricted Italian archives, and even analyze the orally transmitted poems that survivors composed to preserve their own histories. Ahmida gives a more accurate estimate of the numbers as 100,000 people interned and 60,000 dead and confirms that the "death toll was made worse with the decimation of the herds."⁷ Knowledges along with bloodstock conserved across millennia especially for survival in the Saharan extremes were lost there too.

These histories help explain why, unlike many companion-animal stories, al-Koni's novels take a decidedly unsentimental view of human-animal relations. Unfolding through stark and inevitably violent scenes, cross-species relationships signal the endangerment of individuals as often as their unlikely survival and, by extension, the persistence of ancient cultures and species together in their desert homelands. Two of al-Koni's novels that were initially published in 1990 explicitly center on lived relations of interdependence among desert people and animal species. *Al-Tibir*, the English-language version of which appeared in 2008 as *Gold Dust*, follows a loving but doomed relationship of interspecies intersubjectivity shared between a Tuareg tribesman and a camel (*Camelus dromedarius*). Likewise, *Nazīf al-Hajar*, translated to English in 2002 as *The Bleeding of the Stone*, scripts the grim fate of a traditional herdsman with encounters among humans, domestic goats (*Capra aegagrus hircus*), camels, various species of endangered gazelles,[8] and Barbary sheep or mouflons (*Ammotragus lervia*). The last is a large-horned species of wild mountain sheep thought to be an ancestor of all modern sheep, imagined by al-Koni at the edges of extinction and human community alike, and called in the local dialects (as the author prefers) *waddan*.

Elements of these novels' distinctive style, which combines realistic twentieth-century details with ancient aesthetic traditions, loom even larger in the more recent novel *Anubis* (2002, translated in 2005 as *Anubis: A Desert Novel*), including aphorisms, cave paintings, rock carvings, and other antiquities of Saharan country life to prepare readers for pivotal depictions of cross-species transformations in the face of death. While much of this chapter focuses on the first two novels, I start with *Anubis* to establish how the author's distinctive cultural perspective is shaped through select engagements with thanatopolitics, which is to the taking of life as biopolitics is to its maintenance. What distinguishes these novels is their emphasis on reanimating the dead and dying within modern histories marked by organized mass killings of people and other animals in Libya and doing so in ways that represent particular lives on their own deeply enmeshed terms. By focusing on al-Koni's animal stories, this chapter turns necropolitical questioning to more open-ended critiques of biopolitical and what philosopher Roberto Esposito terms "thanatopolitical" theory through fictions of mixed-species communities edging near death camps.

Transforming Lives and Deaths

Tuareg people are known for their veiled men, a practice that reflects their own highly localized adaptation of Islam to a much older matriarchal culture with ancient roots across this region. Tuareg tribespeople historically have inhabited the deepest Sahara, ranging from eastern Libya and southern Algeria to northern Burkina Faso, and their caravans cross most of Mali and Niger in between. Through details in al-Koni's novels, their story unfolds as one of systematic persecution that derives from their allegiance to no single nation but rather to a nomadic pastoral way of life that is inseparable from the grazing animals of the open desert. So the setting of al-Koni's fictions "is not the semidesert conveniently close to major conurbations that most Western visitors to the region get to see but the desolate wastes,"[9] a setting conducive to explorations of cross-species interdependencies as matters of life and death.

In this extreme locale, human-animal encounters become terrific sources of drama and, in so doing, confront readers with a mind-set in which survival entails resignation to an Indigenous desert metaphysics that defies settled reasoning. As one of al-Koni's characters enigmatically explains, the Sahara's vast, inhospitably dry landscapes are "hid[ing] all sorts of treasures, including extinct animals."[10] Steeped in the pastoral nomad's world view, integrations of such aphorisms reveal a distinctive deathly logic; death isn't overrated, in Braidotti's sense, so much as omnipresent. Such a perspective suggests how thanatopolitics might be construed as a profound challenge to urban-oriented senses, let alone sensibilities of life as biopolitically managed or even manageable. What I want to elaborate is how it flags a perspective from which biopolitical philosophy not only appears sexist[11] and speciesist[12] but, more important, does so precisely by avoiding certain aspects of settler-colonialist history. Therefore, it is important to consider carefully the various methods through which the desert dweller's viewpoint both references and extends a thought system that is rooted in shared human-animal lives on the eve of destruction—in other words, an Indigenous desert metaphysics that is the key to survival for the ancient, nomadic peoples and animals threatened with eradication within enclosures peculiar to modern, settled life.

Through references to the jinn—intelligent creatures of Muslim mythology who are not quite angels but capable of possessing and appearing in the shapes of humans and animals—and other multinatural aspects of his own culture, al-Koni develops a thanatopolitical perspective on cross-species companion-ships and the nomadic cultures rooted in them that persists beyond the death camps. In several of his novels, the individual, intersubjective, cross-species relationship becomes one in which whole populations hang in the balance. *Anubis* is perhaps his most ambitious novel in this respect, for it relays the author's version of the founding myth of the Tuareg people's (and therefore his own) divine human-jackal ancestor. Similar elements are present in the other novels; however, the fanciful premise and longer historical sweep in *Anubis* enables al-Koni to craft more deliberately composite critters as integral com-ponents of—or rather, singularities that sustain—the desert dweller.

Within literary studies, such potentials are not so easy to grasp, for the postcolonial frameworks commonly applied to stories of indigeneity tend to reduce singularities like the human-animal relations central to al-Koni's fiction to symbolic extensions of the Indigenous human individual. While not overtly patronizing, some postcolonial critics' interpretations of al-Koni's animal figures and multispecies events strictly in terms of stand-ins for human concerns betray a curiously studied ignorance of what not so long ago were readily dismissed as the simplistic hallmarks of so-called primitive forms, like legends and folktales. Such a myopic interpretive focus is problematic in part because it replicates the "metaphor model" problem in anthropology, through which the agency of nonhuman actors likewise has long been dismissed as a fanciful figure for human action—or in Foucauldian terms, as a substitute for the human subject of anatomo-politics. This way of reading becomes troubling when it underestimates the novelist's role in "link[ing] forms of communication to singular lives open to each other in a community"[13] and thereby securing a space for critiquing relations of knowledge and power that extend far beyond human subjects.

Once lauded as the form that gave voice to the subject of the Enlightenment, the novel has been adapted through the past century to articulate intersubjective human-animal relationality and, along the way, growing awarenesses of the human condition as one of intercorporeality in mixed-species populations.[14] Such developments in fiction mark not a de-personalizing so much as an im-personalizing process. For Gilles Deleuze, fiction can figure forth an "impersonal singularity (or singular impersonality)" that "traverses men as well as plants and animals independently of the matter of their individuation and the forms of their personality."[15] Articulating how his perspective relates life to death, Esposito points to Deleuze's interpretation of the coma-reawakening sequence in Charles Dickens's *Our Mutual Friend* (1865) to illustrate that such a fictional depiction of life at its limit does not illustrate the transcendence of "a norm of life" so much as it crystallizes the Deleuzian sense of "the norm [as] the immanent impulse of life[:] . . . It is this biojuridical node between life and norm that Deleuze invites us to untie in a form that, rather than separating them, recognizes the one in the other, and discovers in life its immanent norm, giving to the norm the potentiality of life's becoming."[16] There is much more to say about the biopolitical "presupposition" here "that any thing that lives needs to be thought in the unity of life"[17]—a "unity" that is at once "a co-belonging of what is different"[18]—not the least of which is that Esposito articulates here some grounds for agreement that the relations of lives in their singularities to the potentialities for collective life are primarily identifiable in fictions of life at the limits of existence.

In a very different context, Michael Hardt and Antonio Negri likewise figure singularity as linked to cross-species relations and fictions. Oriented toward futures that hinge on singularities, whether ones that involve transforming identities, traditions, or forms of resistance to unsettle relations of agency and power, Hardt and Negri point to the contemporary fictions of Indigenous life by writer Leslie Marmon Silko (Laguna Pueblo) as exemplary.[19] A key strategy of conveying what they term "alter-modern senses of singularity" (with "alter-modern" as an alternative to fixed dialectical anti/modern), her novels outline "not simply the preservation of nature but the development and reproduction of 'social' relations . . . between humans and nonhumans."[20] Although their overarching "emphasis on the singularity and commonality of the multitude" becomes problematic from Esposito's perspective—precisely because it "may in fact be an attempt to ward off any suggestion of an underlying antinomy between the multitude as a radically new social formation and personal identity"[21]—all together share a biopolitical sense of singularity as engaging thanatopolitics and, more precisely, as taking shape in certain approaches to fiction writing about death, indigeneity, and companion species.

From this perspective, reading al-Koni's fictions of highly localized knowledges of human-animal relations in the new anthropological terms of an "indigenous metaphysics" helps explain how these fictions deeply unsettle ontological certainties by forcing critical discussions concerning theories of knowledge.[22] Crucial to the process is engagement with creative practices on their own terms, as Baker argues in the context of contemporary art's representations of animals, which offers a "distinct way of framing or unframing issues" that employs "*different* tools for thinking"—albeit tools that are "viewed with suspicion because of their unfamiliarity."[23] At least, this begins to explain the allure and danger for contemporary novelists of narrating the singularities that make Indigenous lives with animals at once both sources of strength and points of vulnerability.

Thinking back to Miyazaki's and Hogan's animal gods, several aspects of *Anubis* seem particularly promising for intervention in stories of genocide and extinction. Incorporated as central components of the stories that define cultures, familiar mythical or legendary hybrid figures bring to his novels long histories of human engagements with other species in particular locales, sometimes long after the disappearance of the cultures and the creatures represented therein. As a mythical hybrid, a supernatural figure uneasily shifting between non/human animal shapes in human imaginations, such a critter cuts across super/natural binaries. *Anubis* moreover explicitly thematizes the loves and losses felt by such a creature, having the god tell the tale of his own emergence through various species and cross-species morphs yet also insisting at many levels that his story can only ever be pieced together through fragments of human experiences that can involve other animals.

The strategy is hard to miss in the author's note that begins the novel, in which al-Koni describes his work as a distillation of the stories of their tribal ancestor Anubi, which is the Tuareg name for the jackal-man god who might be more generally recognized as the Egyptian Anubis. From the outset, Anubi's "legend, one that reach[es] back to primeval times," is difficult to relate coherently because by custom it is not only orally transmitted but also "claimed by several rival peoples alternately joined by alliances and then separated by conflicts" across the ages.[24] The politics of nomadic life are thus introduced in terms of perpetual conflict, into which the nascent novelist was thrust by his early childhood introduction to this god as his own Tuareg tribal ancestor. Reclaiming his own heritage then involved travels that necessarily immersed him in travels and stories: "I made forays in every direction by camel and crossed the desert accompanied by a few of my relatives, visiting the most far-flung tribes in Azjirr, Aïr, Adagh, and Ahaggar, so that I could question their leaders, elders, and sages" for their details and narratives of the god's life, which is also their own.[25]

Hybrid at a formal level as well, *Anubis* is the most blatantly palimpsest of al-Koni's novels. In the opening autobiographical account, which moves quickly from boyish adventure to scholarly journey, al-Koni describes himself more as an anthropologist than novelist, which of course may be read as another fiction. He writes of meticulously collecting stories from every possible source, "from the mouths of matriarchs" to "crumbling leather" manuscripts, including copies of ancient rock inscriptions in the abjad Tifinagh script, and then "devot[ing] an even longer period of time to piecing together the narratives," drafting it first in his native Tuareg tongue, Tamasheq, and many years later translating his own manuscript into Arabic for publication as the novel *Anubis*.[26] Such details relay a sense of his craft as not simply translating between different languages but more profoundly interweaving cultural fragments across distances of many dimensions, including those of geography, history, genre, and species.

This admixture of oral histories, myths, and ancient manuscripts helps explain why reading *Anubis* is a profoundly disorienting experience, and it also affirms that the novel represents a world that is neither purely imaginary nor real. *Anubis* is told from the shifting perspective of Anubi himself, introduced as a prototypic Tuareg youth who is born to a life of exile fated by patricide. Crisscrossing the desert, his wanderings tell the story of the birth of a nomadic people, yet they also are revealing of that people's commitments to pastoralism by insisting on the bare dependence of desert people on even simply the traces of human and animal life. From the journey's start, Anubi must cling to the tracks of camel caravans in order to maintain even the faintest hope of staving off death by dehydration. As one of the many desert aphorisms collected in the novel's final section explains, "Water is blood that has lost its true color,"[27] envisioning its giving and draining of life.

In al-Koni's telling, the god's species hybridization and other animal associations prevent the mythic hero's tale from settling into a stereotypical bildungsroman or any other narrative journey into a fully realized self. The story follows a confused and confusing deity whose bodily form is constantly destabilizing through a series of sometimes bewildering, sometimes revolting human-animal transformations. Along the journey to becoming a hybrid canine-and-divine person who eats and consequently becomes shunned forever by his "animal kin,"[28] the most thickly described of his makeovers center on his prey-animal morphs—that is, the moments when he becomes part-gazelle and part-waddan.

Temporarily morphed into "an ugly, composite creature, half-man, half-beast" who is reviled by shepherds and their terrified flocks, Anubi wanders the desert with "the body of a gazelle and the head of a man," and his return to human form through another transformation is triggered when his mother makes an offering of herself to a priest who then "slaughter[s] her like a ewe on the tomb of the ancestors"[29] in a scene with eerie resonances to the ending of *The Bleeding of the Stone*. Upon learning this, the outraged Anubi stabs and kills the priest, only to learn (many morphs later) that the dead man was the father he had been seeking and that his mother had been trying to save him through (rather than from) cross-species transformations. The trope of transformation as revealing human-animal and immediate-familial relations is one to which al-Koni returns repeatedly to stage profound revelations at pivotal moments in a particular place in the desert in all his animal stories.

Like the gruesome denouements of the 1990s novels, a significant scene in *Anubis* takes place amid the ancient images of the Tassili region at the border of eastern Algeria with Niger, Mali, and Libya, which is world-renowned for its extensive prehistoric frescoes and rock carvings that, in often well-preserved detail, depict humans, animals, and human-animal relationships. Anubi follows a huge waddan ram into a cave only to discover the colossal images, then dwells on the "strangely contrived creatures" they depict, enraptured by the figures of "legendary animals and women" alongside men hunting and dancing and, most compelling to him, "other creatures concocted by matching men's bodies with animal heads crowned with horns or with birds' heads," which he describes as "unnatural, composite creatures."[30] Like characters in al-Koni's other novels confronted with these prehistoric images, Anubi learns there that his fate is sealed between species—in his case quite literally: "I saw I was a monster. I saw I was a freak. I saw I was a creature patched together from two disparate animals. I could not believe that I was still myself, and yet I felt certain my essence had not been destroyed. Only then was I freed. I could feel my body becoming liberated."[31]

Is the god, who is in between cross-species morphs, recognizing the roots of his own legend in long-forgotten people's representations of themselves, even as he sees where his own story is taking him? Significantly, he receives the prophetic vision of his own species hybridity from another "composite apparition," one with a giant gazelle's body and the head of a waddan, who locks gazes with him: Anubi sees "in its eyes the prophetic message, which [he] reads without difficulty although it was wordless."[32] Ancestral continuities shared between the Tuareg and the earlier inhabitants of this part of the Sahara certainly make symbolic or mythical meanings available to the fictional appearance of particularly the wild animals and gods in animal form.[33] What *Anubis* elaborates, however, is how Anubi's real-life counterparts dwell in the company of beleaguered domesticated animals, especially goats and later camels, and are always shadowed by wild ones, especially gazelles and waddan. *Anubis* thus helps explain how, in the earlier novels, these relations provide powerful sources of resistance to the ideologies and conditions of settler life.

Quite different from *Anubis*'s dizzying world of species hybrids and shapeshifters, the novels published in 1990 loft a more realistic vision of the highly culturally specific lived relations of nomadic-pastoral peoples and other animals finding anything but protection from colonial and postcolonial states. Referencing as well as integrating creative expressions like proverbs, rock carvings, paintings, and storytelling, his novels extend a pattern in which literary arts broadly writ provide refuge for collective memories of the colonized. What is more, they serve as a means of theorizing Indigenous experience, providing a critical counternarrative to the disempowering stereotypes of Tuaregs and other tribal peoples as "passive and manipulated traditional peoples with-out history."[34] In *Gold Dust* and *The Bleeding of the Stone*, it is not ancient gods so much as men wielding automatic weapons and four-wheel-drive vehicles that play the role of outcasts—or rather invaders, intruders encountering resistance from deep within local perspectives.

By highlighting certain creative elements of al-Koni's fictions in the more familiarly realistic novels, my point in what follows is to show how they build in ways of reading them on their own desert nomad terms, which in turn sustain ways of knowing that serve as a powerful counter to the postcolonial-critical emphasis on "transcendental"[35] qualities in lieu of the immanence of shared human and animal lives. Viewing his animal representations anthro-pocentrically as stand-ins or substitutes for people proves hard to reconcile with what for many readers makes these narratives so special—namely, their scrupulous attention to the histories and material realities of Saharan life. In the subfield of Arabic literary studies, al-Koni's novels are praised as pivotal for reorienting the novel form away from urban—or "oasis" (another of al-Koni's preferred terms)—settings and toward the desert countryside.[36] Increasingly understood outside Libya as blasting open the ideological fields that otherwise legitimate mass killings, they also offer no sunny escapes to a fantasied idyll before colonialist history but rather work to situate the exterminationist politics of the state amid possibilities for thanatological alternatives. By comparing his representations of humans sacrificing sheep, loving camels, and slaughtering gazelles, in what follows, I elaborate how it is not simply the arid and semi-arid landscapes but rather the multispecies singularities of severely persecuted desert dwellers that make these novels so productively unsettling.

Sacrificing Sheep

Our existence in the desert is delimited. The existence of the desert in us is limitless.

al-Koni, *Anubis*

It is not the arid and semiarid landscapes but rather the rich social fabrics of severely persecuted "desert dwellers" that distinguish the animal novels of this prolific novelist.[37] Scenes of mutual transformations of desert animals and nomadic people, again often under extreme duress, concern traditional knowl-edges and ways of transmitting them. An exemplary moment midway through

The Bleeding of the Stone involves the metamorphosis of a captive man into a waddan, the wild mountain sheep that led to Anubi's understanding of his ancient history, only here providing an escape from a very modern threat:

> [The event was] something the people of the oasis constantly recounted, around which they wove legends. The young men told them how they'd witnessed . . . a man break loose from his captivity and change into a waddan, then run off toward the mountains, bounding over the rocks like the wind, heedless of the bullets flying all around him. Had anyone ever seen a man transformed into a waddan? Had anyone ever seen a person escape the Italians' guns, running on until he vanished into the darkness of the mountains? The wise oasis Sufis [were] . . . convinced one and all that this man was a saint of God. That evening they went to the Sufi mosque and celebrated . . . filled with joy that the divine spirit should come to dwell in a wretched creature of this world.[38]

Relayed through so many interpreters—"young men," "wise oasis Sufis," and other "people of the oasis"—what exactly happens here is difficult to say, but in this telling, the event brings into sharp focus a threat to much more than an individual's life.

Asouf, the man in question, has arrived at this scene as a nomadic herdsman who has lost all his animals to an extreme drought. With no immediate means of sustenance and with no means to replace his animals, he is as good as dead in the desert. But in seeking refuge at the oasis, he inadvertently becomes entangled in a far greater tragedy. The Italian guns refer obliquely to an atrocious and little-known genocide—that is, the Italian colonial authorities' confinement from 1929 to 1933 of what is estimated to be more than a hundred thousand nomadic North African tribal peoples, who were then sometimes hung or shot but by and large starved to death alongside their herds in barbed-wire enclosures later used as models for the Nazi death camps.[39] Other clues in the novel indicate that he arrives in the oasis at just the moment when orphaned male youths of this tragedy were being conscripted to fight Italy's colonial wars in other African nations. Driven by hunger to his "first and last encounter with the oasis people,"[40] at a time and place around which countless others like him died in battles or detainment, the meek herdsman's capture by colonial military forces seems tantamount to a death sentence, from which he is delivered by his fantastic transformation into a waddan. Perceived as "the oldest animal in the Sahara,"[41] once revered for its "totemic, noble significance in pre-Islamic Berber North Africa"[42] and subsequently rendered extinct in parts of Europe as early as the seventeenth century, the waddan seems a fitting metaphor for the destitute Maghrebian tribesman fleeing colonial European forces. But the novel envisions a far more complex situation.

Although the animal that Asouf appears to become in order to escape certain doom is one he himself has known all his life in the Sahara, the waddan erupts as an extremely rare spectacle to the oasis people witnessing the transfiguration. Not exactly innocent bystanders, men in their situation came to use automatic weaponry—upgrades from what they disparage as their own older "Ottoman guns"—and eventually, as the story shows, vehicles like trucks and even helicopters to hunt this kind of animal, along with so many other wild species, to extinction. Amid a novel in which the traditional herdsman comes to believe he was born to protect this severely endangered species and in the end gets slaughtered in place of the animal when he refuses to show hunters where to find the last of its kind, al-Koni introduces a curious flight line through this flickering image of the hybrid human-animal fleeing the circumstances of historic mass killings. One of several similar moments across al-Koni's fictions, it anchors a pattern in which the thanatopolitics of genocidal history are combatted with a multinatural and multispecies singularity through multilayered creative practices.

For instance, into the scene sketched above is built a set of critical forms that exceeds the moment of colonization that it depicts, perhaps most obviously in the mention of the "legends" subsequently relayed orally about how the lone Tuareg man escapes by transforming into a waddan. Legend-spinning also foregrounds a context in which largely illiterate tribal peoples shared knowledges and extended ancient traditions of oral poetry recitation, not coincidentally, to create what is now recognized as "the richest source of Libyan colonial history, especially the history of the genocide."[43] Also important is the multiplicity of perspectives on the event (again "young men," "wise oasis Sufis," and other "people of the oasis") for storytelling in the style of the hadīth literature, a specifically Arabic narrative tradition that layers competing interpretations of what happened into the story itself.[44] Through these tellings, the "wretched creature" to whom the Sufis refer appears at once to be the herdsman, the waddan, and a composite creature. What is more, such a staging calls forth a way of understanding the sequence's ambiguity as having its own aesthetic integrity, an intentional lack of closure that both defies reduction to the analogical aesthetics of Eurowestern literary formalism as well as increasingly characterizes contemporary approaches to artistic renderings of animal life.[45]

Attention to the multilayerings of creative practice additionally reveals how
representation matters to the survival of Saharan singularities in both *Gold Dust*
and *The Bleeding of the Stone*. The plots again are exemplary in this respect: *The
Bleeding of the Stone* is the tale of a herdsman's fatal attempt to physically and
spiritually protect the waddan and himself, amid the period in which the mechanisms were set in place for the extermination of gazelles, and *Gold Dust* tells
the doomed (and, yes, platonic) love story of an exiled man and his precious
piebald camel, set at the twilight of the era in which camels reigned as primary
providers of desert transport and the beginning of an age in which their transformation to meat animals signals the greatest threat to desert biodiversity.
Genocide and its aftermath drive both human characters deep into the desert,
where they are killed by people for wanting to protect their animal companions.

As in *Anubis*, the ancient visual art of Tassili looms large as a powerful tool
with which the novelist opens out multiple interpretive perspectives on the
transformative potentials of human-animal relations in precise locales. Only
in these two stories, they are more deliberately invoked to destabilize distinctions between human and animal sacrifice. Ukhayyad, the protagonist of *Gold
Dust*, briefly escapes the clutches of the bounty hunters hot on his tail when his
tracks are masked by "a huge ram," in a "ghostly encounter" made all the more
uncanny by the millennia-old paintings of waddan hunts that he had just been
pondering on the cave walls of his refuge in Tassili.[46] Just as in *The Bleeding
of the Stone*, the waddan ram takes the place of the Tuareg man to offer a way
out of a condition of "exile" into the open desert and away from Italians who
invaded the country—and again with ambiguous results. To the hunters
who shoot him, the ram becomes their next meal, but to Ukhayyad, who links
his own condition as the hunted with "the exhausted [waddan] painted on the
wall," the actual waddan becomes a "divine messenger," whose death brings
more questions than answers: "Why did the innocent always fall at the hands
of the most malevolent creatures? Why do such people kill every messenger
that is sent to them?"[47]

In its concluding transformation sequence, *The Bleeding of the Stone* uses
many of the same elements to extend this inquiry. Through the vision of the
meat-crazed hunter Cain Adam, who emerges through the second half of
the story as his mirror-opposite, Asouf for one final time morphs into not only
a waddan but also "a sacrificial animal."[48] And it is a vision rendered more
visualizable by the exact positioning of Asouf's body atop a rock carving, in
precise alignment with the figure of a waddan in the process of being sacrificed

by a priest wearing a mask: "His body was thrust into the hollow of the rock, merging with the body of the waddan painted there. The waddan's horns were coiled around his own neck like a snake. The masked priest's hand . . . touched his shoulders, as if blessing him with secret rites."[49] Just as "great drops of rain" begin to fall at the end of the novel, "the blood of the man crucified" and ultimately beheaded by the craven hunter is described as dripping onto a stone on which is inscribed "in the mysterious Touareg alphabet" the prophecy that the bleeding of the sacred stone waddan will bring redemption in the form of a deluge in the desert.[50]

Most readers of the novel see the passive Asouf as having sacrificed himself here in order to secure the safety of the live, rare waddan, who has become habituated to himself and his beloved goat herd. After all, these animals are his only chosen companions at Tassili, for he shrinks from the company of other people, especially after the oasis incident. Read alongside the similarly staged conclusion of *Gold Dust* as well as the sacrifice "like a ewe" of Anubi's mother, however, the scene raises further questions about how "the earth will be cleansed"—and of what—through the carefully delineated human-animal relationships of love and slaughter. What gives here, in Esposito's terms, to the norm of the potentiality of life's becoming? Even as they spell out many horrific ways to die, these stories also explain how the lives of desert dwellers persist, perhaps most surprisingly, with love shared across species lines.

Loving Camels

A tomb in the desert is everlasting sleep in a paradise of nonexistence.

al-Koni, *Anubis*

The singularity of certain human-animal relations is established earlier in all three texts through depictions of cross-species codependence in extremity, fostered amid the exceptionally harsh realities of dehydration to the point of death. Interwoven into such scenes are aphoristic descriptions of "thirst" as "the worst enemy one can have in the greater Sahara" and water as "the most potent source of protection in the desert."[51] At particularly grim moments, for instance, characters lost in the desert resort to licking their own blood and tears or even animal urine—worst of all, camel pee, a "thick, salty, and syrupy" liquid.[52] These interactions are presented as signs of not debasement but rather enlightenment to the potentials for companion-species relations, whose values gain greater significance in the stories when articulated in terms of kinship.

Dangling with one precarious handhold on a cliff after his lone, failed, adolescent attempt to rope a waddan ram leaves him entirely unable to get a foothold, Asouf fears thirst more than exhaustion and proceeds meticulously to lick his tears, then to suck the blood from wounds on each hand in turn and, "when there was nothing left to suck, [finally to bite] into his hands with his teeth to suck more blood and moisture."[53] Thus he manages to survive in a wavering zone or "third condition"[54] between life and death, until a rope miraculously drops to let him pull himself up to safety—and consequently face-to-face with "the same waddan. His victim and executioner. But which of them was the victim, which the executioner? Which of them was human, which animal? . . . Suddenly, in the dimness of the [dawn], he saw his father in the eyes of the great, patient waddan. The sad, benevolent eyes of his father, who'd never understood why man should harm his brother man, who'd fled to the desert, choosing to die alone in the mountains rather than return to men."[55] Through this multifaceted transformation—involving both a father who had vowed to never teach his son to hunt the waddan due to an eerily similar experience and again references to having fled Italian-colonial genocide—Asouf becomes unable to palate meat and remains vegetarian for the rest of his life.

Ukhayyad is also profoundly altered through a perilous life-threatening situation in which he is dehydrated to the point of being "perched between consciousness and oblivion," inhabiting "that interval between life and death"—only in order to live, he must lick the urine dribbling down the thigh of his camel, a creature introduced as no ordinary animal but rather as a rare thoroughbred, a "mahri" piebald, who has been the man's companion since childhood.[56] Lost together in the open desert as a result of Ukhayyad's efforts to heal his camel of a disfiguring and possibly deadly skin condition, it is with a sense of relief that readers are told, "It had been divine inspiration to tie his hand to the camel's tail" and so to maintain access to the liquid that he needs to live through this precarious episode.[57]

As in all the man-waddan transformation scenes, the human-camel fusion is presented as a possible pathway to divinity, in this case leading to a more literal vision of heaven on earth. When the camel finally leads the desperate man to a well, he reattaches himself by the foot to the camel's tail and plunges in, trusting the camel to "carr[y] out his unspoken command" and "pull . . . him out of that freshwater sea" even as death approaches with a vision of "the houris in paradise."[58] The animal rescuing the human again is explained in terms of cross-species kinship bonding, only more directly, for they "spoke to one another as brothers, by way of gesture."[59] Fatherly and brotherly love only approximate what these novels are trying to convey in visions of people coming to understand themselves through their companion species singularities, a point underscored by a similar scene in *Anubis*.

More deliberately, *Anubis* calls into question perspectives from which the animal-urine-drinking nomad dehydrated nearly to death might be pathologized as degraded and delusional. When Anubi follows a hare only to lose all signs of the caravan trail he had been following, likewise becoming blinded by thirst in the desert, he luckily stumbles across a puddle of gazelle urine and, in drinking it, regains his vision in time to look into the eyes of its source. He knows he ought to be wary. "Gazelles," his mother had told him, "are the livestock of the spirit world," by which she means the animals ridden by the jinn, who are themselves hybrid creatures with spiritual powers but physical needs. However, he finds that this silent exchange of looks enables him to recover a peculiar sense of spirit along with life: "I found within me the ability to comprehend the forgotten language, which reconciled my tongue with that of the gazelle's, united my destiny to the gazelle's, and created from my spirit and the gazelle's a single spirit."[60]

Like so many similar incidents across al-Koni's novels, a human-animal singularity emerges at a moment of utmost duress and leads to a revelation about nonhuman interdependence as a basic condition of the desert dwellers' existence. In *Anubis*, it goes over the top—Anubi spies in the gazelle "a splendour that we observe only in eyes that have gazed into the eye of eternity till absence becomes second nature to them"[61]—but only to emphasize the sublime and unspoken communications shared between species. Together, these close encounters with oblivion averted through the help of members of other species clarify how the thanatopolitics of the death scenes that conclude *The Bleeding of the Stone* and *Gold Dust* are in turn encircled by other potentials. Particularly in light of their ancestor's invocation of memory, language, destiny, and spirit as recovered through a meaningful exchange of gazes that seal blood ties between species, Ukhayyad's and Asouf's fatal attachments to animals appear to be grounded in unique sources of strength.

Such extreme forms of kinship bonding contribute to a deep unsettling of conventional understandings of "domestication" and other processes whereby, for example, the human introduction of camels into the region proved crucial to the flourishing of decentralized social structures of pastoralism. Conventionally portrayed in strictly utilitarian terms—"the major source of transportation as well as a source of milk, meat, and clothing"—camels in recent years gain historical interest as having enabled flourishings of cultures in the region.[62] Such a recognition is critical to the question of historicity in these companion-species relations because the migrations away from droughts and ensuing famines, the establishment of trade routes, the accompanying spread of Islam, and other culturally complex conditions that could be credited to this human-animal relationship are scrupulously written out of earlier histories that depict nomadism as riding camelback in lawless intrusions on agricultural society. Because such disregard has enabled Eurocentric historians to "disparag[e] the precolonial period as 'barbaric and stagnant,'"[63] reading al-Koni's representations of camel-human relations as sympathetic and complex also cultivates a decolonial perspective.

What is more, recent transformations to the ways in which people and camels live and die together inform the precarious futures for human-camel melding as depicted in *Gold Dust*. Authors of the 2006 UN report *Livestock's Long Shadow* point to semiarid places—like the fragile valleys upon which al-Koni's human and animal nomads cling for their life-giving vegetation—as the environments most endangered by the soaring global markets for meat. Exponentially expanding scales of traditional cattle, goat, and sheep herding explain one dimension of the problem. A more difficult aspect to grasp is the transformation of camels to primarily meat animals, which was escalated quickly with the normalization of Libyan-Chadian relations since the 1990s, where "overstocking and overgrazing" particularly has accelerated "desertification" in the region depicted by al-Koni.[64]

Although, as extremely rarefied racing animals, a few special mahris continue a tradition in which camel ownership signals prestige and political independence, the status of the vast majority of camels has changed abruptly from the valuable "ships" or "freighters of the desert," powering the sort of caravans on which, even before his vegetarian conversion, Asouf relies for trading his goats for supplies of barley and wheat. Now overwhelmingly serving as commodities herded to market on foot over East African deserts, often by ill-equipped young men who all too frequently "lose their way in the desert and perish together with their herds,"[65] camels have become a "symbol of backwardness" for nations in the Arab Middle East, whose governments remain actively interested in settling nomads within their borders.[66] This precarious, ancient-to-contemporary set of associations adds a special sense of singularity to Ukhayyad's declaration concerning his near-death experience with his own mahri: "The hardship we shared transformed us from two creatures into one."[67]

Coming together in this way, man and camel are not simple expressions of nostalgic sentiment. Nonsexual cross-species companionship is an affective bond through which people organize their ordinary lives, and even in urban-industrial environments, some additionally experience such intimacies in terms of a radical intervention into the isolating and otherwise disempowering structures of normativity.[68] In the struggle to articulate the difference between the generalized attempts informed, for instance, by feminist care theory to empathize with animals and the experience of shifting a sense of one's own subjectivity across species lines, Kathy Rudy persuades that the experience of "falling in love with a particular animal" leverages a critical shift, a singularity that is "not something that can happen abstractly or universally, but only something that happens particularly."[69] Singularities in love may never simply be correctives to genocidal or ecocidal impulses, but al-Koni's staging of affective bonding across species lines as forged by mutual dependence for survival in hostile environments offers some insight as to their relevance for thanatopolitics.[70]

Notably, the brotherly bonds shared by Ukhayyad and his special camel are not shared by other characters within the novel, who see the mahri as a piece of saleable property and his poor owner's love for his camel as the source of his own downfall. Their bond gains more legitimacy when compared across novels with the descriptions of Asouf's father, who likewise cares with "great tenderness" for a piebald that he too speaks of as a "noble camel."[71] Young Asouf scoffs at how his father "spoil[s] his camel quite outrageously, even letting him drink from his own scarce supply of water" until schooled by his father on the survival and other advantages of shared cross-species affection: "Always take the greatest care of your camel. If you don't love him, he won't love you. If you don't understand him, he won't understand you—and then he won't save you when the going gets rough. Animals are more faithful than people."[72] Lest readers are inclined to dismiss such statements as the misanthropy of a misguided animal lover, al-Koni clarifies earlier that the source of the family's extreme social isolation was that the father had "lost his connections" to people in the oases when "the Italians had invaded their shores," because "they'd enter every tent" that they could and inflict the "shame" of imprisonment on whomever they caught.[73] Again, the death camps loom at the edges of these scenes, underscoring a context in which love between species secures the

survival of nomadic pastoralists who are otherwise severely socially isolated
from kin and kind by colonial-Italian genocide.

Whereas Asouf is simply left alone among animals following his parents' death, Ukhayyad cuts a fiery swath from his patrimony by marrying a poor woman—and more. While his own father maintains to the end a "noble" status among his own and other tribespeople for his leadership in "repelling foreign invaders from the Sahara," eventually dying of thirst while leading the tribes' last coordinated stand against Italian colonization,[74] the by then socially out-cast Ukhayyad is confronted with the ignoble fate of so many more landless and herdless Maghrebi refugees to oasis communities: sharecropping while starving. If his human family is seen as tying him to conditions surrounding a genocide as part of which "a third of the total population—a half-million people—died in battle or from disease, starvation, or thirst" while a quarter million more were forced into exile,[75] then his nonhuman kin seem in contrast to provide a mechanism of deliverance from doom.

Perhaps most tellingly, the special man-mahri bond troubles conventional commodity relations. Amid the ceaseless wailings of their starving infant son, Ukhayyad yields to his wife's pleas to sell his camel. Better than any of Ukhayyad's human companions, the camel proves his love by faithfully return-ing, again and again, only to be beaten back by hired herders who nonetheless observe the intensity of the animal's "pining" when separated from his lifelong human companion and conclude, "He's a human being in a camel's skin."[76] Neither a substitute for human love nor a mere means of transport, Ukhayyad's mahri is carefully drawn together with him in terms of "companions," com-pelled by a shared desire to wander away from their separate miseries in the oasis and to light out together to the open desert. The novel's exact wording asserts a sense of circularity even in their ill-fated final voyage, insisting that man and camel are fated to "depart together, and together . . . return to their original state, to what they had been before birth."[77]

Through such descriptions, the singularity of human-camel "brothers" may exceed Eurowestern readers' comfort zones, yet they also open up a space for thinking through enduring desert lifeways. It is a sensibility conceptually barred, in Esposito's terms, by the "biojuridical node between life and norm"[78] and materially broken in al-Koni's novel through the trading of bodies for the titular metal. The man-camel idyll ends when Ukhayyad is driven to a murder-ous rage by rumors that he has gained back his camel by taking gold in exchange for his wife and son from the cousin who offered them refuge from destitution.

After killing the cousin, Ukhayyad has a price on his head, and his only option is to flee into the open desert. Commodification of life likewise informs a range of far more exploitative human-camel relationships within the novel, including the unremarkable plow camels Ukhayyad is briefly hired to drive as part of his sharecropping work, the meat camel bought to sacrifice for his wedding feast, and last but not least, the pair of riding camels to which the bounty hunters horrifically bind Ukhayyad by hand and foot, in order to draw and quarter him to death in the novel's conclusion.

Because he has "plac[ed] his heart with the piebald," Ukhayyad's human hunters can smoke him out of his mountain-cave hideout by burning, cutting, and otherwise torturing his beloved mahri, whose screams Ukhayyad proves unable to endure.[79] As both novels are at pains to elaborate, such affective responses are neither psychological projections nor substitutions but reciprocated feelings that seal cross-species singularities that, in turn, in better circumstances guaranteed their mutual survival. Love between man and camel may be doomed, but as *The Bleeding of the Stone* makes even clearer, the fate of interspecies relations also bears heavily on the threatened populations that sustain them, an understanding that tentatively arises in that novel through the stories of animal mothers.

Slaughtering Gazelles

The desert is a homeland that has migrated.

al-Koni, *Anubis*

More clearly fleshing out the perspective of *Gold Dust*'s "malevolent creatures" who kill the waddan—who is in the end and elsewhere aligned with the mahri as "a messenger sent from on high"[80]—the second half of *The Bleeding of the Stone* tells the story of Asouf's nemesis among the Tuareg, Cain Adam. Like his Biblical namesakes, this character appears cursed. He is orphaned as an infant only to be briefly adopted by a couple who, in their last act before dying of thirst in the open desert, feed newborn Cain Adam the blood of a gazelle. How does the couple manage to kill a gazelle when they are too weak to save themselves? In "The Covenant," the lone chapter in which an animal speaks in these novels, al-Koni offers a curious answer through an animal mother's tale of sacrifice.[81] Telling her calf the story of how they gained protective magic, a gazelle speaks of the death of her mother, who martyrs herself so that just such a dying human baby might live.

Choosing to write from a nonhuman perspective is nothing new in literature in Arabic or European languages, and in doing so, critics note that "al-Koni continues a tradition that goes back to *Kalila wa-Dimna* and Hesiod" of "animal-told tales."[82] But his avoidance of it except in this one chapter adds interest particularly because it voices nonhuman perspectives on the cross-species kinship bonding that emerges from moments of extreme duress in the desert. Through a gazelle daughter's perspective, her own mother's act of self-sacrifice forges kinship between species, a singularity that the daughter explains to her own calf in terms of brotherhood: "My poor mother! She did it for my sake and yours, so our progeny would enjoy safety through all the generations. Her blood made a bond of brotherhood between our kind and humankind. We and humankind, I say, are brothers now. And this bond of safety was bought with cruel blood."[83] The gazelle's perspective mirrors that of Asouf's father, who, along with promulgating man-camel love, sees gazelles as embodying the "magic" and "spirit of the desert," a paradoxically "impossible . . . freedom." Hence his outrage at people for gazelle hunting: "Why should this wicked creature man chase such an angel? . . . Why should man be so hungry that he feels he has to spill the blood of this lovely creature?"[84] Thus this particular mise en abyme pinpoints the most ambitious dimension of *The Bleeding of the Stone*'s thanatopolitical project, clarifying cross-species singularities shared not simply between individuals but also at the species level and revealed at such only when death becomes certain.

Readers are informed that Asouf's father is himself not innocent. Providing for his family off the land means that he hunts and eats gazelles, but he strictly limits his bag to one per hunt, not simply to conserve the numbers but also as an act of faith. He must choose his prey carefully, for "to hunt a pregnant animal from the herd was a great sin."[85] By exercising restraint, he is following not just Tuareg custom but more deliberately the guidance of a mystic who long ago convinced him that it will strengthen "the soul of the gazelle" as part of a conservation practice that combines "the shield of the Quran" along with "the talismans of magicians and amulets of soothsayers" as well as "the incantations of devout sages."[86] Invoking the range of natural and cultural practices integral to Tuareg belief systems, the self-exiled man shares with his son a respectful vision of gazelle-human relations that both includes the possibility of killing and legitimizes the gazelle mother's belief in reciprocity. *Gold Dust*'s highly personalized, intersubjective man-camel singularity is thus, early on in *The Bleeding of the Stone*, open to the thanatopolitical negotiations of impersonal singularities at the species level. As the ending of the gazelle narrator's own story later comes to clarify, the stakes of these negotiations are no less than the survival of species and cultures.

In this context, Asouf's choice to become vegetarian seems a logical next step against which the likewise desert-born but oasis-raised Cain Adam's relentless and wasteful hunting strictly to feed his greedy meat cravings appears to be a retrograde turn, as it leads to the destruction of humans and animals and, along with them, that of intrahuman and human-animal relationships. The novel gains an eerie resonance decades later, for one result of the Libyan Civil Wars beginning in 2011 and their consequent redistributions of power and weaponry has been the decimation of gazelle populations. Their dwindling numbers worldwide are an ecological tragedy that scientists have been tracking across decades,[87] but the losses have been severely accelerated by the removal of hunting restrictions on the three remaining wild gazelle species from what had been their last large de facto refuge in central Libya.[88] Obliquely introduced through the shadowy cousin in *Gold Dust*, the base consumerism of oasis dwellers that brings a totalizing sense of death to al-Koni's desert dwellers is fleshed out in *The Bleeding of the Stone* through the character of Cain Adam.

Cain Adam chases down the elderly Asouf at Tassili, where he is told that the legendary man who transformed into a waddan can be found and almost upon meeting him announces, "I'm proud to say I personally ate the last gazelle in the northern desert."[89] It is one of the first things readers learn about him, and because Cain Adam's story is told largely in the second half of the novel, it sets him up to be remarkably unsympathetic. The book is divided between the stories of these two characters, leading with Asouf in a way that fosters a sense of sympathy for the old hermit with his herd and interrupting the mad Cain's story with that of the gazelle mother in a way that undermines the legitimacy of his position. But through these intersecting trajectories, blood lust appears less a universal condition and, like Asouf's vegetarianism, a diametrically opposite but no less conditioned response to the legacies of settler colonialism.

As a twice-orphaned infant in the desert, Cain Adam was a foundling awash in the blood of a self-martyred mother gazelle, whose story is hard to read as anything but the self-sacrificing mother in "The Covenant." Alongside the baby are the corpses of his would-be foster parents and the gazelle, but no sense of obligation follows. Raised henceforth by a rich man amid the trappings of oasis life, the adult Cain Adam's inexorable pursuit of gazelles attracts the attention of John Parker, an armchair Orientalist seeking a dubious sense of enlightenment through the consumption of bushmeat. The latter's position as a US colonel stationed to protect petroleum interests in Libya provides deadly access to the modern military resources that in by-then expert hunter Cain Abel's hands spells doom for gazelles, if not Asouf's rare waddan as well.

The prescience of this novel, published twenty years before the Libyan Civil Wars and their present-day toll on already-beleaguered gazelle populations, is perhaps most appreciable in the final discussion of Cain Adam and John Parker. Although each point out the other as most responsible for rendering gazelles extinct—"the hateful crime he'd committed against one of the loveliest of creatures"[90]—the novel clarifies that the military-industrial colonizer has the power to withhold the tools but chooses instead to let them be used for his own self-serving greed, ironically for a spiritual understanding like Asouf's. Only Cain Adam, onetime child of the desert and tribesman by birth if not by upbringing, appears capable of the transformation to loving kinship that might prevent it.

Searching together by helicopter for the last gazelles, who seek a final refuge in the mountains—an unusual migration route that "according to the sages . . . [is] a sign of doomsday"[91]—a mother and calf catch Cain's eye. In terms familiar from al-Koni's other scenes of humans exchanging gazes with waddan, camels, and gazelles, they exchange looks that are "intelligent, speaking some unknown language," immediately after which Cain becomes aware that he has "seen a human in a gazelle's body" and questions his own grip on reality: "How could he, Cain, have held back from pressing the trigger, when a graceful gazelle stood there in front of him? Had she really been a gazelle at all? And was he really Cain?"[92] Perhaps because the human gets to decide the fate of the animal, and not the reverse, this time the cross-species encounter fails to result in love or enlightenment. Urged on by his human companions, Cain looks away but nonetheless shoots, a wild but devastating shot that kills both calf and mother. Before she dies—and in a gesture that again links back to "The Covenant," only here with a profound sense of violation—the gazelle mother shocks them by howling in protest over her slaughtered child like a "wolf," yet no transformations, magic or otherwise, can save them. In the end, Cain "didn't just kill his sister. He ate her flesh too."[93]

Within the novel, this scene marks the tipping point in the modern hunters' story toward the fatal pursuit of waddan, and consequently Asouf, at the same site where cross-species love is even more spectacularly destroyed in *Gold Dust*—for once again, al-Koni leaves us ultimately at Tassili, where the stones are "bleeding" with representations of cross-species relations that are wounded, dying alongside their referents. At a rare speaking engagement in the United States in 2011, al-Koni explained his constant integrations of these monuments into his stories by recounting his own journey to view the Tassili petroglyphs and paintings, which, though difficult to date, are estimated to be at least ten thousand years old. Noting that the artworks are supposedly protected as part of a UNESCO World Heritage site and located nowhere near any modern battles, the novelist recalled asking at the time why several of these ancient images obviously had been defaced by bullets, only to learn that in recent years, some of then-leader Muammar al-Qadhdhafi's soldiers had intentionally shot at them. To al-Koni, this kind of artistic defacement is deeply disturbing, "destroying the heritage of mankind, a message from mankind to mankind" sent from the earliest times to the present, and in such a way that is "killing humanity" and "not just humanity, but also plants, animals, and stones."[94] In Libya as well as Afghanistan, Iraq, Syria, the United States, and many more sites worldwide, such defacements continue to become interlinked with histories of killings on massive scales, and through them, al-Koni's aesthetic choices gain wider resonance.

For the novelist al-Koni, the problem with such histories is not that they are unrepresentable, as is so often claimed of genocides. Rather, it is that their representation in strictly human terms only ever insufficiently accounts for the more profound, ongoing threat coconstituted by the nomad forms of desert species. Though shaping their destinies, the death camps are never visited by al-Koni's protagonists, which helps emphasize how the perseverance of Tuareg people is not simply like but also intimately bound to that of the waddan, the gazelles, the goats, the camels, and all those adapted over the long *durée* to desert life together. It is a perspective voiced by the ancient Tassili artists that al-Koni continues through modern methods of storytelling, enlisting multi-modal creative practices toward a focus on death as nonexistence.

If, as I suggested earlier, art provides an especially useful way of thinking differently about the relations of endangered populations by using unfamiliar tools that lead to surprising outcomes, then how might it intervene in the biopolitics and thanatopolitics of companion species? More crassly put, what do al-Koni's fantasied transformations, sacrifices, loves, betrayals, and slaughters have to do with the historical records of real peoples and animals pushed together to the brink of oblivion? Although the complexity of the stories defers any easy answers, reading these novels together indicates how fiction itself can serve as a mode of intervention.

In a very different context, Deborah Bird Rose illuminates the resiliency of some traditionally nomadic Australian Aboriginal cultures as rooted in storytelling, particularly "stories [that] constitute more-than-human geneal-ogies that enmesh people in cross-species transformations."[95] Just as al-Koni's stories of human-animal morphing reflect a "wild and crazy ethic" that defies Eurowestern rational sense at the same time that they instill a shared sense of cross-species "brotherhood" and even kinship at the species level and across natural and supernatural boundaries, the stories that Bird Rose shares from Yarralin and Lingara communities in the Northern Territory at once reflect a system of values that enables life to go on in the face of genocide and anthro-pogenic extinctions. More precisely, they voice an ethic that is rooted in love "as fierce as death" and that in our current era of mass killings of humans and especially animals on ever-increasing scales is needed to counter the forces "drawing life out of earth, unmaking the fabric of life, severing the bonds of connectivity."[96] What al-Koni's novels illustrate so well, I think, is a compet-ing approach to death as nonexistence, a generative sense of the extremities of desert space that is profoundly disruptive to the settler-colonialist mind-set. "Patriots boast of their affiliation with a homeland. The desert dweller boasts of his affiliation with nonexistence,"[97] is one of the aphorisms listed in the conclud-ing chapter of *Anubis* that captures what is at stake in countering that mind-set.

Concerned with relating the thanatopolitical to the biopolitical, theorists like Esposito smartly gravitate toward the negative "immunizing" forces charac-terizing the modern politics of death in general and genocide in particular. But engaging with al-Koni's attempts to articulate an ancient, ongoing nomadic per-spective on the peculiar horrors wrought by European colonialism in the Maghreb makes me wonder more recklessly instead about the forces of infection—or rather, in Donna Haraway's terms, "the potent transfections"—through which we are always linked symbiogenetically to our own and others' livings and dyings.[98] How else to declare affiliation with nonexistence in the twenty-first century? Like many contemporary Libyan authors, al-Koni uses human-animal bonds to explore "the present through the primordial,"[99] but absence, nonexistence, and the systematic destruction of desert dwellers, human and nonhuman alike, appear to concern a much more enduring struggle between nomad and oasis or, in conventional terms, Indigenous and settler-colonialist state forms of power.

In their "Treatise on Nomadology—the War Machine," Deleuze and Guattari take up the problem of the origins of the state, the political form so often cast as using capital to organize and ultimately disband more fluid social forms like clans or tribes. Conversely, they insist, the inverse is conceptually more plausible, because it is so clearly in the interest of the "primitive societies" to keep the formation of the state at bay. In other words, these other social forms are primitive in the sense not of locating origins or reflecting a lesser status but rather of operating with a tactical simplicity to resist "the formation of a State apparatus" at every turn, even to wield the power of "making such a formation impossible."[100]

Their "nomadology" thus begins to explain why novelists like al-Koni reference the horrors of genocide and extinction obliquely in stories that end not in death camps but rather in a killing of humanity of a far different order. At the conclusion of both *Gold Dust* and *The Bleeding of the Stone*, men who have tried to live in the desert fail to protect animals or even themselves, slaughtered by killers who have betrayed their birthrights and are motivated by the all-consuming desires that define oasis life through Eurowestern colonialist history. Put another way, the stories concern ongoing failures to decolonize imaginations and the total destructions that inevitably follow. Setting up these contrasts, al-Koni makes embracing "nonexistence" appear to be a desirable alternative.

The cross-species singularities on which nomadic desert lifeways depend do not illuminate the crushing impossibility of postcolonial subjects, the "'all or nothing' problem of unified subjectivity that also haunts" religious as well as subaltern studies,[101] so much as they pinpoint the struggle between the ideology of the modern state (in which power is vested only ever in human subjects) and that of nomad systems, which rely on the sort of shifting sovereign, biopolitical, thanatopolitical, necropolitical, and other fields and forms of power envisioned through these fictions. Appreciating the formal hybridity of al-Koni's work as exemplary for prompting new thinking about the various narrative traditions contributing to the Arabic novel's inception, it becomes possible to see that what is at stake is the very "linkage between developing notions of modernity (and the identification of those who are entitled to define it) and what can be termed pre-modernity."[102] To think through how there can be more to follow might involve reading through nomadology, attending to the ways in which these fictions seem to question such historical progressions by casting the state's subject (an agent of sovereign power) in an enduring struggle with the nomad (an interstitial figure navigating multiple modalities of power).

But I think al-Koni's storytelling asks more: envisioning an ongoing struggle wherein, surrounding the subject of the state (in the terms of al-Koni's aphorism, the "patriot" tied to the "homeland"), ranges the nomad of the intermezzo, the vagabond of no-man's-land, locked in an embrace with "nonexistence" and like Anubi endlessly metamorphosing in "a fuzzy aggregate" across species lines.[103]

The picture that emerges of Saharan human-animal relatings enables what Braidotti terms "nomadic becomings," a kind of "emphatic proximity and intensive interconnectedness," to operate as a deconstructive element not only in the Eurowestern concept of human subjectivity, as she argues,[104] but also at the heart of its thanatopolitical critique, through the visioning of singularities that come to concern the futures of populations forging blood ties to create and sustain multinatural and multispecies communities. The elements that anchor these sensibilities in al-Koni's animal fictions underscore how these relations might reveal the state to be at best merely the regulator of its subjects, its own forms of power. Not so much in opposition as in excess, nomadic human-animal relations give rise to other formations, including positive and productive ones that to varying degrees in *The Bleeding of the Stone*, *Gold Dust*, and *Anubis* situate historical horrors amid ancient and ongoing struggles to assert the validity and vigor of lives that continue to be shared at the edges of nonexistence. After all, as one of al-Koni's aphorisms declares, "The desert is a paradise of nonexistence."[105]

The next chapter turns to another culture whose wandering ways became even more radically disrupted in the twentieth century through enduring the genocidal practices of a settler-colonialist state. The stories at its core are more direct representations of atrocities but share important similarities in articulating as well a metaphysical perspective through which traditional human-animal relationships remain at the center, defining a uniquely resilient culture while making possible a way of life in an extremely harsh environment. Again death and other losses detail an understanding of life with animals before and beyond market forces, a knowledge made manifest in a spiritually and physically sustaining love that is not easily grasped by outsiders; however, in this case, the circumstances in which they are told ensure that they will have real-world political consequences that resonate far beyond the affected communities.

Arctic Nomadology

Inuit Stories of the Mountie
Sled Dog Massacre

In the late 1950s, anthropologist Toshio Yatsushiro was hired by the Canadian government to study the impacts of "settlement" on Inuit people in Qikiqtaaluk. A first-generation Japanese American who had been imprisoned in and then hired to study an internment camp during World War II, he knew well how racism and xenophobia factored into forced relocations.[1] Yet what Yatsushiro found in Canada was so shocking that he was compelled to go public at the cost of his job. In a national magazine article arguing for Inuit self-rule, he pinpointed what would become a most controversial aspect of how settlement signaled irrevocable changes to Inuit lifeways.

In the article, Yatsushiro notes that police shootings of dogs deemed "a menace to the community, especially the white residents," left the Inuit unable to "travel or hunt in the winter" and illustrates the traumatic effects of this policy by citing the firsthand account of an informant named (not in the article but in his notes) Jamesie. After his dogs were killed by a cop, Jamesie recalls, "First I thought of killing the policeman. But I don't mind now. Maybe afterwards there won't be so many dogs, since the police are shooting them. In five years there may be none at all. Maybe the police will kill Eskimo then, just like the dogs."[2] In Jamesie's view, lines blur between not just himself and his dead dogs but also all Inuit and all their dogs, an affective reality that follows from Inuit traditions of human-canine interdependence.

A half century later, anthropologist Lisa Stevenson tracked down Jamesie's initial moment of disclosure, and her transcription of Yatsushiro's audio recording of the ensuing conversation proves even more revealing:

"Policemen kill Eskimo, next time."

"Eskimo . . ." begins Yatsushiro, sounding unsure. "Policemen kill Eskimo? Or Eskimo dogs?"

"The same as Eskimo, same as dogs. Policemen kill," explains the translator. [. . .] "Dogs, same thing, Eskimo," adds the translator emphatically, but Yatsushiro still wonders if he has misunderstood.

"Oh, Eskimo will shoot their own dogs."

"Eskimo dogs same thing. One," says the translator forcefully.

"Same," repeats Yatsushiro, the realization of what Jamesie is saying breaking over him.[3]

What Yatsushiro is witnessing in this moment is how the killing of dogs by Canadian government officials was experienced as a devastating attack on a community, a special form of terrorism that exploits the unique traditional relationship shared between Inuit (in Inuktitut, literally "people") and their *qimmiit* ("many dogs").[4]

Before the advent of snowmobiles, qimmiit were viewed as essential to Inuit lifeways. For an Arctic people who traditionally did not use snowshoes or skis, qimmiit provided a crucial means of mobility and, along with it, a source of livelihood, protection, and even identity, as they continue to do, only for more Inuit in Greenland than Canada today. Conflicting views of these dogs map readily onto insider/outsider cultural positionings, but all who have experience living with them agree that such dogs are not stereotypically dependent companion animals, nor are they akin to the free-ranging "street dogs" who are fixtures of urban histories. Rather, Inuit sled dogs thrive in a special sort of working partnership of people and dogs, enabled by highly specialized adaptations to subsistence living in the Arctic. How they will continue to do so remains an open question.

Traditionally, a person is a dog's *inua*, a word that is "formed using the radical *Inu(k)* (person) and the grammatical affix *a* (possessive), and [that] literally translates to 'my own self.'"[5] Though often interpreted as a dog's "owner" or "master," *inua* is the same word for the animal god or protective spirit specific to every other animal species and so grounds "strong affectionate bonds" in a unique sense, both physical and psychic, of "symbiosis between dogs and men."[6] The devastation of Inuit culture through the rupture of these relations lies at the heart of the story of how qimmiit today has come to designate both a site of highly endangered knowledges about precontact life as well as a rallying point for Inuit resurgence.

Within the past decade, through official investigations and a ground-breaking truth commission project, the series of events popularly termed "the Mountie Sled Dog Massacre" has become documented far more extensively and with far-reaching consequences. Starting from the question of why indigenous North American dogs disappeared from Canada's eastern Arctic region, the Inuit-initiated and Inuit-administered Qikiqtani Truth Commission (QTC) resulted in a series of reports that assemble firsthand accounts of how a unique kind of cross-species relationship is a flash point for documenting the devastating interventions of the state into Indigenous life. Addressing allegations that Canada led a systematic campaign in the mid-twentieth century to exterminate Inuit via their sled dogs, the testimonies gathered by this self-organized First Peoples justice inquiry provide incontrovertible evidence of cultural genocide and more.[7]

Weaving people's stories together are expressions of feelings for what it meant to have and to lose the dogs without whom self-sufficient life on their lands and waterways became impossible, a profoundly "emotional and affective identification" for Inuit dogs at the heart of Inuit culture.[8] Personal stories contribute to a larger narrative of how epistemological differences factored into the mass killings, signaled in the title of the Inuit-produced documentary, *Qimmit: A Clash of Two Truths* (2010), which I discuss at the end of this chapter. The film intercuts often intensely emotional footage of QTC testimonies with settlers' responses along with historical reenactments, highlighting how the official Canadian and Inuit accounts of the disappearance of the dogs become irreconcilable. But I think the film's sources in QTC documents are more helpful to those outside the community for understanding how the strong feelings are intimately related to crimes committed in the name of settlement.

Considering the myriad of ways that Inuit people have depended on these dogs, the story of *qimmiijaqtauniq*—meaning "many dogs (or dog teams) being taken away or killed" and frequently translated now as the Mountie Sled Dog Massacre, or more simply "the dog slaughter"[9]—that emerges through the records and reports of the QTC is exceptional for many reasons. A rare large-scale project in which people take charge together in decolonizing their own history, the QTC resulted in the public reconstruction of an oral history of exterminationist practice, one that accounts for how a community's dogs became explicitly identified and consequently feared as a threat to settler colonialism. Including testimony from hundreds of Inuit about dog teams intimately identified with particular people in family groups, the project prompts broader concerns about how abstracting notions like the "breed" of the dogs in question—whose uniqueness long predates the science of animal husbandry—close down ways of seeing animal and human lives as together sources of political power and, perhaps more important, as limits to neoliberal globalization.[10]

During the same period that Deleuze and Guattari first touted the potentials for people becoming-animal with a pack or a "demonic multiplicity" to topple the psychic subject of capitalism,[11] Inuit people living along with their packs of sled dogs appear to have been similarly identified with danger by the agents of expanding market forces. In their cases, however, such associations largely led to separation, detainment, and victimization by the state, respectively in the name of becoming enfranchised voters or immunized animals (biopolitics becoming quite literal through the contested issue of dog vaccination).[12] The Inuit perspectives coordinated by the QTC articulate how having become who they were through working partnerships with qimmiit inadvertently set them up for exploitation as cheap labor in the Arctic, then utter dependents once those ties were severed in settlements from which dogs were eradicated.

By turning to peoples' nonfictional representations of their own stories, of suffering with their animals, I am acutely aware that this chapter risks extending histories of exploitation—that is, that I am open to critique for dipping my pen in others' blood, as the expression goes. Yet reading and watching the testimonies reveals that so much about Inuit dog-keeping practices is not just unique but also remains unsaid in that context, with no need for people to explain key details to members of their own community, who are their primary audience. While the omitted details are an important reflection of ongoing cultural integrity, they also serve as a provocation to outsiders like me to educate ourselves and each other in order to appreciate how actions against the dogs implied actions against people, who in some cases had friends, relatives, or were themselves the dogs' protectors, even namesakes, in itself a highly significant relationship in Inuit culture that I explore in this chapter.[13] Recovering the details of why and how great quantities of these dogs died within a couple of decades therefore entails telling a complex story of Canadian nationalism, capitalism, and globalization as profoundly challenged by Inuit culture's vibrantly mobile potentials through life shared between species. I am compelled to piece the story together from the outside because, of all the cases collected in this book, the QTC's narratives justify hope that narrating human-animal relationships can be generative of world views along with sustaining multispecies justice.

Lamenting the ghost dog is not the QTC's point. Just as Inuit testators' stories resist straightforward celebrations of qimmiit as demonic or menacing figures of multiplicity, they describe lost dogs as collective figures evoking specific emotions for people whose everyday lives with them are likewise gone, as specific dog teams who remain only in their memories. Leaving the animals unnamed for culturally specific reasons detailed below, the testators' stories of their deaths also gain much wider significance because they invoke "the animal specter," only in a way that avoids the trap identified earlier in this book because the material substance and historical specificity of the dogs wavers between complete anonymity and individual animal subjects.[14] Relaying how a particular kind of dog together with a profoundly changing culture became perceived as heading for extinction by outsiders, the starkly contrasting perspectives dramatized in the film *Qimmit* anchor different ideas too about their affective potentials. Human-animal storytelling in this way emerges as a means of resistance to exterminationist and other rhetorics of erasure and collectively illuminates the QTC's refusal to reduce the dogs to destroyed property requiring compensation. By reading testimonies in the larger context of autobiographies, fictions, films, anthropological studies, and other narratives of Inuit sled dogs, my point is to show how their stories come to loft an interspecies version of Shukin's vision of a "heterogeneity of protesting subjects struggling to articulate alternatives to the present"[15] by recalling human-animal relationships beyond the killing fields of a haunted past.

Unsettling Histories

The Federal government operated [in the mid-twentieth century] under the belief that traditional Inuit culture was *doomed to extinction* and that the best solution for all concerned would be to integrate them as quickly as possible into the Canadian "mainstream" by creating a healthier, better educated work force for future economic development.

Marc Stevenson, *Inuit, Whalers, and Cultural Persistence* (emphasis added)

The difficulty for Qallunaat (non-Inuit) settlers to grasp the nature of the atrocity known as qimmiijaqtauniq begins to explain why it has taken so long for these events to gain national attention in Canada and why it remains little-known abroad. Five years after the first formal requests to review this history at the national level were submitted by the Qikiqtani Inuit Association and the Makivik Corporation,[16] a Canadian House of Commons committee in 2005 listened to elders who testified that "to diminish our numbers as Inuit, our dogs were being killed" by Royal Canadian Mounted Police (RCMP) from the 1950s into the 1970s.[17] Under orders from Ottawa, the RCMP subsequently submitted to Parliament the 2006 *Final Report: RCMP Review of Allegations Concerning Inuit Sled Dogs*, summarizing a self-study by the police that exonerated themselves from the accusation that actions of its officers caused a precipitous decline of the dog population in the region from an estimated tens of thousands in the 1940s to a few hundred in the 1970s. The disappearance is not disputed by anyone, but the cause has been hotly debated.

Responsibility for qimmiit deaths, not their consequences for people, was the narrow focus of the RCMP's investigation. Ballyhooing terms like "a massive dog pogrom" and "a sled dog holocaust,"[18] the mainstream Canadian press accordingly entertained only to dismiss the possibility that their government committed acts of genocide in the Northwest Territories (NWT) and Arctic Québec in the twentieth century. Lost amid their hype was the key detail that the RCMP in its *Final Report* concedes that only 8 Inuit are represented in the approximately 150 eyewitness statements that they reviewed in order to draw their own conclusions.[19] In short, Inuit versions of events were conspicuous by their absence from the first official account of how the area's qimmiit disappeared.

Starting in 2007, the QTC documents of qimmiijaqtauniq collected accounts from more than 350 Inuit through written testimonies and many more interviews and statements recorded at public hearings, providing a compelling counternarrative and moreover identifying a motive that is intimated by Yatsushiro's characterization of the dogs as a "menace to . . . white residents." Released in 2010, the *QTC Final Report* explains, "Government records, police patrol reports, scholarly research, newspaper and magazine articles from the 1950s, 1960s and 1970s show that dogs were killed in the Baffin Region often without due regard for the safety of and consequences on Inuit families and because Qallunaat were scared of dogs."[20] Never simply countering the RCMP's review of the facts, the QTC paints a richer picture of the regional introduction of a disproportionately powerful minority charged with settling a historically seminomadic people within spaces that once provided them with freedom—ironically in the name of assuring their political freedom to participate in federal democratic processes that largely failed to materialize. In the process, the QTC also quietly outlines profoundly different views of the human and animal life at stake in this fateful transition—more specifically, the differences peculiar to a kind of human-animal relationship that holds the potential to maintain a way out of entrapment in the market economy.

When RCMP officers and other governmental officials shot dogs according to policies that were created with no Inuit input—often "at random, without warning, and without consideration of the consequences"[21]—independent hunters report that they were initially shocked and immobilized, and thenceforth reduced to lives of dependency and menial service in settlements in which they were effectively silenced by a combination of fear of reprisals and grief for dogs whose identities were intimately intertwined with their own. Achieving *saimaqatigiingniq*—peace with former enemies, reconciliation among equals, or literally, "when past opponents get back together to meet in the middle to become calm and peaceful with one another after a conflict"[22]—is the QTC's overarching purpose, and like all key aspects of the project, it foregrounds that it matters most to individuals and cultures shaped by shared experiences of enduring harsh conditions.

Since expanded to include the entire affected area, the QTC's initial focus on Qikiqtaaluk, formerly known as the Baffin region of eastern Arctic Canada, is one of the project's strengths because it is by far the area where the most intense effects of settlement were experienced during the time in question. Gathering the stories of often elderly eyewitnesses and of the dead through their surviving family members, the QTC qualifies the numbers with detailed personal narratives of lives and livelihoods lost as a direct result of dogs being killed. The project's stories remain irreducibly collective at every level in part because no one laments the loss of any individual Inuit sled dog (*qimmik*) as an end in itself; instead, the focus remains on groups of dogs who traditionally are connected to a person providing for a small and family-centered community. Interstitially, the plurality of qimmiit takes shape as a membership missing from lives that in canine quantity and human quality became obviously diminished by permanent settlement.

Inuit continuance evinces exceptional cultural adaptability.[23] Deep social disruption was already well under way by the 1950s due to Christian missionaries' discrediting the role of *angakkuit*, or shamans, in providing spiritual guidance to maintain law and order. The distinct political culture in the region today was shaped more directly still by the systematic disenfranchisement of the genera-tions of Inuit who directly experienced qimmiijaqtauniq. Singled out from all other Indigenous peoples in Canada, Inuit alone were denied the right to vote for decades by federal bureaucrats who pointed to their seminomadic conditions and paradoxically "portrayed . . . the grounds for their exclusion . . . as practical rather than ethnic."[24] Consequently, the creation story of Canada's newest province could be told as an eastern Arctic spring of sorts, in which democracy flowers with the formation of Nunavut—literally "our land"—except that the territory was any-thing but ceded in 1999 to Inuit residents as a result of the 1993 Nunavut Land Claims Agreement (NLCA). The NLCA includes a controversial extinguishment clause, a mechanism by which Aboriginal peoples cede any title claims to the land, "often to receive the much-needed economic benefits associated with set-tlement and the right to develop and co-manage lands and other resources," and by which governments in turn frame "comprehensive claims as fundamentally contractual matters, despite the fact that treaties and comprehensive land agree-ments now have constitutional status and protection" in Canada.[25]

Another important dimension to the QTC therefore has been establishing a community basis for reframing discussions as nation-to-nation negotiations with the Canadian government, a process that concerns as-yet-unmet obli-gations to Inuit as well as First Nations and Métis people across the country. Writing about the larger Truth and Reconciliation Commission (TRC) of Canada that followed the QTC, political scientist Glen Coulthard (Yellowknives Dene) notes the difference between a pacifying approach to reconciliation, which sets colonial atrocities as harms suffered by individuals in the past, and a politically revolutionary view of the colonial relationship as an ongoing harm in need of transformation; the difference is signaled in these movements by a stymying *ressentiment* overtaken by a rallying resentment.[26] The challenge is to stay focused on what in particular is resented, by whom, and on whose behalf. Shifting knowledges of global climate change add a sense of urgency to advancing these discussions, as well as to respecting how exactly melting ice, accumulated contaminants, and nonhuman population freefalls are felt as extensions of the colonialist legacy by locals in Nunavut.[27]

Starting in the early twentieth century, policies were instituted to create the informed electorate that the Canadian government ostensibly desired, only with-out taking into account even advice from Inuit. These mandates often directly resulted in coercive or forced relocations of families to isolated settlements, the removal of children from their families and their abuse in schools, and most visibly, the destruction of qimmiit. The QTC thematic report devoted to the question of the dogs, *Qimmiliriniq: Inuit Sled Dogs in Qikiqtaaluk*, documents how "wave[s] of killing" immediately followed relocations of large groups of people to permanent settlements where they were no longer permitted to keep dogs in the old ways.[28] In the history of settlement, the same forces enlisted to organize representative government thereby came to undermine the Inuit's traditionally nomadic and communal culture, which at the time was already troubled by a century of habituation to the whalers, Christian missionaries, and company stores, the last of which is most directly responsible for promulgating still more conditions of shared human-animal tragedy by encouraging Inuit to shift from subsistence hunting to collecting animal pelts for trade.

Among other possible motives for forced settlement was the international-scale embarrassment for Canadian officials following the catastrophic collapse of the fox-fur trade in the 1940s.[29] Members of the US military sent to Arctic air stations that were established to move planes to aid the Allies reported an utter lack of services provided to starving and sick Inuit, who were left with no one to exchange pelts for food when the traders abruptly abandoned their posts. The continuing postwar US presence further "raised concerns about *de facto* Canadian sovereignty," according to a 1994 report on the relocations authored by the Royal Commission on Aboriginal peoples.[30] As practices instituted in the name of expanding human rights that more clearly served Cold War military interests, the relocation policies lend credence to ongoing resentment because they ensured cheap "labor or 'company' for military" manning the radar stations of the Distant Early Warning Line that was erected in the 1950s to watch for incoming Soviet nuclear weapons.[31] As the QTC testators explain, for Inuit, these moves often were devastating, and even when people survived them, for their dogs, they proved overwhelmingly fatal.[32]

Many signs point to the ongoing settler legacy in Canada's eastern Arctic. Far closer to the averages in Indigenous communities worldwide than to those of other Canadian communities, Nunavut's residents' continuing "drug and alcohol abuse, high unemployment, family violence, high suicide rates, and a large gap in understanding between generations" trouble any triumphal narrative of peaceful transition to home rule.[33] However, the strong persistence of the traditional language Inuktitut provides an indicator of the ongoing cultural retention of the values and attitudes favoring community that are embedded in their ancient culture.[34] Among Nunavut's Inuit majority, attempts to honor the enduring legacies of traditionally shared and sharing lifeways require a reframing of the story outside the terms of empire—more specifically, in the case of the QTC, the recasting of qimmiit-Inuit relationships from a source of past shame and pain to one of healing, strength, and even cultural resurgence.

An unsettling local history in every sense, the QTC's construction of the story of qimmiijaqtauniq compels a rethinking of how intimacies that roam across species lines trouble the very terms of globalization. One of several truth-and-reconciliation efforts of the sort identified by Hardt and Negri as a "symptom of passage" from national- to global-scale imperial forms, the QTC project might be expected to produce the singular truth of the multitude, by which Hardt and Negri mean the gathering forces of opposition to the global spread of capitalism. More complexly, the stories of qimmiijaqtauniq posit a representational challenge that involves not so much battling the capitalist subject as keeping open flight lines to a condition that precedes and exceeds the spheres of market economies, in whose interest it lies to render such formations physically and normatively extinct (a point to which I will return through the film *Qimmit: A Clash of Two Truths*).

Decoupling the extinctionist ideologies that portend the end for Inuit dogs and cultures alike following relocation to settlements in Qallunaat histories, the stories of QTC testators extend and enrich the descriptions of academics, artists, and others regarding how carefully cultivated relations of mutuality operate as a cornerstone of Inuit culture. A recovery effort with far-reaching implications for the future of Nunavut, the creative constitution of a collective narrative that concerns more-than-human worlds thus frames an affirmative answer to the pressing question posed by literary theorist Scott Richard Lyons (Ojibwe/Dakota) for Hardt and Negri: "Is it possible today to envision the survival of indigenous identity, culture, and nationalization in a nonessentialistic manner?"[35] Positioning material relations of immanence—rather than those of spiritual transcendence—might seem an unusual route to this goal. But to the previous chapters' discussions of the active presences of animal gods and ghosts, stories of the QTC add the further complication that death can occur to spirits as well as bodies.

For Inuit, sled dogs play a special role in spiritual well-being. Traditional Inuit aver that, in addition to immortal spirits and mortal bodies, humans have *name-souls* that embody and shape character traits and can live on when the name is transferred to another.[36] Inuit culture's ritualized, gender-neutral[37] naming practices encourage newborns to be bequeathed the name of another, often elderly or dying person; a baby gains "the identity of the spirit associated with it" and eventually "become[s] that person in adulthood."[38] Name-souls are an essential mechanism for Inuit maintenance of a sense of kinship beyond blood ties.[39] Qimmiit were given human names for many reasons—to maintain intimacy with far-flung relatives, to bear human grudges or illnesses, even in the common case of children giving their own names "because they are very infatuated" with their first dog and because it fosters mutuality in loving bonds[40]—but in the old days, in conditions conducive to low birthrates as well as high risks of untimely demises, dogs became essential as keepers of the names of dead people that could be passed on later when infants were forthcoming. Understood yet not elaborated by the QTC testators, the cross-species name-soul sharing is one of many culturally specific traditions that help explain why dogs hold such a special place in Inuit society and why their random indiscriminate killings by outsiders continue to hurt.

In beginning to relay these specificities, I do not want to downplay the hazards of extending a long and problematic history of outsiders generally representing Arctic cultures as "remote, strange, and 'natural'"[41] and of academics specifically institutionalizing "white lies about the Inuit," which are legion.[42] As someone who has long been studying stories of *Canis lupus familiaris*, our default accomplice in replacing wolves of all species as the most widely distributed four-footed creatures around the globe, my entry point is curiosity about how the uniquely shared human-canine relationship captured in the Inuktitut term *qimutsiit*—referring to sled dogs and people as an irreducible team[43]—has become a site of endangered knowledges and cultural resurgence. Patching together the longer story of how to live nomadically in the Arctic in interdependence with dogs who are neither wholly domesticated nor feral but of necessity somewhere in between, I mainly want to qualify the QTC testators' insistence that there is much more to the project than memories of dogs being killed, in the next section adding details about the dogs themselves, their training, and ultimately the profound disruption to their special bonds with Inuit hunters.

From Qimmiit to Qimutsiit: Arctic Dogs and Human-Dog Teamwork

The Canadian Eskimo Dog [also known as qimmiit, or Inuit sled dog] is *on the verge of extinction* with estimates of three hundred or less pure CKC registered dogs left in the World.

Canadian Eskimo Dog Foundation website (emphasis added)

Because the polar bear, or *nanuq* (*Ursus maritimus*), is widely seen as the iconic image of the endangered Arctic environment,[44] it was no surprise that the newly formed government of Nunavut initially opted to maintain a version of the NWT's iconic *nanuq*-outline license plate. But more meaningful relations inform the territory's legislators' vote in 2000 for qimmiit as the official animal symbol of Nunavut. One of the earliest political gestures of the new assembly, this decision remains largely symbolic because this kind of dog no longer exists as it once did in terms of quantities or quality of life. More a tribute to the sled dog's historic significance as a partner in independence for Nunavut's people, the gesture honors the fragile interdependence of culture and environment—in this case, local memory and global conservation efforts targeting what some see as the rarest registered breed of dog in the world.

Only "breed" is a dubious way to define these dogs—and not simply because of recent genetic research that identifies evidence of a consistent pre-Columbian lineage that long predates the modern breed divisions of qimmiit into Inuit sled dog, Canadian Eskimo dog, and Greenland dog, as well as distinguishes this "group" of dogs from all others.[45] The three breeds have been biologically redefined as the same subspecies of dog (*Canis lupus familiaris borealis*), notwithstanding the breeders' interests in keeping them apart.[46] Pace historian Harriet Ritvo's argument that the modern notion of breed began innocuously with the eighteenth-century documents of English foxhound pedigrees,[47] the institutionalization by national kennel clubs of breed names like "Inuit sled dog" and the more offensive moniker "Canadian Eskimo dog" underscore how the concept requires biopolitical regulations of dogs' bodies through colonialist and racist projects that affect animals as well as the people associated with them. To understand exactly what happened to these dogs in the NWT, however, it may help to follow the lead of postcolonial theorist Kalpana Seshadri to focus on breed as a eugenicist phantasm, in the sense of an "ontological essence" expressed in "the violent extirpation of human or animal identity (or property) that was never fully possessed to begin with."[48] In the case of Canadian qimmiit, breed status emerges late and as a compensatory gesture, one that reflects Qallunaat attitudes.

Registered under the unfortunate name "Canadian Eskimo dog" by the Canadian Kennel Club (CKC), the few hundred so-called purebred qimmiit remaining of the twenty thousand estimated to have lived in the NWT half a century ago are largely credited with having been "saved" from absorption into the mixture of breeds accompanying Qallunaat settlers to the NWT by the dedicated efforts of a handful of enthusiasts. Coinciding with the end of qimmiijaqtauniq, the jointly government- and territory-sponsored Eskimo Dog Research Foundation's efforts began in 1972 and are rivaled only by those of Brian Ladoon, of the privately run Canadian Eskimo Dog Foundation (CEDF), whose story of starting a little later in the 1970s and amassing the largest genetic stock colony of qimmiit is the subject of the documentary film *The Last Dogs of Winter* (2011).[49] Utterly reliant on "Inuit who owned good dogs and sold them" at the outset,[50] these organizations attest to an acute Qallunaat awareness of the devastation of Inuit dog populations yet remain suspiciously silent about culpability for its causes as well as consequences for Inuit people. The CEDF website melodramatically laments that, with "estimates of three hundred or less pure CKC registered dogs left in the World," its own work is a last-ditch effort against "extinction" of this particular kind of canid,[51] despite the fact that the greatest problems with keeping such dogs among people remain not biological or ecological so much as cultural.

Most agree that it is impossible to go back to the old ways that dogs and humans coevolved in order to survive better together in the Arctic. Partly the challenge in living among qimmiit is that the very qualities that make these dogs distinct ensure that they will not be easy dogs to home, in the sense of placement as a pet kept in a house. Traditionally never tied except in harness, Inuit sled dogs were left to fend for themselves during periods when their work was not required for specific tasks like portage and hauling, practices that favored canine self-selected breeding for year-round survival in Arctic conditions. Keeping them as semiferal working animals was not a sign of neglect but of ethical know-how:[52] "Inuit knew that qimmiit needed constant exercise; tying them up weakened them."[53] Unlike lighter-boned breeds favored in modern sled dog racing, qimmiit are not that kind of elite athlete so much as all-around survivors.

Genetic studies debunk fantasies that qimmiit are wolf-dog hybrids, but their tendency to wolf anything resembling food, their eerie wolf-like vocalizations, and somewhat wolfish appearance ensure that the longstanding stories of their essential wildness linger on. Turn-of-the-twentieth-century Norwegian polar explorer Otto Sverdrup waxes poetic as he attempts to capture what makes this kind of dog so special: "It has the persistence and tenacity of a wild animal, and at the same time the domestic dog's admirable devotion to its master. It is the wildest breath of nature, and the warmest breath of civilization."[54] A fierce love is at the heart of such descriptions.

More prosaic accounts identify qimmiit as extremely active as well as highly reactive to any stimuli—qualities guaranteed to make them either neurotic pets in cities or excellent company in bear country—and as highly social with their own pack and people, although aloof with outsiders. With these qualifications in mind, the characterization of qimmiit as "primitive" in the CKC's official breed description may be intended as both a compliment to a kind of dog that is unilaterally praised for superior physical and mental fortitude as well as a warning to prospective owners, who are advised in its breed guidebook that they are at best "a companion for adults, and . . . not to be considered a child's pet."[55] Between the lines of such descriptions hovers the recognition that traditional practices of training and keeping Inuit sled dogs allowed them to realize such a particular set of potentials.

Managing dogs is a central component of *Inuit Qaujimajatuqangit* (IQ), a distinctly Inuit Traditional Ecological Knowledge. According to literary critic Keavy Martin, IQ requires intense experiential efforts to achieve "a state of *silatujuq*—having wisdom—which aligns itself practically with a close understanding of one's *sila*, one's environment."[56] Because qimmiit provide invaluable support for hunting large and formidable animals like seals, caribou, and polar bears, skillful handling is so essential to IQ that it maintained an Inuk's high social value, even his masculinity, within his culture. "In the past, a man without dogs wasn't a man," according to Paulusie Weetaluktuk of Inukjuak, an elder cited in the Makivik Corporation's report that inspired the RCMP and QTC inquiries.[57] Dog keeping was considered men's work, but everyone was involved in maintaining their welfare. Hunters needed dogs in order to become providers, and dogs needed human protection in order to become something more than easy prey for hungry people and other large mammals.

Exactly how they came together to work so successfully has not been easily or comprehensively documented, making the QTC archives a treasure trove of information about this aspect of Inuit lifeways. Papikattuq Sakiagaq of Salliut offers an exemplary description, cited at length in the Makivik report:

> In our customs there were a lot of regulations, though it seems typical that the Inuit don't have regulations, but in spite of that assumption, we did have a lot of regulations. For example, in raising a dog team, while they're still puppies we had to stretch the legs, and rub their underarms, tickle them in order for them to get used to the harness. . . . While they're becoming adolescent dogs, we would have to take them for walks with their harnesses on. If they are not tamed that way, they cannot become

anything. I mentioned about tickling because when they are harnessed they are irritated if they were not tamed in this way while they're still puppies, and they are not comfortable to run if they are not used to being stretched on their forepaws, and feeding them with soup, making sure that they don't get into the habit of being hungry . . . that was how it was.[58]

Sakiagaq's framing of the narrative pushes back against the assumption that Inuit had inadequate regulations particularly for dog keeping—hence the need for Canadians to develop and enforce policies for maintaining order among them—and it also gains interest in light of Cherokee literary scholar Daniel Heath Justice's point that of the many "toxic" potentials in storytelling, "the most corrosive of all is the story of Indigenous deficiency."[59] Sakiagaq's recollections here explicitly begin by calling attention to misperceptions of the disciplining of Inuit sled dogs.

Such accounts are important because they also reveal that key details are missing from scholarly records. Anthropologist Kerrie-Ann Shannon's mid-1990s study of traditional knowledges of dogs in an unnamed Northwest Hudson Bay Inuit community notes a curious pattern of reticence among her anonymous informants. "Frequently, respondents did not reveal the names of dogs they had owned in the past," which Shannon accounts for as one of the kinds of traditional knowledges that are not shared with nonkin.[60] Other anthropologists note how Inuit naming patterns traditionally reflect the intensity of interfamily relationships,[61] a shared name being seen as an *atiq*, or name-soul, that is both gift and obligation of the dead or dying to the *saunik*, or namesake.[62] Because qimmiit are the only nonhuman animals to whom the Inuit extended this practice, particular dog names can be touchy subjects,[63] and any given dog may be given multiple names to serve different purposes. In the context of the QTC, it becomes clear that another more devastating reason for the reticence noted by Shannon may be the losses of particular familial and community connections to name-souls through the haphazard ways in which dogs were dispatched during the height of the slaughter.

How many name-souls were lost forever because there were no namesakes to take them when dogs were abruptly killed, with no warning? How painful, even impossible, was it to name the names that no longer have any bearers, that were unable to be transferred from the dying to the living? Conducted when few outsiders saw any basis for the Inuit-initiated inquiries that were then just beginning, Shannon's study includes no mention of the dog slaughter as a silencing factor, but she identifies and attempts to address sled dog training as a huge gap in scholarly understanding of the culture, especially given the "great amount of traditional knowledge being built up around the subject of dogs . . . [and] dog teams."[64]

Even to describe this terrific sense of interdependence when times were good appears to have been a persistent and formidable challenge to the imaginations of Qallunaat observers, who return almost compulsively to particular, lived examples in order to convey their sense of wonder at the achievements and risks that such relations entail. Glimpsing what such a life entailed in the early decades of the twentieth century, artist and writer Rockwell Kent's memoir *Salamina* (1935), about his years living among Greenlandic Inuit or Greenlanders around a Danish colonial trading post, illustrates the centrality of highly skilled work with sled dogs as a necessary survival skill. He describes a celebrated Greenlander hunter named David encountering dangerously thin ice and stopping the sled in order to lead the way home on foot: "I have spoken of the obedience of Greenland dogs at such a time: it is impressive. David with a low whistle would signal them to stop. They would instantly halt and lie down, watching him placidly as he went ahead in the darkness [to test the thickness of the ice]. At another almost whispered sign they'd jump to their feet again and set out after him, again to halt at his low sign."[65] The scene evokes QTC testator Isaac Shooyook of Arctic Bay's memory of qimmiit who "could lead [him] home without giving commands,"[66] an especially handy skill in the whiteout conditions of blizzards.

On treacherous ice, it is not a bullying style of command but rather the quiet understanding shared between the human and animal members of a qimutsiit that proves essential to safe passage, just as it is to successful hunts for the winter staple of seal. Then as today, the whip is viewed as "an important part of training dog teams,"[67] but it is also used sparingly, because (through Kent's eyes, at least) "nonchalance and effortlessness in driving are established as good form."[68] Dogs in harness may be brought into line, but like modern guide dogs, they are encouraged to exhibit "intelligent disobedience," or the refusal to follow a command that might lead to the endangerment of the person issuing it.[69] As the description of David's dogs illustrates, qimmiit instantaneously can exhibit collective intelligence like a bird flock or bee swarm, to all outward appearances sharing one mind.[70] While an excellent trick to get off suddenly breaking ice in time to avoid the whole harnessed-together pack being killed along with its driver, allowing dogs to use their common sense is a tendency as likely to inspire awe as terror in people unused to such behavior.[71] On the flip side, poor sled dog management proves a perennial source of drama even in the Euro-American literary canon, whether it is due to negligence, as in the frame story of Mary Shelley's *Frankenstein* (1818),[72] or deliberate brutality, as in Jack London's *Call of the Wild* (1903).[73]

Because they are deliberately stripped of such melodrama, however, the sled dog scenes of *Salamina* highlight fragile dependencies central to the old communal lifeways—lifeways that Kent prefers to what he terms the elusive "Progress" promised by colonial and later global trade systems, despite his detailing of many examples that echo what QTC testators say again and again—namely, that life on the land and ice was never easy. At the crux of the story, Kent himself skirts death when lost in thick fog on melting sea ice, only to be saved by his dogs. The homing instinct frequently noted in descriptions of qimmiit is all the more incredible in this situation because, as Kent notes, those particular dogs "never before traveled within many miles of the route we that day followed. I spoke of it to [another Inuit hunter named] Rudolf the next day. 'Yes,' said Rudolf, 'good dogs know.'"[74] Underscoring the hazards of the subsistence hunter's life, such details also paint a vivid portrait of what it takes from both people and qimmiit in order to "*fit* that life,"[75] a quality presented by Kent as hard-won, enviable, and for those of us not raised within it, ultimately elusive.

In the same year, Danish anthropologist Peter Freuchen recorded how sales of dogs in the central Arctic were never final because the *inua*-dog bond made it so that the people who raised them could reclaim dogs at will.[76] What such customs also reflect is that while outsiders like Kent might be able to purchase established teams of qimmiit, developing the IQ to raise them to the tasks of providing for one's own community is the work of a lifetime. The QTC's *Final Report* cites Pangnirtung resident Pauloosie Veevee's eloquent description of how hunters were judged on the basis of whether their dogs "looked well-fed and well-mannered" because the assumption was that the "performance, appearance, health, and endurance" were distributed across the species lines of qimutsiit; keeping a dog team was not for every man, but not doing so left the impression that "he was not yet quite a man," for without one, he couldn't be much of a hunter.[77] Such a deep sense of identification between dog and man left an Inuk psychologically, physically, and socially vulnerable when harm would come to his team, for Inuit culture placed the highest importance on their mutual success.

Part hunting buddies, part survival tools, qimmiit were never simply the property of hunters, who necessarily would care for generations of dog families that were deeply integrated with their own, functioning as elders beyond the conventional species boundaries. Bonds were forged from the earliest days of both puppies' and children's lives, and the Makivik Corporation's report notes that "many of the elders interviewed noted that as children, they had spent much time playing with puppies."[78] The memoir of early twentieth-century missionary Samuel King Hutton of his stay in Labrador describes how even an outsider can see how a sense of mutuality becomes ingrained: "The boys train the puppies, and teach them how to do dogs' work; and the training is a training for the boys as well, for they copy all the tricks and mannerisms . . . [that] they see their fathers do in the real work of the daily life."[79] Playing with puppies was a mainstay of Inuit childhood for the practical reasons that each became well versed in their roles and their particular interspecific relationships to each other.

Not in spite of but because the dogs remain dangerous to anyone who is slight of build or otherwise appears weak, those early bonds were necessary because they ensured the socialization of particular dogs and people to each other and thus the formation of a family unit that extends across species lines. "Our dogs used to be gentle to our children because they recognized them as part of the family," observes David Oovaut of Quaqtaq.[80] Ownership was shared within and across family generations, as testator Ludy Padluk explains: "They were family dogs. My wife and my kids owned the dogs. One person doesn't own those dogs. If I talk to my brother today, he has a dog-team; he would say 'our dogs.'"[81] Free-ranging dogs not only stuck around people they recognized as food providers from their earliest memories but also sounded the alarm when they perceived intruders, whether human or nonhuman animals, and therefore contributed to tremendously important safety systems for living in remote locations.

Before the twentieth century, Inuit most often chose to live in kinship-defined groups of at most thirty people with slightly larger numbers of dogs. Only with the intensification of the fox-fur trade in the early twentieth century were dogs kept in teams of ten or more.[82] The logistics of providing for—let alone keeping order among—ten times as many dogs as people appear to have been enabled by their customary geographic dispersal, along with very precisely cultivated sentiments. Kent elaborates that qimmiit "like their masters and they don't too much hate man. [Reciprocally,] men like their dogs. . . . They don't *love* dogs. That is perhaps a blessing to the Greenland dog and an expression of men's common sense."[83] While I understand his distinction, I think it needs to be challenged. A far cry from London's fictional sled dog Buck discovering "genuine passionate love"—a kind of "love that was feverish and burning, that was adoration, that was madness," for his white "master" in the Klondike a generation earlier[84]— Kent's description speaks more realistically of the unique way in which dogs and people maintained working relationships with each other through powerful affective bonding, which does not negate so much as very precisely delimits love between the species.

Neither pampered pets nor entirely free-ranging dogs, qimmiit traversed in-between spaces, functioning as powerful dogs fed in exchange for seasonal work for humans and all the while taking any opportunity to forage. Dogs themselves were eaten as a second-to-last resort, just before eating leather and fur clothes, which dogs could also be counted on to steal away with and eat at all times, given any chance. Working in Sugluk in the 1950s and '60s, anthropologist Nelson Graburn notes that many elders' stories highlight periods of starvation, noting "the loyalties and hostilities revolving around food" as characteristic of "a kind of life we and the younger Eskimos cannot even imagine" except when observing dogs.[85] The downtime of qimmiit, loose and out of harness, would be occupied chiefly with looking to keep themselves fed and to maintain their places in a pack, which meant outbursts of vicious fighting and opportunistic feeding were always a potential.

For Qallunaat, this aspect makes them particularly scary. Kent relays, "Grown dogs are best avoided, though if one walks straight at them with a manly stride they'll generally slink away."[86] A weak or unwary person can fall prey to the working dogs, simply by falling down among them,[87] an exceedingly rare but plain fact of life, just as in the past, people in dire situations turned their dogs and still more rarely their clothes and, at the worst extremes, each other into food.[88] Even in harness, they are not to be trifled with. Hutton describes stumbling over the dogs' traces, and "the whole team was on [him] with a pounce"; he was only saved from "snarling, fighting dogs" by the quick action of their "shouting, kicking drivers," who then instructed him "never to go among the dogs" without holding a whip.[89] It seems likely that Kent's and Hutton's anecdotes of living among qimmiit feature happy endings because both narrators have learned enough Inuktitut to be able to be taught by their Inuit companions how to avert danger over the long haul.

In contrast, as the QTC's *Final Report* notes, the overwhelming majority of Qallunaat who came to the NWT during the period of qimmiijaqtauniq stayed at most for three years, "some for an adventure, but almost all as a way to advance their careers quickly" to get better jobs in southern Canada and therefore saw no reason to learn the local language or customs.[90] Even more directly contributing to the setting and enforcing of policies that proved socially destructive to Inuit, this willful ignorance ensured that Qallunaat would be menaced by qimmiit, if only in their imaginations. In this way, the QTC's unique focus on the dog slaughter opens a distinct and understudied dimension of exterminationist politics.

As literary critic Anat Pick identifies in the context of Europe, holocausts concern not simply "crimes against humanity" but a more "fundamental unraveling of the human" from humanist ideals—in her terms, a stripping down to "creaturely fellowship grounded in the vulnerability of living bodies."[91] I would add that something even more complex comes undone in human-qimmiit history, for that which was once a source of cultural strength becomes also a point of weakness with the dog slaughter. Emerging through the QTC's telling of the history of qimmiijaqtauniq is that this terrific sense of power and love in the relationships of qimutsiit was enhanced within traditional Inuit groups but then became a point of vulnerability when these groups were relocated to the larger, mixed communities characteristic of settlements.

From Qimutsiit to Qimmiijaqtauniq: Killing Teams

"And what do people's names look like?"
"Like souls, only smaller still." . . .
"And where do the names go after people die?"
"They float miserably in the air till they find new bodies to house in. That is why you must always give new-born babes or dogs the names of the dead."

Hans Ruesch, *Top of the World*

Born of a culture of hunters more than gatherers, the old Inuit ways favor the sharing of resources as the surest path to making a living off the unforgiving Arctic land and sea. In conditions where meat is a mainstay as well as a difficult thing to procure and cache, it is not simply an altruistic act but, more important, a collective survival strategy to distribute food across one's own group, which requires that dogs too be fed, at least when they are unable to feed themselves. Mobility is the mainstay of all nomadic peoples, and traditional Inuit life without dogs meant no way to get across the snow and ice to hunting and fishing grounds in a countryside that provides precious little nonanimal foodstuffs.

Consequently, the loss of dogs for any reason amid relocation to settlements that were otherwise approachable only by planes and later snowmobiles became indistinguishable from subjection to a concentration-camp-style existence. The QTC's *Final Report* notes, "Many men were unable to hunt after their qimmiit were killed because they were simply stuck in the settlement. Others were fortunate enough to be able to share dog teams with close family members and, by the late 1960s, some people were using snowmobiles. Those Inuit who lacked qimmiit or snowmobiles to access the land felt that life in the settlements was a form of imprisonment."[92] Not all the dogs were killed by human outsiders. Qimmiit showed little resistance when exposed to deadly diseases that caused major outbreaks before inoculation campaigns were instituted by the RCMP, not so much ironically as coincidentally. Vaccination for distemper and rabies was a practice that likewise benefitted Qallunaat dogs, like the Siberian huskies who were favored for transportation by the RCMP, not to mention people because, as zoonotic diseases, they also make us susceptible to deadly infections. That said, the official reliance on culling and immunization during disease outbreaks remains controversial because it contrasts sharply with the IQ approach to sick dogs. An unnamed QTC testator reflects, "Some [dogs] were recognized as dangerous or certain to die, and quickly dispatched. In others the disease was allowed to run its course, in the expectation that most would die but enough would survive for rebuilding teams."[93] Although Inuit were prepared to work with the forces of natural selection to produce disease-resistant dogs, the settler ideology of wholesale culling and replacement with immunized dogs prevailed. Also, Inuit understandings of sick dogs as capable of bearing illness away from human individuals and communities were utterly disregarded, all of which contributes to ongoing problems with dog management in Inuit communities today.[94]

Quite apart from viral infection, which was a predictable consequence of contact between settler and Inuit dogs, many more deaths followed from policies that enabled the control of humans through their dogs. Some Inuit shot their own dogs in advance of relocation when informed that the teams would be prohibited or unworkable in the settlements, and others evacuated for medical treatment were forced to abandon their teams on short notice.[95] Some even had guns put in their hands and were commanded to shoot their own dogs for reasons unknown. But more testators recount how subtle strategies of coercion sealed their fates. Lured by promises of jobs, housing with modern conveniences, and education that would lead children to a better life, altogether too late they realized that they lost far more than they ever imagined they could gain. Padloping native Jacopie Nuqingaq succinctly explains of the family's relocation to Qikiqtaɩjuaq, "When we got here, our dogs were slaughtered, and we had no choice."[96]

How exactly the dogs came to be slaughtered within settlements involves an equally complex convergence of factors, as the QTC clarifies. Amid the many pressures to assimilate, it becomes more readily understandable that some Inuit attempted compromises—for instance, to supplement life on the land with wage income during off-seasons, a plan that precariously hinged on both flexible employment as well as the adaptation of qimmiit to settlement life. All too often, hunters who became wage-laborers stopped feeding their dogs within the settlements—only not seasonally, as in the past, but when they inevitably ran out of time and meat to keep them properly. Amid the steadily growing crowds, a new situation emerged.

Some dogs must have starved, but because opportunistic scavenging out-doors year-round is part of the qimmiit way of life, leaving such animals to fend for themselves in settlements with open dumps was not an automatic death sentence. Indeed, the QTC cites Yatsushiro as concluding from direct obser-vation that such practices were "perfectly reasonable,"[97] because the dogs were sure to die without the chance to forage, plus they cleaned up meat scraps and other garbage that otherwise attracted more fearsome wildlife like bears and wolverines. For RCMP officers and others charged with maintaining public order, however, these advantages were outweighed by the significant risks of daily living around semiferal qimmiit on their own terms.

Citing evidence that dogs were shot "by the hundreds [and] perhaps thou-sands," the QTC's *Final Report* again identifies a major factor to be "Qallunaat [who] considered the dogs to be a danger to inhabitants" of their communities.[98] The RCMP's *Final Report* lends credence to the fear factor with descriptions like the following: "The Inuit sled dog is a large and aggressive animal that can pose a danger to public safety, particularly when diseased or starving."[99] Still, there were RCMP members working in the region during the early years of the time in question who owned and cared for sled dogs and clearly rec-ognized the value of qimmiit; some officers provided their own husky dogs'

144   pups to Inuit families left destitute when their dogs died, and they inoculated thousands of qimmiit to fight their abundantly clear decimation from newly introduced diseases. Yet the RCMP report notes too that the period in question was one in which the government was phasing out sled dogs from official duties,[100] making it an open question whether the presence of Inuit sled dogs became equally devalued by Qallunaat as these changes took effect.

The history of dog regulation in the region is telling. Although dog attacks were extraordinarily rare, considering how many people were living in close proximity with them, increasingly severe governance provisions followed swiftly on the heels of incidents in which people were mauled or killed, particularly when the victims were white women or children.[101] The first, 1920's misleadingly named Ordinance Respecting Dogs, was seen as the official response to a white trader's young daughter being killed by dogs. Racist fantasies of imperiled white femininity traveled wider as dubious justification for the killing of dogs. The QTC records several testimonials from people who were told that their dogs had to be shot because a local policeman's wife had just been killed by dogs, only the historical grain of truth in the story of Maggie Clay, the lone policeman's wife who died of injuries from a dog attack in the region, occurred decades earlier.[102]

A series of regulations instituted largely as amendments to the Ordinance Respecting Dogs, the laws authorizing qimmiijaqtauniq ranged from coercive to confusing from Inuit perspectives.[103] The requirements to tie or muzzle loose dogs on pain of ruinously high fines to be paid within very short allowances of time seem lifted straight from more overtly colonial contexts in which the effect similarly is to privilege non-Aboriginal dogs and to make it virtually impossible for Indigenous people to move into settlements while maintaining dogs in the old ways.[104] In the area that became Nunavut, these policies moreover reflect at best ignorance of and at worst an active menace to local lifeways, such as the dogs' need to have their muzzles free to eat snow in order to hydrate themselves, never mind to eat, to clean themselves, and to protect themselves from predators. Inuit testimony that dogs entitled to a period of impounding instead were often shot point-blank, sometimes in harness, contributes to lingering senses of confusion and resentment.

Even for Inuit trying to follow the letter of the law, tying their dogs was not a viable option. Not only were chains expensive and often unavailable; they were also destructive to dogs whose social and other intelligences are sharpened by the ability to stay free-ranging in their time out of harness.

The QTC clarifies, "Inuit were particularly critical of Qallunaat who had no knowledge of the impact of chaining dogs on the behaviour of working animals,"[105] but there is evidence that some knew well what the outcome would be. The Makivik report includes the following quote from Northern Service officer W. G. Kerr's letter dated 1960: "I personally do not think that 'wandering' dogs create any greater hazard than does the normal automobile traffic of southern Canada. . . . It is also my experience that a tied-up dog, if approached by children, is more dangerous than a 'wandering' one."[106] Far less able to fend for themselves and far more vulnerable to attacks by dogs and other animals, tied dogs also tire more easily in harness, as many testators note. It does not take much familiarity with dogs to guess how many formerly free dogs put in chains became neurotic, self-destructive, vicious, and otherwise unworkable.

What does remain unfathomable, particularly to eyewitnesses, is why many dogs kept in compliance with the Ordinance Respecting Dogs were also shot. Igloolik resident Thomas Kublu's story is illustrative:

> In the spring of 1965 while I was at work all my dogs which were chained up were shot. . . . I never understood why this happened. I thought, "Was it because my hunting was getting in the way of my time as a labourer?" . . . This was very painful to me as I needed to hunt and because I was alone with no relatives to help me out with my responsibilities as a hunter and wage earner. . . . Since I had grown up hunting with a dog team and I so enjoyed hunting, a major part of my livelihood was taken away from me, my identity and means of providing for my family.[107]

Fleshing out the general sense of dog killing as a form of retributive punishment for Inuit, his story helps explain why the testimonies given as part of the QTC often include versions of the sentiment "I remember the day my dogs were shot" or "I remember when my father's dogs were shot," as well as why these lines are frequently spoken "through tears."[108]

The timing of key amendments to the Ordinance Respecting Dogs specifically to widen authority to kill dogs adds to a sense that the dog slaughter was a calculated strategy. The 1950 amendment sanctioning any RCMP officer to kill without any prior authorization coincided with the need for laborers in building the Distant Early Warning Line, and the area of coverage for its enforcement was expanded dramatically to include these communities in 1955, when DEW was activated and permanent workers consequently required. Another wave of dog killing followed the creation of some permanent settlements where people could keep living with their children attending day schools—but only if they agreed to kill their dogs.[109]

The RCMP officers' descriptions of killing loose dogs further help explain why these scenes still traumatize people fifty years later. Retired staff sergeant Mort Doyle laconically recollects, "It was unpleasant as the first shot very rarely killed the dog outright."[110] For Inuit, the incidents additionally mark the moments at which poverty became destitution, if also sometimes the motive for an endangered community to rally together. "It came to a point where I couldn't even sleep at night trying to keep the dogs alive," reported Eli Qumaluk of Puvirnituq, as cited in the Makivik report: "We used to watch out for each other's dogs and avoided getting them shot and killed and that is how we limited the killing of our dogs."[111]

Reports of more indirect measures lend credence to the conclusion that the culture was in the cross hairs along with the dogs. Another QTC testator, Kaujak Kanajuk of Pond Inlet, vividly remembers that qimmiit were an explicitly forbidden topic for children in school: "We weren't allowed to draw dogs or tell stories about them, anything that had something to do with being Inuk, about igloo or anything."[112] Of course, such details pale in contrast to recollections of the severe physical abuse meted out to children who failed to learn English quickly—not to mention the psychological, sexual, and other abuses suffered by children isolated from their families and sent to live in residential schools or with southern Qallunaat—or those of families forced to relocate to settlements often too quickly to pack survival gear and simply because they refused to be separated from their children. Presented by the QTC together with testimonial evidence of cultural genocide and other atrocities, however, the attempts to erase knowledges of qimmiit marks a tipping point for a generation promised opportunities for better lives but provided instead with experiences that "left them ill-prepared for a life of self-reliance and self-determination in either the modern wage economy or the traditional economy."[113]

"A flash point in Inuit memories," according to the QTC *Final Report*,[114] qimmiijaqtauniq illuminates one of the most controversial and coercive settlement tactics for relocating people from traditional life on the land. For people who, less than a century ago, lived largely on the move in small kin-based, self-sufficient groups between *ilagiit nunagivaktangit* (a term that encompasses seasonal camps along with special places like family burial grounds or

particularly favorable hunting areas[115]), relocation to permanent communities   147
of strangers and settlement amid relationships overwhelmingly defined by
institutionalized dependency was felt as a form of incarceration—and more.
Disturbing the platitude that Inuit went from "the stone age to the space age in
one generation,"[116] the QTC voices this transition firsthand in terms of a peculiar
form of violence that was inaugurated by the deaths of the dogs, inspiring the
wide-ranging grassroots response manifested by a unique truth commission
years after their culture and canine companions alike were said to be con-
demned to extinction. Moreover, by creating an archive through which Inuit
can assemble, share, and otherwise come to grips with their own history for
years to come, the QTC models an Aboriginal-led rarity among comprehensive
social justice inquiries, one that forges important new links to futures in which
knowledges of interspecies life are no longer endangered but rather inspiring
new narratives, such as the film *Qimmit*.

Specters of Multitudes

"Gradually, most of the dogs faded into history. And on came the onslaught
of skidoos," according to retired superintendent Clare Dent, as cited in the
RCMP's *Final Report*.[117] Painted in shades of nostalgia, his is a view that tellingly
pits machine against animal in a scene featuring no people, a story that sounds
way too good to be true. Working in the 1950s and '60s in a community where
he witnessed the number of dog teams drop from thirty-five to one within a
decade, Graburn (who was a student of Yatsushiro) offers more details about
the effects on Inuit culture of the introduction of the snowmobile—including,
for instance, that hunts were greatly reduced in frequency, scale, and nature
because walrus meat was no longer needed as dog food. In exchange, people
gained new risks like getting lost, stranded, or frostbitten on a "machine [that]
cannot smell its way home [or] . . . be eaten in emergency" and that proves both
ruinously expensive and unreliable.[118]

"No need for search and rescue," Nutaraaluk Iyaituk from Akulivik recalls
of the time before snowmobiles. "Nobody got lost. The dogs always brought
us back."[119] Still, the numbers indicate that machines are what people chose to
replace, not their dogs. Speaking to Graburn at a time retrospectively identifiable as the height of qimmiijaqtauniq, an unnamed Inuk elaborates: "a strange
sickness visited the teams every few years cutting down the numbers and

148   causing great hardship."[120] Maybe his description is not meant to be metaphorical, but it certainly lodges a protest within the narrative of skidoos as simply replacing qimmiit in the area that became Nunavut, albeit one that can only be read as such retrospectively through the specter of the multispecies multitude that emerges through the QTC.

Conceptually, *multitude* has a long political history of signifying a mass of people sharing only the bare facts of their existence, which in recent critiques of globalization presents a uniquely untethered source of strength to those who identify in such formations: the capacity to assert their own constituent projects quite apart from social contracts with sovereign political bodies. Multitude is a difficult enough concept to apply to people, so my extending it to situations where people are only one among other interdependent species is risky. But it is also necessary for thinking through the potentials for critique of exterminationist politics that are raised through the spectacle of humans in partnerships with dog packs.

Albeit in different ways, the film *Qimmit: A Clash of Two Truths* illustrates the "two truths" of settlers and the unsettled with a shared sense of uneasiness around representations that are violating a dog, a kind of dog, and a population of dogs—or, more specifically, images that deconstruct an animal variously perceived as a human ego projection, a cultural symbol, a demonic multiplicity, and all three at once. Through halting figurations in *Qimmit*, the very particular ways in which Inuit lived off the land and sea for millennia emerge as dependent on a special cross-species partnership with dog packs. The film both shows the very particular ways in which Inuit lived with dogs and makes the case for why it is important to see dogs as working not for or as individuals but rather at the center of communities.

Released as the QTC was producing reports, *Qimmit* opens with the spectacle of feeding the dogs what looks like seal meat on the ice, which is carefully explained as an ongoing practice and one that traditionally is central to the lifeways of Inuit together with dogs. As part of achieving the uniquely shared human-canine team relationship of qimutsiit, they must be unleashed daily and allowed to sort themselves out among themselves as well as with people and other animals. As he works together with another person to feed them in the old way in the film's opening sequence, their Inuk musher—who is also the film's codirector Joelie Sanguya—explains that such care is essential to the team's cohesion, both to ensure their immediate survival as a human-canine working group on the open sea ice and, traditionally, to build their long-term resiliency as seminomadic cohabiting critters.

In addition to the documentary-style illustration of culturally specific practice, some video testimonies compiled by the QTC are woven into the film along with white settlers' perspectives. Thus it explains what happened to specific people and highlights never-before-recorded instances of cultural genocide and consequent denials of responsibility from former government officials. Because the names of particular qimmiit are not shared, what happened to individual dogs proves much more difficult to say. Finger-pointing figures into some of the testimonies, but there are no easy answers. Before the opening credits roll, select previews of the stories that are featured clarify that the film attempts a balance of perspectives on what exactly happened, with clips of Inuit as well as white people voicing the "two truths" of the subtitle. A key strength of the film is that these bits of typical talking-heads-style documentary footage of people telling their stories are interwoven with representations of dogs that provide more than just stylistic contrast.

Throughout, we see different people struggling to share their experiences of the time of the dog slaughter. They are frequently shown to be prompted to tell their stories by interlocutors, sometimes as official QTC testimony and sometimes in their homes or public settings. More often than not, they have to be prodded to provide further details and analysis of what are very obviously difficult memories of "loss, shame, and puzzlement."[121] Moving as these sequences are, the film's representation of the dogs' fate holds a special poignancy, for their stories require more than just words. Real-time footage of the speakers is intercut with old photographs as well as with reenactment sequences featuring dogs as present in human lives only to be violently erased from them. The overall effects of this approach include ensuring that no one person dominates the narrative and that, alongside survivors, the long-gone dogs and people whose stories they tell become materially present, if also ghostly presences, within the story.

Voiced-over by people's recollections of shootings, qimmiit are shown trying to slink away or cowering before their shooters. When depicted as dead, their tongues roll out of their mouths, and it becomes easy to see why the filmmakers preface the film with the prominent statement that no dogs were harmed in the making of the film (whatever that might mean in this context). But it is also important to note that lamenting the ghost dog is not the point, nor are qimmiit celebrated as demonic or menacing figures of multiplicity, in Deleuze and Guattari's sense. In the main, Inuit describe specific dog teams as having been with them as coprotagonists and covictims in shared family histories. Again for reasons that are not clarified in the film but highly charged to anyone conversant with the culture, they are never named as individuals but nonetheless lovingly described as highly localized collectives working in support of human family and friend groups to make lives together.

The dog sequences underscore this point because they are often visual reenactments of deeply shared losses that announce themselves as such through the cut from full-color, present-day documentary footage to a past signaled with black-and-white images that feature old-timey feathered edging. Released in both English and French-dubbed versions with an eye to pan-Canadian and wider audiences, the film's presentation of people speaking in Inuktitut includes subtitle translations that clarify that the shooting of the dogs that we see reenacted meant a loss never simply of a pet or working animal but of relations built on trust with dogs who had to be constant companions within human families in order for them all to be able to subsist from hunting. The contrast of audio testimony of palpable love for qimmiit and visual presentations of violence committed against these dogs is one of the most powerful ways through which the film confronts viewers with not simply the difference between the two truths but also the struggle to articulate alternatives to the present situation.

While uniformed white men figure largely as the shooters in these stories, the most poignant examples do not necessarily divide people along obvious racial or colonial lines. A central sequence involves multiple Inuit witnesses to the same incident and is intercut with their individual testimonies, old snapshots, and reenactments. Only this time, fictional sequences of younger versions of the people are contrasted with current footage of the same people going back to reconstruct an event that profoundly affected their small group of families when staying at a seasonal camp decades earlier. Children at that time, they return to what feels more and more like the scene of a crime when they talk together as adults about how one of them was effectively deputized by a white man and ordered to shoot multiple families' dogs while their adult relatives were away from camp. Confusion and hurt are everywhere: among the now-adults who are all weeping, in the faces of the child-actors portraying them, and in the faces and bodily gestures of the dogs portraying the lost qimmiit, who submit to or fail to flee from the gunman. Blinking back tears, one summarizes, "I think, 'Those goddamn people did it.'"

Shown some of these video testimonies, a Qallunaat who is a former mayor of a settlement proclaims in another sequence, "I have never heard such crap in my life." The white man's angry tone and defensive body language mirror that

of many of the other retired government officials like him whose stories balance the film's overall take on the dog slaughter. But this man goes on to speak
to the difficulties of regulating a fast-growing settlement, where the very qualities that made qimmiit valued traveling companions prove impossible for him to
reconcile with the task of managing settlement life.

Illustrating the risks of living together with another species and how they
were compounded through colonization, he goes on to tell of the tragedy
of an unnamed young Inuk being killed and partially eaten by free-ranging
dogs in his own community and the subsequent problems of enacting and
enforcing colonial rules that dogs must be tied. His story takes a strange turn
as he recounts that the only dog he knew to have been shot by a trigger-happy
government official was his own Newfoundland dog, the only pet and the only
named dog in the film. Additionally, he is the only animal mourned as an
individual, a local celebrity commemorated in a poem presented as published in
the local newspaper. That the pet is named "Dog" ironically works to reinforce the
overarching story that each is always one of several dogs whose fates were tied
to their canine and human communities alike. With the film's concluding shots
of qimutsiit tearing across the frozen landscape to the tune of a song celebrating
the joys of traveling by dogsled, the multispecies multiplicity comes together in
Qimmit to present a timely and emphatic counter to the fantasy that the dogs
just faded away, replaced by individuals' choices to upgrade to motorized sleds
and otherwise assimilate to the cultures of modern conveniences.

Admittedly, my reading depends on whether and how you see one or several dogs in these stories. Colin Dayan in *The Law Is a White Dog* offers a
different take on the problem of seeing dogs as existing at all in the first place:
"Inhabiting this intermediate space between person and property, between
the most loved and the most disdained, the dog exists nowhere in itself. In the
law this seeming paradox becomes the working definition of dog: so empty of
substance that it can accrue to itself all kinds of properties, no matter that they
are paradoxical. . . . The flesh-and-blood dog that cares, suffers, reacts, and
remembers no longer exists."[122] Dayan is concerned with the legal problem that
the reductive construction of "the dog"—rather like Derrida's problematization
of genericizing "*the* animal"—remains insufficient.

Conceding her point, I would add only that the broader cross-cultural challenge of *Qimmit*'s two truths remains to envision how dogs have always enabled
people a way out of conflicting alternatives and, in the case of Inuit sled dogs,
more broadly to pursue historical and material alternatives to the symbolic

152 abstractions that imagine them into becoming obstacles in the fabled progress of capitalism. Drawing from the QTC's tales in both form and content, in this respect, the film's overarching story hinges on the dissolution of lone characters into a pack that itself is shaped by irreducibly human-animal relationships. In this emergent cinematic vision, the presence of dogs becomes haunting because it is framed in the context of mass killings and cultural genocide, bringing into the picture the absence of so many more who are dead.

In Nunavut, the immediate problems of large-scale human suffering that continues as a result of the transition to settlement life begin to explain why there is no mention of qimmiit in the concluding recommendations of the QTC's *Final Report*. Instead, the case is made by Inuit sled dog enthusiasts. In the pages of *Fan Hitch: Journal of the Inuit Sled Dog International*, an editorial statement urges the Canadian government to "encourage action be taken to secure a place for the Inuit Dog in Arctic Canada, while the gene pool is still viable and knowledgeable elders are still available to consult" and, more precisely, to "extend the necessary support to an Inuit-generated program which will assure a future for the Inuit Sled Dog in the north."[123]

In 2008, the federal government of Canada officially apologized to Aboriginal peoples for the residential school system, reiterated in 2015 upon the delivery of the *Final Report* of the Truth and Reconciliation Commission of Canada, yet to date, it remains silent about the fate of Inuit sled dogs. In 2011, an agreement signed between Québec's provincial government and the Makivik Corporation indicated some movement forward along these lines. Premier Jean Charest issued an official apology for the slaughter of Inuit sled dogs. Plaques were installed in each of the Inuit communities of that province to commemorate the tragedy. And Makivik dedicated part of the restitution monies to organizing sled dog races in Nunavik, the Inuit region of Québec.

Across the border in Nunavut, where fan-hitch sledding largely persists as a tourist attraction, these were not outcomes sought by the QTC. Elijah Grey, a resident of Kangirsuk, indicates why: "Personally, I believe we can get the dog teams back if we try. However we can never get back the same ways the dogs had at that time. I think we would not be able to train the dogs properly as in today's world I don't think we could give them an undivided attention as we used to in the past."[124] Restitution in the broadest sense is not an option for lives once shared so intimately between species. What remains instead is to articulate the vulnerabilities as well as to assert the strengths of a culture shaped by lives shared with qimmiit and, in so doing, reassert the community values rooted in multispecies multitudes long coadapted to local survival, all of which has been spurred by the QTC's efforts.

In search of saimaqatigiingniq, Nunavut's Inuit have created a collaborative project that reflects and reinforces their culture's unique and historic engagement with sled dogs. In recording a history of tragedy for both people and dogs, the project also collects and details knowledges that are not otherwise noted in the literature. "It was a great pleasure to travel by dog team," explains Peter Stone of Kuujjuarapik,[125] a sentiment reinforced again by the ending of the film *Qimmit* and by other testators who see no contradiction in their interdependence with dogs as securing their independence.

Distinct from the conventional truth-and-reconciliation structures ordinarily erected in pursuit of human rights or environmental justice, the QTC documents the rupture and recovery of the value of human-canine interspecies love at the heart of the culture. More distinctly than al-Koni's narratives, it lofts hopes alongside warning of dangers for a multispecies multitude—namely, that human-animal relationships felt as historic and vital to a seminomadic culture can provide important material as well as ideological means of mutual escape from the forces of settlement that would otherwise will them to enslavement and eradication. Inuit efforts through and beyond the QTC to record and honor sled dog love as vital links to life before and after encounters with settler colonialism are adding an important dimension to a wide-ranging grassroots movement, whether locally to reclaim Arctic land and sea before they are plundered for shipping and resource extraction or to enact more widespread movements for pan-Indigenous resurgence efforts like Idle No More. The latter certainly help clarify how and why love matters to these stories. Begun by a handful of women in 2013, Idle No More might be seen as continuing the momentum of the TRC of Canada, the QTC, and other earlier efforts—not to mention those that have come after, like the 2016 film *Angry Inuk* and consequent #Sealfie social media campaign, both of which focused attention on Indigenous women promoting awareness of the ongoing problem of how colonial attitudes toward seal hunting are hurting Northern communities.

Feminist scholar Dory Nason (Anishinaabe) identifies at the core of Idle No More "the boundless love that Indigenous women have for their families, their lands, their nations, and themselves as Indigenous people" as their primary motivation "to resist and protest, to teach and inspire, and to hold accountable both Indigenous and non-Indigenous allies to their responsibilities to protect the values and traditions that serve as the foundation for the survival."[126] As part

154 of this work, it is important to identify and value the particular affective bonds at the heart of the decolonial efforts that are gaining great strides. Yet thinking back to the difficulties of taking cross-species love seriously, it is also important to consider why animals are not explicitly in her list. Calling out uneasiness about the rarity that is love for Inuit sled dogs must be reckoned with as both part of the problem and part of the solution to their disappearance.

Coulthard echoes Nason's concern that love is mobilized by the women of Idle No More at the risk of a dangerous backlash that in turn is revealing of how "the violence that they face is both systemic and symbolic."[127] The threat explains why animals are not explicitly encompassed by otherwise "boundless love."[128] And it also begins to clarify why none of the QTC documents include any mention of the human-dog bestiality stories that once tantalized non-Inuit ethnographers, which are "almost completely based on hearsay," according to anthropologists Frédéric Laugrand and Jarich Oosten, who nonetheless document several versions of an origin story involving a dog's human wife.[129] As documented in my previous books, affective ties to animals have long been derided as signs of sexual perversion in Eurowestern traditions, but the targeting of women with sexualized violence by the end of the twentieth century becomes a severe drawback to any possibilities for empowerment that such relations also bring. Avoidance is not just understandable but also possibly a survival strategy. Yet as author and artist Leanne Simpson (Mississagua Nishnaabeg) suggests, such omissions serve the "gender violence" that empties out a sense of agency in animals, plants, and peoples severed from lands in processes of colonization and commodification.[130]

Whether feared (as bestial, violated, dehumanized) or revered (as platonic, pure, transhumanist), sexist, racist, and colonialist fantasies can obscure many more narrative potentials available to the polymorphous affective intensities anchored in material relations shared between species. A critical dimension of telling stories about the sufferings of endangered populations as shared across species lines concerns "the invention of improbable manners of being," the same creative work of posthuman and queer pluralizings of beings and worlds that matter.[131] Turning more explicitly to Indigenous, feminist, and other writers' depictions of nonhuman, gynocentric communities under threat, the next chapter explores some possible pathways through which violence threatens connections of communities across species lines and how storytelling itself signals ways out.

The Birds and the Bees,
or Life After Sex

Like birds, bees have long played special cultural roles in the generation, illustration, and transmission of stories of sex. One of the most famous literary examples is Samuel Taylor Coleridge's 1825 poem "Work Without Hope," in which birds and bees provide a point of contrast to the human on this point, enacting a heteronormative ideal of nature that eludes the lonely Romantic artist:

> The bees are stirring—birds are on the wing—
>
> .   .   .   .
>
> And I the while, the sole unbusy thing,
> Nor honey make, nor pair, nor build, nor sing.[1]

Despairing of being "unbusy," Coleridge's narrator seems like an outlier in a tradition that more often encourages people to get busy, conflating the senses of working and fucking. So birds and bees come to serve as ordinary reference points for the business of life—that is, until now.

In the twenty-first century, fear of a world without their work as animal pollinators enters even into animated feature films like *Bee Movie* (2007). Riddled with goofy anachronisms like male worker bees and a penultimate courtroom drama that features an insect suing successfully for the rights for bees to keep their own honey, the film contributes to a problematic tradition of animation's lack of fidelity to bees' and other social creatures' particular politics, only up to a point.[2] When the liberated bees then inadvertently trigger a worldwide die-off of unpollinated flowering plants, the story of queer bees mastering legalese swerves toward a heavy message about life after sex assisted across species lines. The film's vision of a gray, mostly dead world to follow is a devastating prospect, one that in the real world is becoming ever more possible.

Once an English-language euphemism for sexual knowledge, "the birds and the bees" has become a dead metaphor with dying referents, whose passings portend an apocalyptic vision like no other. The past twenty years alone have witnessed the greatest waves of honeybee die-offs ever recorded, and since Coleridge's time, the disappearances of bird species have steadily increased to numbers that are thousands of times greater than ordinary extinction rates. Because the forage of many bird species both depends on and includes bees and other insect pollinators, their declines are all the more rapidly accelerating.

Amid current conditions, "the birds and the bees" might well become a genteelism for extinction, not least because so many others depend on the increasingly fragile interdependencies of so many of them. As animate creatures who assist in the sexual reproduction and genetic outcrossing of most vegetal species—an estimated 75 percent of crop plants, including most fruits, vegetables, nuts, and seeds as well as 90 percent of wild plants worldwide[3]—their disappearances can never be just ends in themselves. As *Bee Movie* indicates, a grim landscape awaits in a future without pollinators, requiring a reckoning with our histories with social animals, particularly those who flock and hive. Our dependence on the literal fruits of their labors, not least to create and replenish seed stock, suggests a way of thinking of the reproduction of life as managing as well as managed by multiple populations—in other words, the ordinary ways in which biopower has always been nonexclusive to humans.[4]

Fictions of the twentieth century reflect a growing recognition of the ecological uncanniness of the birds and the bees. First fueling their figurations as a chaotic menace in horror films like *The Birds* (1963) and *The Swarm* (1978), the growing awareness of our greater vulnerability to "beemageddon" or "beepocalypse" informs abrupt shifts in narratives of the social lives of pollinators. In light of the mounting ecological evidence of the consequences of bird and bee endangerment and extinction for plants, humans, and other animals, this chapter explores a couple of narrative routes through which they take wing in sympathetic narratives that reflect and influence growing perceptions of them as endangered communities not just like but deeply entangled with human ones. Hovering at the edges of previous chapters are potential reconceptualizations of the relationship of materialist to what were once called animist perspectives—possibilities that Indigenous metaphysics allows for the simultaneity of both—and this chapter brings them to the fore by considering stories of collective intelligences that extend beyond and reveal vulnerabilities of our own.

Tracing flight lines above and beyond the built-over world intensively occupied by all things human, the spectacle of migrating flocks increasingly appeals to a rising sense of the precariousness of migrations, whether in terms of dwindling bird flocks or growing waves of human refugees.[5] As a sense of urgency rises around the fate of honeybees, bee swarms similarly gain interest for being fragile social bodies held together by negotiations that exceed our intelligences and, moreover, for revealing how animal and human colonial histories intersect amid the rise of biopolitical structures. This chapter focuses largely on two fictions—Louise Erdrich's *A Plague of Doves* (2008) and Douglas Coupland's *Generation A* (2009)—that connect birds and especially honeybees to modern histories of North American Native peoples. Both novels are haunted by horrific events involving animals and humans: in Erdrich's, a multiple lynching that becomes eerily redressed in part through a deadly bee sting and, in Coupland's, an attempted cultural suicide of a tribal nation imagined at the site of the world's last honeybee hive. Connecting fraught bird-and-bee histories with those of humans in the Americas, this chapter more deliberately than the previous ones taps the potential in literary animal studies to advance a genuinely decolonized Indigenous politics, one that is recuperative, as opposed to restorative or reconciliatory, through alignments of human along with bird and bee populations as superorganisms.[6]

Simply because pollination's players can be so varied, their narrative scope ranges far beyond the subject of this chapter, but some representational continuities are worth noting up front. In addition to birds and bees, pollinators include certain species of flies, beetles, ants, and wasps (invertebrates stereotypically viewed as pests) as well as bats, possums, lizards, and other vertebrates viewed as rodents—that is, all kinds of animals that are all too often earmarked for extermination. Even charismatic pollinators get caught in deadly representational patterns. Amid an ongoing history of killing butterflies, moths, and hummingbirds as exotics for natural history and art museum display,[7] appeals to a sense of visually attractive pollinators as passive victims appear to inform otherwise well-intended yet dubious conceptual migrations of species like monarch butterflies (*Danaus plexippus*) toward symbols of protest against agricultural genetic-modification technology.[8] Whether by reviling, revering, or pitying, diminishment of pollinators to dead bodies props up a deceptive sense of human control over their far-ranging capacities for social action.

In novels ostensibly concerned with the legacies of settler colonialism in the era of globalization, the birds and the bees not only figure in threats of global ecocatastrophes to entire species, including our own. They also illustrate that the recovery of all sorts of endangered populations hinges on humans becoming proactively creative in engagements with the sentiences of others (not to mention less procreatively active among ourselves). Rethinking our own "selves" as heterogeneous assemblages, whether of micro- and macroorganisms or of neurons and other cells, becomes easier through recognizing how other organisms more visibly organize life through collective formations. This is what I mean by thinking of them after sex: no longer wildlife observed for our instruction or amusement, "do[ing] it like they do on the Discovery Channel,"[9] pollinator stories of endangerment and extinction concern the management of life as a more-than-human set of responses and responsibilities. Particularly in fictions where they operate as superorganisms—bird flocks and eusocial bees—whose disappearances intersect with profound disruptions to Native North American communities, pollinators emerge as biopolitical negotiators for whom looking out for their own interests always involves interventions into the futures of other populations. They thus help frame ethics of engagement that apply to relations across cultures and species.

The recognition of the birds and the bees as not just biopolitical subjects[10] but also biopolitical brokers follows from scholarship at the crossroads of literary, Native American, and human-animal studies, though much work remains to demonstrate how fictional representations foster sympathy with animals together with Indigenous peoples struggling in changing environments.[11] While consensus is emerging about animal storytelling as one of what queer and Native American theorist Mark Rifkin identifies as "modes of indigeneity . . . that defy state narratives and survive despite being targeted for eradication,"[12] how exactly cross-species "ethical intersubjectivity" is promoted through modern Native storytelling requires further elaboration.[13] In the profoundly altered ecosystems that typically follow Eurowestern contact,[14] it becomes ever more important to recognize when and where the symbolic bleeds into materiality and to cultivate the world views that allow for such recognitions.

Multispecies ethics are the stakes of indigenous bird and especially bee stories. Bookended by stories of bird flocks and bee swarms, Erdrich's novel gains interest in relation to other novelists' similar uses of these critters to explore the politics of extinction in contemporary antiracist and anticolonial struggles, in part because she explicitly engages with what might be called animist materialism. Pursuing a theory of the "animist unconscious," African literature scholar Harry Garuba frames it as "a form of collective subjectivity that structures

being and consciousness" that is not only specific to historically and "predominantly animist societies and cultures" but also structuring abstract belief as
materialist realization.[15] Foregrounding the centrality of oral storytelling and
its representation to animist-materialist politics, Coupland presents an even
more explicit depiction of honeybees as disappearing—and in a way geared to
test how animist materialism relates to humans' very capacity to exist as social
creatures. In other stories, too, I show how narrating birds and bees as brokers
of indigenous life and thus as agents of social justice proceeds from a startling
correlation of human attunements or responsiveness to communications of
superorganisms that follows from catastrophic losses of particular populations.

Amid a broader rhetorical shift across otherwise disparate theories of political scientists, biologists, and media theorists, birds and bees more generally
are gaining new interest as conceptual figures for advancing social thought
about populations as exhibiting collective intelligences. Through their social
phenomenon of swarming and their industrial role as pollinators, bees lend
themselves more readily to elaborating such inquiries, which begins to explain
why representations of them are growing more elaborate, accurate, and meaningful in contemporary fiction. At the heart of these stories, I identify the urgent
questions framed by writer and beekeeper Heather Swan of how we might build
communities of "love and respect" with bees: "In a world obsessed with profits
and computer screens, how might we rekindle or create a sense of belonging
with the nonhuman members of our larger community? Especially with something as alien as an insect? How can we create connection and intimacy?"[16]
Forces larger than all of us compel me to add, What can we learn about the
biopolitics of love as well as sex from them?

Flocking to Traditional Knowledges

One of the many things that interests me about Garuba's animist-materialism as
applied to fiction is how it messes with the typical literary strategy of dividing
metaphorical and material animals, in part because that division helped me
in *Animal Stories* map transformations in urban-industrial cultures that have
little relevance to those at the heart of this study. Garuba's reframing of figures
and matter as entangled within Indigenous metaphysics strikes me as exactly
the sort of maneuver implicit in what Glen Coulthard argues is necessary for a
truly decolonial politics, where resilience gives way to resurgence. The trick is

The Birds and the Bees, or Life After Sex

positioning fusion as a starting point that is held together by Indigenous logic, and contemporary stories of nonhuman superorganisms like bird flocks and bee swarms follow the earlier ones of Inuit sled packs in the previous chapter to suggest that these intelligences can be shared across species lines.

This is not to say that metaphor is anathema to critiques of colonialist history. A limiting case that correlates symbolic and material conditions of indigenous critters across species lines outside of the animist unconscious, the title story of Thomas King's (Cherokee) collection *A Short History of Indians in Canada* (2005) crafts a devastating metaphor through the spectacle of migratory bird flocks in a modern city. In the story, a businessman visiting Toronto asks a doorman where to go to see something special and is directed toward a downtown neighborhood where he instantly spots "a flock of Indians" smacking into a skyscraper. To his delight, he discovers that it is a common occurrence, around which a whole system has been developed to identify bodies "by their feathers," as cataloged in "a book," a sort of field guide.[17] "Toronto's in the middle of the flyway," the tourist is told by a special team of workers who attend to the injured ones. "The lights attract them."[18] Long aligned in the Eurowestern taxonomizing imagination, "feathered beings and feather wearers"[19] here collapse into one superexoticized migratory form rendered vulnerable in the city. The material fact that the erection of brightly lit skyscrapers in avian flyways results in pileups of bird bodies[20] here bleeds into the conceptual erasure of Native peoples from cities, what Cherokee writer Marijo Moore symptomatizes as the "genocide of the mind," contributing to the bleak view in King's story of the postcolonial condition of Canadian First Nations Peoples.[21]

In *The Truth About Stories* (2003), King posits that the history of photographer Edward Sheriff Curtis's attempt at the turn of the twentieth century to document North American Indians that he believed to be "poised on the brink of extinction" directly follows John James Audubon's methodical killing of rare wild birds to document disappearing species: the one follows the other not just in terms of historical sequence but also as materially and ideologically "help[ing] them on their way."[22] King's concern with the politics of tribal enrollment and other policies aimed to regulate who and what counts as culturally Native might explain why he focuses on parallel or sequential ruptures of nomadic lifeways— only I would add at the expense of how they are experienced across species lines. To take up Garuba's challenge to merge the material and the metaphorical within Indigenous ways of knowing, I turn instead to Erdrich's novel, which likewise enlists the specter of species extinction to revisit genocidal histories but turns to yet another nonhuman superorganism in the end in order to outline a decolonial land ethic.

A long and complex novel, *The Plague of Doves* depicts not only birds but also bees as eusocial beings whose experiences are coshaping those of the Ojibwe and (as most characters in the story come to be across the generations) Métis, "mixed-bloods" of European and Native American descent. Within the story, relations of animals along with people and things manifest Erdrich's long-standing interest in personhood as a more-than-human concept from a distinctly Anishinaabe perspective.[23] Only in this story, superorganisms enable a subtle strategy more sharply geared to clarify how mixed-species social contexts support indigenous knowledges that tie people to things and other forms of life, taking Erdrich's career-long explorations of her own mixed-blood heritage in a distinctly animist-materialist direction.

Not without controversy,[24] Erdrich has cultivated a complex aesthetic since the 1980s that uses multiple strategies relentlessly to resist and roll back the erasure of Indigenous peoples and cultures.[25] One such strategy in *The Plague of Doves* involves a distinct departure from the metaphors, shapeshifters, and other extraordinary depictions of animals typical of her earlier work and to Native American fiction more generally.[26] Humor persists as a strategy through which her fictions suggest comparison with King, Vizenor, and other contemporary Native North American writers—nowhere more clearly than in the novel's titular event. Foregrounding how birds have come to signal the limits of our knowledges of other species life,[27] the "plague of doves" later becomes identified as the last great return of passenger pigeons (*Ectopistes migratorius*) to Ojibwe country in 1896, as witnessed by the character Seraph Milk, who is referred to only as "my Mooshum," or grandfather, by Evelina, one of the novel's several narrators.

Young Evelina delights in Mooshum's tales of the arrival of the birds in the racially divided community of his North Dakota childhood at the turn of the twentieth century. We see him through his granddaughter's eyes, as an old man telling stories from his youth, when the differently styled homes of "mixed-bloods" and "blanket Indians" alike suddenly collapsed under the weight of massive amounts of passenger pigeons. Their crop seedlings are consumed alongside those of racist Norwegian settlers, who "disregarded everybody but themselves."[28] In other words, white settlers might have seen themselves as separate and elevated, but they were leveled with all their neighbors from a literal bird's-eye view.[29] All of the people try to net, slaughter, eat, and even preserve the pigeons for later consumption, but the mass killings do nothing to stop the birds' destruction of everyone's crops. So Mooshum's brother, "one of the first Catholic priests of aboriginal blood," organizes his congregation to walk the fields together in an attempt to "pray away" the birds that the priest insists are "doves."[30]

The humor of the scene turns on the misperception of species and their associated iconographies. The Old Testament's avian messenger who brings the olive branch to Noah to signal the end of the flood, the dove signifies peace in Judeo-Christian traditions. Moreover, in Catholic iconography, the dove represents the Holy Spirit, or the third person of God. Mooshum's story of doves as wreaking rather than resolving havoc and of the priest as exhorting his own flock to drive them out multiplies inversions of bird meanings—and more. Erdrich's depiction draws from a much older dichotomy—"doves = good / pigeons = bad"[31]—that explains the identity transformation of the introduced "rock dove" (*Columba livia*) to the default North American "pigeon," today's ubiquitous urban "flying rats."[32] Plus, it finds support in historical accounts that clarify that passenger pigeons appeared similar enough to have been mistaken frequently for mourning doves (*Zenaida macroura*), another species indigenous to North America that was once thought to be its closest relative.[33] The consequences of the mass killings for passenger pigeons as a species and, along with them, for the peoples for whom their appearance traditionally had been celebrated as a great windfall haunts the scene as well. But it takes the novel a while to get there.

Unlike the usual stories of the passing of the species, which circle around Martha, the last-known living passenger pigeon who died in the Cincinnati Zoo,[34] Mooshum's doves remain an unindividuated flock who may or may not have been divine messengers. Devolving to romance, the novel's opening anecdote introduces them primarily as a plot device, a cover for Mooshum to run away with the love of his life. Only a more profound connection between the Anishinaabe man and the birds, "whose numbers were such that nobody thought they could possibly ever be wiped from the earth,"[35] takes shape through the doves' return—much later in the novel and at the scene of the lynchings that he witnessed right before their arrival, for what he is fleeing in the initial scene turns out to be the terror of his people that would follow the slaughters of people and birds alike.

While acknowledging her grandfather's tendencies toward inconsistency and embellishment, Evelina identifies as one of "the facts" of his storytelling that "those doves surely were the passenger pigeons of legend and truth."[36] Literary scholars seem less sure. Despite Evelina's clarification, Erdrich's play with the revered/reviled animal meanings contributes to critical confusion—and in ways that underscore the limits of reducing fictional animals to stand-ins for human meanings and interests. Critters explicitly identified as "brown doves"[37] are read metaphorically as stand-ins for "an excessively large, migrating, white mass of life clamping down on the landscape, overusing the land and starving out the indigenous population."[38] How Indigenous birds dubiously "plaguing" settlers and Indigenous people alike equate to a racially white menace boggles my imagination, but the persistence of such interpretations cautions against writing about animals without learning something about them from those who have lived with them.[39] How might attentiveness to animal life and death instead enhance the ethical complexities of Indigenous literatures?

Another important detail that Mooshum withholds from his granddaughter is the fact that the birds arrived immediately after three Native friends were wrongfully accused of murdering a white settler family and hung by their white neighbors, who were enacting their own frontier justice. Mirroring a historical incident, the youngest victim was a thirteen-year-old boy named Holy Track.[40] Only years later and from a descendant of a member of the lynch mob does Evelina learn that the victims were fingered by Mooshum, for whose drunken reveal of their having all stumbled together upon the crime scene he too had been threatened with being hung, only to be cut down at the last minute; he is thus left as the only nonwhite eyewitness, presumably to terrorize all Natives in the area. Evelina, as the novel's voice for "how history works itself out in the living," has by this point in the story acknowledged that "mixed in the spring of our existence [is] both guilt and victim."[41] So when she confronts the elderly Mooshum with the self-incriminating details left out of his version of the story, there is no big emotional outpouring, just a desire to visit the hanging tree.

Evelina describes the hanging tree as "always full of birds" and adds that, upon her arrival with Mooshum, "a thousand birds startled up at the same instant," then "disappeared, sucked into the air."[42] Mooshum sees the animals more specifically, he says, as "doves . . . still up there."[43] Unlike in the inaugural incident with the passenger pigeons raining down on the land, by this point in the story, it is clear that Mooshum's innocence has long gone the way of the passenger pigeon, "the New World dodo."[44] He has also lost faith in the institution of Catholicism. Yet as Evelina explains, he continues to believe in the doves' existence as "endless," as if "the blanket of doves has merely lifted into the stratosphere and not been snuffed out here on earth."[45]

Fluttering somewhere between passenger pigeons, the Holy Spirit, and wholly Indigenous spirits, Mooshum's final vision of the doves presents no easy metaphorical equivalence but instead provides one of many living embodiments of the relational matrix that anchors a traditional sense of personhood throughout the novel. Drawing from anthropological accounts, literary critic Catherine Rainwater identifies individual animals and even things as "nonhuman persons" animated in the novel according to traditional Ojibwan belief.[46] A rare reading of the novel on its own terms that attends to animist ontologies, Rainwater makes the persuasive case that the story consistently thwarts Eurowestern expectations by depicting characters only ever relationally, caught up with each other in stories in which things play active roles. I would add that Mooshum's returning flocks of doves indicate that more can be said about how nonhuman beings shape the story, particularly as they enter in collective forms like bird flocks and bee swarms that extend beyond the ethical-intersubjective ideals of personhood and, in the case of bees, challenge identifications of and with endangered indigenous creatures.

A quick comparison with another contemporary American novel suggests that birds may be too overdetermined as figures of extinction to realize the possibilities set in motion here by bees. Although equally elaborately embroidered with human family dramas of violence amid US imperial wars, Jonathan Franzen's best seller *Freedom* (2010) includes the cerulean warbler (*Setophaga cerulea*) as "not only a beautiful bird but the fastest-declining songbird in North America" today.[47] Introduced as the target of a neoconservative character's conservation pet project and later embraced in the story as the poster child of a popular campaign to curb the human population, the cerulean warbler ultimately serves in the novel as a symbol of an environmentalism that fails to take into account human and animal needs and consequently reduces the bird to a victim of corrupt capitalist, racist, and patriarchal politics.[48] When actual birds eventually arrive in *Freedom*, they serve as points of contrast to human characters, interjecting "a tiny plot in which there are no individuals at all."[49] More effectively than the green-leaning set speeches sprinkled throughout the novel, Franzen's depictions of severely endangered birds as active presences emphasize the effects of fatal habitat destruction on a handful of remaining species of "migrants exhausted by their five-thousand-mile journey compet[ing] with rivals who arrived earlier for the few remaining scraps of territory."[50] Yet persistence in decline is all that the story allows for them, in eerie alignment with the novel's only nonwhite US-immigrant character, whose untimely death after reproductively silencing herself inspires the creation of a commemorative and quite plausibly simply symbolic bird-conservation sanctuary. As in *Freedom*'s intertext, Thoreau's *Walden; or Life in the Woods* (1854), the physically present birds slide into storied forms to be elegized[51] and, along the way, eclipse histories of human migrants.

However, in Erdrich's novel, European honeybees present no easy metaphorical equivalence to any kind of person in the story but instead imbue the relational matrix with evolving Indigenous senses of personhood, which in turn leads to a commitment to justice on tribal terms. Accurately to the mid-twentieth-century time period it depicts, *The Plague of Doves* does not introduce honeybees as a threatened population so much as a social group through which people come to recognize and articulate Native American world views. Judge Antone Bazil Coutts, another one of the novel's mixed-blood narrators, finds a sense of pride and purpose in his Ojibwan heritage through living with a hive of feral honeybees. More specifically, at a point at which the bees are forced to leave their hive, Bazil discovers through them an empowering sense of communication with nonhuman others. In ways that build on similar moments in postcolonial fictions of the preceding decade, encountering the intelligence of bee swarms helps the individual gain critical distance from histories of human oppression.

Reflecting on his young adulthood, Bazil recounts his torrid affair with Cordelia, a white woman eventually revealed to be the lone, infant survivor of the family murder that inspired the lynchings. Cordelia is known by everyone else to be "more than [a] garden-variety bigot," but Bazil takes a long time to realize why she otherwise has no dealings with Native people in her personal or her professional life as a physician: "I'd always be her one exception. Or worse, her absolution."[52] During their breakup years earlier, though, all he knows for certain is that she has married a white man while stringing Bazil along. Meanwhile, Bazil let his ambitions to study law languish to the point that he can no longer afford to keep his childhood home, the back wall of which he "let . . . go to bees," in part because their "hum made the whole house awaken."[53]

But the hive proves a special link to the Ojibwan relational matrix in a way that leads to a greater affirmation of Indigenous knowledges. After reluctantly selling his home to Cordelia's husband, Ted, a real estate developer keen on teardowns, Bazil moves into a shabby bluebird-themed motel, only to find that "guilt at having abandoned the bees" fosters a change of heart. More profoundly, bees help him sense his house as alive: "It was as though the house was calling

out to me, telling me that it loved me, that its destruction was a cruel and unnec-
essary adjunct to my decision to break things off with C[ordelia]."[54] Upon Bazil's
arrival with Cordelia to save the house, Ted responds to her pleading with anger,
smashing the bee wall, and immediately the white couple are "swarmed by the
bees" and covered in "massive amounts of stings."[55]

The bee nerd in me has to add that technically, they are not swarming (a phenomenon I explain a bit later in the chapter), but more important to my argument
are the differences in how honeybees respond to Native and European American
characters, through which the story lends them a political intentionality—or at
least a sense of poetic justice. Bazil carries Cordelia away, and her witnessing his
comparatively callous disregard of Ted's suffering spells the end of the affair. The
fact that only two bees sting him with no apparent malice—"I think . . . [they
were] young bees that did not know me"[56]—sets an even stronger contrast with
Ted's death a year later from anaphylactic shock caused by a single bee sting. But
the swarming rhetoric proves misleading; rather than true swarming behavior, it
recalls a scene from a different postcolonial fiction in which a native bee colony
attacks another character bearing a heavy settler legacy.

In J. M. Coetzee's semiautobiographical *Boyhood: Scenes from Provincial
Life* (1997), the English-speaking white boy John visits his Afrikaans grandfather's farm in the Karoo region of South Africa and approaches a wild hive.
Attracted to the "fierce little, black bees," a description that identifies them
as the native Cape honeybee subspecies (*Apis mellifera capensis*), John fails to
get the bees to see that he is different from those who have robbed them before;
he wishes them "to recognize that he, when he visits, comes with clean hands,
not to steal from them but to greet them, to pay his respects" but is promptly sent
"running off ignominiously across the veld with the swarm behind him."[57] Again
the term "swarm" is inaccurate to describe defensive behavior, and perhaps in
this skewed perception, Coetzee's honeybees invite alignments of Indigenous
peoples and bees, writing histories of violent displacements of populations as
continuing through the failed negotiations across species differences. Like the
stinging death of Erdrich's Ted, it is at best ironic, a backfiring of colonialist history as embodied by colonial animals. Only the fate of Erdrich's swarm suggests
a radical rethinking of politics, literally from the ground up.

Quite apart from the romantic fallout of the incident itself, the perspective that the bees help Bazil gain in *The Plague of Doves* guides a new
course for his life and that of his people. The disrupted hive's action proves a
major turning point for Bazil, who immediately commits his career to Indian

law and eventually moves to the neighboring Anishinaabe reservation, where his mother grew up. There he eventually is appointed to serve as a tribal court judge and commits his career toward a greater goal of securing tribal sovereignty, as detailed in Erdrich's sequel, *The Round House* (2012). At the end of *The Plague of Doves*, upon returning to the gardens in flower at the site of his old house, Bazil finds that the bees truly have swarmed after all—and in a way that allows them to flourish. Although highly implausible because European honeybees are not ground bees, the relocation of the swarm to the town cemetery where they build a hive "beneath the earth" and get busy "filling the skulls with white comb and the coffins with sweet black honey"[58] has again a certain poetic logic, given Bazil's specialty in land claims. For Bazil's interpretation of sovereignty guards "tribal law on tribal land," grounded in ownership as interpreted not by US law so much as by "a historical Native continuum"[59]—again a relational matrix of humans, animals, and things—that his own gentle relations with the bees and their shared home bodies forth.

Foreshadowing the fate of the bees, Bazil quips early on, "The ground swallows and absorbs even those who form a country, a reservation," just as it fosters the traditional tribal "love and knowledge of the land and its relationship to dreams."[60] The honeybees who prop up a social matrix that fosters his home-love in turn embody the responsiveness required of responsibility to the land and all its inhabitants, which is nothing so patronizing as environmental stewardship nor objectifying as ownership. That they persist in doing so as invasives, where passenger pigeons have gone extinct, says much more about why bees more than birds prove useful to narratives like Erdrich's that explore complex questions of indigeneity across species lines.

Why More Bees Than Birds?

The wild animals most frequently encountered by people today, birds claim a special role in perceptions of shared multispecies worlds that range far beyond the dynamics of pollination. Of all categories of animals, their literary history is also the most far-ranging in terms of symbolic and other human-centered meanings.[61] As literary critic Jeff Karnicky observes, the "notion of birds as either a means of appreciating nature or of understanding the human place in the world is a common thread that runs through the history of much American writing on birds," including that of Audubon and Thoreau.[62] While some see their prolific representational history as an opportunity to restore an ecopoetic sensibility of what birds used to mean in people's everyday lives—a route that risks racist fantasy through conflations with Traditional Ecological Knowledges[63]—Erdrich's novel offers a special challenge to such conclusions by aligning material sensibilities of the extinction of passenger pigeons with settler-colonialist atrocities and the persistence of "Native ways of knowing" with nonnative honeybees.[64] But again, the burden is on the reader to bring knowledges of other species to the text.

Like dogs, birds' accrual of cultural roles and meanings presents challenges to seeing and thinking about them differently. The colloquial persistence of "birdbrain" to mean a scatterbrain or stupid person reflects a serious challenge to taking avian intelligence seriously. Relayed in her best seller *The Alex Studies: Cognitive and Communicative Abilities of Grey Parrots* (2002), animal psychologist Irene Pepperberg's work with Alex the African grey parrot (*Psittacus erithacus*) popularizes scientific understanding of birds' capacities for great-ape-level cognitive tasks,[65] and it reflects a recent and far more comprehensive transformation of perceptions of who is physically capable of intelligent life according to neuroscience.[66] Intertwining cases of human brain-trauma survivors with the endangerment and fraught conservation of sandhill and whooping cranes (*Antigone canadensis* and *Grus americana*), Richard Powers's novel *The Echo Maker* (2006) explores further how new neurophysiological identification of the similar workings of the human amygdala and the brains of birds has benefited medical caregiving for human head-injury survivors. In the novel as in life, the accumulating evidence, such as that the brains of pollinators like some species of parrots contain as many or more neurons than those of primates (in the forebrain, concentrating two times as many as primates[67]) does not stop developers from destroying the habitats of bird species, setting them firmly on course toward extinction.

As environmental philosopher Thom van Dooren argues, narrative can be enlisted in different ways to highlight how the species extinctions especially of birds involve a distinct and often "slow unraveling of intimately entangled ways of life" that evolved over millions of years. Such work gains increasing urgency as their passings become more and more unevenly experienced as tragedies.[68] But there is something to be said about how bee stories mark dramatic shifts in recent decades toward appreciation for the role of microfauna in improving human lives. As old associations with fecundity give way, beepocalytic fears shape sympathetic narratives informed by their imbrication in modern human foodways. Although honeybee hives have a long symbolic history as utopian alternatives to human societies, growing understanding of their biopolitical significance as eusocial pollinators shifts them into closer alignment with human worlds in which their biopolitical histories as colonial animals encounter friction with those of Native peoples.

Indigeneity immediately raises the question, Where do honeybees belong? In most places where they live today, honeybees are not native and not wild, complicating associations with invasion along with environmental concerns about their impending doom. Because the Western or European honeybee (*Apis mellifera*) constitutes the main pollinator population being systematically monitored, they have come to serve as the proverbial canaries in coal mines, indicating alarming rates of their own decline, along with those of wild bee and other pollinating species, particularly in recent decades.[69] As animate creatures who assist in the sexual reproduction and genetic outcrossing of most vegetal species, their disappearances can never be just ends in themselves.

First observed in 2006, the phenomenon now known as Colony Collapse Disorder (CCD) in commercial honeybees marks a tipping point in terms of mobilizing public efforts to stem a tide of die-offs, including US president Barack Obama's 2014 executive order to address the "breadth, severity, and persistence of pollinator losses."[70] Yet the health of the pollinating species responsible for so much crop and wild-plant diversity was not a major conservation consideration until the mid-1990s. Stupefying in retrospect, public interest lagged years behind commercial beekeepers' initial reports of massive losses that at the time sounded a global alarm among apiculture scientists.

Even today, effective actions continue to be hindered by the fact that science and industry have been parts of the problem all along. Although Assyrian and Mayan texts aver ancient knowledges of the importance of winged creatures to flowering-plant health, scientific misconceptions and prejudices long hampered the development of pollination ecology, a field also known as anthoecology.[71] Meanwhile, industrial-scale agriculture—propelled by the doubling of the world's human populations and increase of our caloric consumption by almost a third, all within the past fifty years—has grown to depend on monocrop fertilization through commercial apiculture.

While scientists fail to identify a single cause, the CCD crisis increasingly appears to be the tip of the iceberg, a symptom of the highly contingent and unsustainable dependence on a peculiar form of animal farming, or "apis industrial agriculture," in which we consume not their bodies but the products of their labor.[72] A dizzyingly amped-up version of modern apicultural practice, commercial beekeepers' constant movement of their hives follows the money from one kind of crop planting to another rather than allowing bees the diverse forage they evolved to consume. A poor diet consequently makes parasites and diseases endemic in the species most commonly in use, the European honeybee—hence "the best-known insect on the planet"[73]—just as it has helped them inadvertently hurt wild insect pollinators by spreading infectious pathogens.[74] Efforts to restrict uses of neonicotinoids and other toxic pesticides do not address the fundamental problem that pollinators have been made to suffer the injustice of our greed.

Calls to liberate these "lilliputian livestock"[75] are equally problematic for failing to appreciate the particularities of our shared situation. Never simply confined, dominated, or exploited, European honeybees are self-organizing societies that can thrive in symbiosis with humans—or more precisely, in the care of skilled, diligent beekeepers who can try to secure access to sufficiently diverse quantities of flowering plants. Averting a growing crisis that at once concerns food security and the futures of global ecologies in the current situation of pollinators requires that the complexities of cross-species sociality be reframed beyond animal rights and economic wrongs and instead through questions of cultures and capacities that cross species lines.

Amid a newfound sense of urgency about their fates, interest is growing in long-term studies of bees that, like the bird studies, are revealing their astonishing intelligences. Pursuing the earlier findings of Karl von Frisch and Martin Lindauer about honeybee communication through what they called the waggle dance, entomologists-turned-popular-science-writers like Thomas Seeley, Bert Hölldobler, and E. O. Wilson clarify the analogy between a hive's bees and human brain cells—in which, "in both cases, a constellation of units at one level of biological organization cooperate closely to build a higher-level entity"[76]—and are credited with influencing popular novels like Laline Paull's *The Bees* (2014). But they account for only part of bees' stories in contemporary fiction.

Literary critic Sean Meighoo compares how the early findings of bee ethology became strategically interpreted as communicating code but not language—"a closed language of signals," not "an open language of symbols"—through the wide-ranging arguments of Jacques Lacan, Émile Benveniste, and Martin Heidegger.[77] Through them, conceptual along with experimental violences are directed at bees that cumulatively reinforce a sense of human exceptionalism ironically at the heart of self-proclaimed antihumanist thinking.

As Meighoo notes, the regular cycles of mass death now normalized in industrial apiculture are among the many commonplace examples of "massive forms
of human violence against nonhuman animals."[78] Erdrich's novel suggests
that situating Eurowestern thinking amid humans' and bees' colonial histories, broadly writ, sets another story line in motion with living, nonhuman,
collective alternatives. More comparisons with increasingly realistic fictional
representations of swarms that also revisit horrific human histories help clarify
the multispecies indigenous politics at stake in contemporary fictions that
more explicitly and accurately present swarms as forms of expression of honeybee intelligences.

Swarming Girls

While bird colonies are usually selected as prime nesting spots inaccessible to
humans and other predators, honeybees operate in colonies more like human
colonizers, as mobile and adaptable societies founded on the division and dif-
ferentiation of labor. Because their "model form of social organization . . . has
inspired every possible political theorist,"[79] entomologists still struggle with
terms to make sense of bees' social life. To correct the modern misperception
captured in Charles Butler's 1609 title, *The Feminine Monarchie*, Seeley in particular draws from extensive studies of the phenomenon of bee swarming—the
unique behavior through which bees collectively choose a new home from
among several options—to make the case that it resembles a peculiarly US
model of democratic negotiation, with different options presented and voted
on by the entire group. Yet the royal-family discourse persists in obscuring the
distribution of power in the hive in much the same way that settler family lore
of being descended of an "Indian princess" distorts histories of Native North
American contributions to modern democracies[80]—notably the historical influence of the Iroquois Constitution, or Great Law of Peace, in the formation of
the US Constitution, ironically the basis on which Native American sovereignty
later became eroded and genocide enacted as official policy. Looking more
closely at how bee and human colonial histories come into friction in contemporary fiction and in ways that mess with gendered hierarchies, it becomes
clear that swarms gain interest as much for what they undo as for what they do.

Quite apart from the reactionary attacks represented by Erdrich and
Coetzee, swarming is a peaceable if mysterious process. When a hive decides

that it's big enough, the old queen leaves with more than half of the worker bees to form a new colony. Terms like "queen" belie the fact that, once a swarm alights at a temporary location, they are organized communally, taking the form of protracted deliberations. In a healthy hive that reaches the critical mass, around half stuff themselves with honey and depart with the old queen in a sudden swarm formation, which quietly settles in a spot from which scouts go out, returning to share information about different nesting options through dances. The swarm concludes with a collective decision to move into a permanent home (all will die if they do not come to an agreement). An eerily similar process to what goes on between the neurons in our brains when we make decisions, swarm negotiations demonstrate the defining hive-mind quality of a superorganism.

In recent fictions, realistic depictions of swarms increasingly call attention to the complex roles of nonhuman intelligences in mediating Indigenous pasts and futures. Three feature not boys but girls attracted to gynocentric communities who find themselves at the center of the bees' activity: swarms literally settle on their bodies. Each novel is ostensibly about the girl's coming to terms with the racist and colonialist legacies of her own human community and features a swarm as triggering key transformations. By the end, each girl is moved to become a beekeeper and actively to distance herself from settler inheritances. What is perhaps most curious is that across the decades, this character type increasingly, if haltingly, is also identified as Indigenous.

In David Malouf's critical success *Remembering Babylon* (1993), the girl Janet eventually lives as a nun in a convent, a situation ripe for interpretation as a beehive metaphor, except that she also works there as a bee developer or breeder of international standing. Her decision to hybridize indigenous Australian stingless with imported European honeybees figuratively folds back on her youthful love for Gemmy, who is a white man assimilated to Australian culture in an Aboriginal community as well as the historical figure at the heart of the story. In early discussions of *Remembering Babylon*, an exclusive focus on human dimensions fueled critiques of Malouf's silencing of Indigenous people's voices in favor of spinning a pastoral idyll that privileges European viewpoints. More recently, literary critic Clare Archer-Leane links the novel's concerns with human animality to its visualizations of human-animal encounters in order to show how the story deconstructs romanticized nature in order to introduce a more explicitly "post-pastoral" vision.[81] Her argument builds from an animal-centered reading of the novel by Graham Murphy, another literary critic who persuades that Gemmy unwittingly calls attention to "uncomfortable truth" of the common human animality of colonizers and their "others."[82] As encounters that do not idealize or transcend their conditions, other narrative moments featuring human-animal intimacies reveal struggles to articulate new ways of relating—most clearly in the depiction of Janet's bees.

European honeybees kept harmoniously alongside stingless native varieties invite yet another kind of symbolic reading as utopian-animal alternatives to the novel's fraught human-colonial politics. But the particulars of Janet's bee encounters layer in a practical transformative potential that leads her off course from settlement life, perhaps most significantly because Janet is the novel's only major white character born in Australia. She initially laments that she cannot share directly in her parents' nostalgia for their Scottish home, but as the story unfolds, their expressions of longing lean toward the replication, even parody, of European pastoral ideals. Like Erdrich's Bazil, Janet introduces a different relation to nonhuman personhood and Indigenous land claims, and the swarm scene explains how. Suddenly finding herself covered in bees, newly pubescent Janet remains uninjured not simply because she remains still but, more important, because she melds with the hive mind, engaging with swarm consciousness: "Her mind had for a moment been their unbodied one and she had been drawn into the process and mystery of things."[83] Suggesting more to the coincidence that the typical bee swarm weighs exactly the same as the neurons in a human brain (3 pounds, or 1.5 kilograms), the scene is also a rare literary attempt to represent swarms as thinking.

In the absence of any all-knowing leader, planner, or even supervisor, the twenty to eighty thousand bees of a hive govern themselves collectively, a process that becomes all the more critical when several thousand peel off to found a new colony. Whether bees or brain cells, the individual unit contributes limited information or intelligence to a process that results in decisive action on the part of the whole superorganism. Seeley's studies of how bee swarms almost always choose the best available nesting location lead him to conclude that they serve also as communicative models "for building groups far smarter than the smartest individuals in them."[84] Because this all-important deliberation happens only after they have left their old home, the waggle dances through which bees share and deliberate options are performed atop each other's bodies, in a swarming mass. Janet thus becomes conscious of something greater than she could ever have known as the bees repurpose her body as a temporary communication platform.

The Birds and the Bees, or Life After Sex

Seeing herself afterward "through Gemmy's eyes," in "his astonished look,"[85] Janet knows instantly that she has become permanently altered by her sense of communication within the swarm. The novel does not clarify whether the swarm is of imported European or native stingless bees—and among the latter, whether it might be one of the most common two Australian honeybee species (*Tetragonula carbonaria* or *hockingsi*), which in itself seems significant for blurring the nonhuman lines of native and colonizer, just as Gemmy does in the human realm. As a first-generation settler, Janet's life with hybridized bees allows her to body forth an alternative to the displacement and destruction that is the fate of Gemmy's adoptive community at the hands of other white people—he is later murdered alongside his Aboriginal family—and one that casts her in an unlikely alliance among the old and new natives of different species.

In Sue Monk Kidd's best seller *The Secret Life of Bees* (2001), the swarm experience inspires the girl Lily to flee from a brutal father with her African American nanny Rosaleen, who in the Jim Crow–era Deep South is threatened with lynching for registering to vote. Reminiscent of Bazil's house in Erdrich's novel, the bee swarm originates from a hive within an outer wall of Lily's childhood home and in a way that leads to a reframing of personal suffering within political issues. Like Janet, Lily becomes "the perfect center of a whirlwind cloud"[86] of bees, only one that quickly disappears, indicating a rare split decision that can result in the failure to form a new colony. With the girl as its sole human witness, the swarm arrives here too as an inspiration for socially progressive change. Lily and her nanny run away and quickly find shelter in a community of African American women who worship with honey in the tradition of their slave ancestors, and Lily eventually learns beekeeping from their leader.

More a commercial than critical success, *The Secret Life of Bees* inspires far more explicit accusations of cultural theft[87] than *Remembering Babylon*, though along similar lines. The events of 1964's Freedom Summer, a pivotal moment in African American history, are reduced to a backdrop for a white writer's story of a self-identified white girl becoming profoundly changed by being welcomed into an intimate group of black women. Trading in racial stereotypes, the novel introduces all of the black women as caricatures—whether mammies, haters, or nutters—but importantly does not leave them there.

That all the central female characters eventually and explicitly question racist reductions of people to type aligns them with Evelina and Bazil, Gemmy and Janet, as complicated, changing, and changed characters in (rather than caricatures of) painful social legacies—in this case, the US history of slavery and segregation. While Janet gains a sense of female empowerment and appreciation for others' indigenous knowledges, for Lily, intimacy with the bees begins a process that leads her to embrace her newfound life with "all these women, all this love."[88] And undermining Lily's first-person narration, all along the novel hints that the girl is being kept from knowing that her long-dead mother wasn't white and that she may be directly descended of the bee-loving black women. Though the evidence is vague, the girl's embracing their honeyed goddess alongside them additionally may represent her finding her own Indigenous African roots.

Such a possibility is more explicitly pursued in Lindsay Eagar's *The Hour of the Bees* (2016), in which adolescent Carol comes to embrace her heritage through witnessing her grandfather's fanciful stories of bee swarms coming true. The narrative mostly centers on the Chicana protagonist's dramas with her sister and other schoolgirls but is punctuated throughout by her grandfather's insistence that they embrace their "Spanish" heritage in the New Mexico desert, where his son is pressuring him to sell his farm to developers. Just as in Paull's Apis-centric *The Bees*, another novel set and published in the twenty-first century, humans and honeybees alike are slated to fall victim to the displacement of Jeffersonian yeoman-farmer ideals with the dubious progress of capitalism. As part of learning to appreciate what bees can do, however, Carol intervenes on their behalf and in a way that ultimately saves the family farm because she comes to value her heritage, which includes the great love shared by her grandparents, as signaled by her final embrace of her birth name, Carolina, the only name with which her grandfather ever addresses her.

Moreover, by the end, evidence arrives via a swarm of bees that his tall tales of being on the land for more than a thousand years may be true and that they are therefore also Native Americans. Although an inverse affective setup to that of Erdrich's Evelina, the granddaughter again holds space for the continuity of animist materialism, only here through a more direct encounter with a nonhuman superorganism. Her experience of being covered by a swarm results in her family's decision to keep the grandfather's family farm, sparing it from developers, and their consequent collective decision to become beekeepers there. Unlike in *The Plague of Doves*, extinctions of nonhuman organisms are not explicitly of concern, yet the repeated staging of an at least partly Indigenous child learning to value a traditional grandparent's perspective certainly concerns endangerments with consequences that extend beyond the human realm. Although the cultural reference points otherwise remain vague, the explicit admixture of Anglo, Chicana, and Indigenous elements that Gloria Anzaldúa identifies as harbingers of the new mestiza[89] are dramatized in a coming-to-consciousness with the help of bees. This aspect seems all the more compelling in light of Anzaldúa's insistence that social change first has to be imagined before it can be materialized. While more fancifully sidestepping the fraught questions of land ethics after settlement than in the other novels, the swarm-girl relationship seems ever riper for articulating complex negotiations of indigeneity across cultural and biological borderlands.

Through these multiplying examples, an animist-materialist narrative of the swarm is seeming to write itself, but under what conditions? When bees move to the center of the story, as in bee-centric narratives like Paull's *The Bees* and Jay Hosler's graphic fiction *Clan Apis* (2000), readers are invited to learn about life in the colony from bees' perspectives—only the present-day conditions of disaster increasingly enframe them in a severely depleted industrial-agricultural landscape. Spinning out this trajectory, when honeybees themselves are threatened with extinction, a more profoundly transformative potential appears to emerge in unlikely community bonding in *Generation A*, where the future of bees themselves becomes more explicitly uncertain on a global scale.

Living After Sex

Intersecting with hopeful stories of honeybees en masse, another narrative that more explicitly links collective life and death follows more directly from the development and disastrous escape of a hybridized European-African strain dubbed "Africanized honeybees" or "killer bees" in Brazil in the 1950s. With their slow northward territorial expansion, tracked through the Cold War and into today's War on Terror, Africanized bees range ever farther across the Americas even as they gain a special hold on US racial and colonial imaginaries. Produced by researchers in South America who bred different European with African subspecies of *Apis mellifera*, killer bees' official moniker—Africanized honeybees—signifies more than just remarkably prolific intraspecific hybrid bees that respond comparatively faster and in greater numbers in defense of their hives than their ancestors.

"You know what I know about bees?" says Nigerian-born US émigré Moji in Teju Cole's 2011 novel *Open City*. "That the name Africanized killer bee is a piece of racist bullshit. Africanized killers: as if we don't have enough to deal with without African becoming shorthand for murderous."[90] The weirdness of the term "Africanized" draws attention to killer bees' eerie similarities to descendants of other populations relocated across the Atlantic in the colonial period, whose darker bodies and defensive behaviors likewise are often perceived as signs of aggression, provoking responses that all too often turn lethal for them.

However, in Cole's novel, Moji's comments inspire the narrator instead to turn their conversation to the topic of Colony Collapse Disorder—about which another friend interjects, "That sounds like something out of imperial history. . . . The natives are restless, Your Majesty, we can't hold on to these colonies any longer"—in order to hold forth with his theory that because contemporary people "lack familiarity with mass death," we are "an anomaly in human history. We are the first humans who are completely unprepared for disaster."[91] Therefore, he posits, "Maybe [bees] are connected with us in some essential way that we haven't figured out yet, and their death is a warning of some sort to us, like the canaries in a coal mine, sensitive to an emergency that will soon be apparent to dull, slow human beings."[92] Douglas Coupland's *Generation A* explores just this possibility in greater detail, more explicitly entertaining animist materialism in order to position the biopolitics of love in non/human collectives still more explicitly through indigenous frictions.

Published a year after Erdrich's *The Plague of Doves* and arguably the most extensive contemporary fictional treatment of the looming global threats accelerated by the commercialization of honeybee pollination, *Generation A* considers how honeybee extinction might work as an act of communication between different species of superorganisms. The premise is that, after their sudden disappearance from the entire planet, a handful of honeybees miraculously reappear seemingly just to sting one person each in five different locations scattered around the world—random incidents that due to their extreme rarity are treated as major global events. The narrative begins as a string of recollections about each incident from the victim's perspective, thus setting up a polyvocal structure similar to Erdrich's novel as well as narratively driving the eventual gathering of these five otherwise-unrelated characters who suddenly find themselves in weird relation to each other through the actions of a "supposedly extinct bug."[93]

Departing from the model set by Coupland's *Generation X* (1991), there is no frame story. Readers only learn obliquely about the bees' all-but-extinction between the lines of first-person trauma narratives[94] of five people who initially seem to have nothing in common. Yet their stories reveal that, prior to the stinging incident, each person had been loveless or lovelorn. Each was "deeply isolated," with no prior adult experiences of meaningful intimacy and, at the momentous event, caught in acts that express a longing to connect on a grand scale, to be "involved with the planet—[Zack] using satellites to do sketches [with a mechanical harvester] in an Iowa cornfield; [Samantha] making Earth sandwiches [with a smartphone and a stranger pinpointed exactly across the globe from where she is] in New Zealand; [Julien] being expelled from virtual gaming worlds in Paris; [Diana] being excommunicated from the afterworld [by her preacher and philandering lover] in Ontario; . . . [and Harj] simply participating in global consumer miasma in Sri Lanka."[95]

The world and world views imagined by the novel initially are not hopeful. In their lifetimes, honey, apples, and almonds have become extremely high-end, black market fare, amid a new norm characterized by rapidly deteriorating transportation, communication, and economic systems. When faced with the question of what they feel about bees, the stinging victims voice a mixture of remorse for what people have done and nostalgia for what life used to be like, often expressed through a primal pollination scene featuring bees and wildflowers. These connections prompt their development of farther-reaching narrative potentials as their stories converge.

Teams of scientists whisk each stung person away to sterile laboratory environments. Testing determines that the bee-sting victims—or, as Julien dubs them, the "Wonka children"[96]—share a rare aversion to a highly addictive new drug called Solon that promises to correct the modern maladies of loneliness and boredom by making people crave solitude, and making time seem to pass more quickly because, as a "chronosuppressant," it makes past and future alike seem irrelevant. Even before they are stung, the characters have experienced alienation from the Solon users in their lives, perspectives inflecting postmodernist aesthetics' flattening out of any sense of history with a queer absence of futurity. Only the pharmaceutical company leaders know that, wherever the drug is produced, bees and other insects disappear; beepocalypse proves just a symptom of farming's impending pharmageddon—that

is, the agricultural-pharmaceutical industry's profit-driven, global-scale ecocide. Through the novel, Solon's story emerges as that of a vicious cycle of
ameliorating the "collective fear about food" amid the "massive crop failures"
of the ever-growing pollination crisis, which is both propelled by the drug's
production and a main reason for its ever-growing popularity.[97]

According to Harj, the group's eternal optimist and the lone survivor of
his entire family's death in the 2004 Indian Ocean tsunami, the sudden self-
resurrection of their individual bees is meant to call attention to more than just
the Wonka children's natural resistance to the drug. He thinks that honeybees
want "to let the world know that the bees are still around" and, "in a highly
visible manner that seemed entirely calculated . . . to give humans hope and
encouragement."[98] More clearly than Cole's narrator, Harj affirms an animist-
materialist perspective from which the stinging incidents become a benevolent,
swarm-like communicative act across species lines. Causing the five to connect
with each other, honeybees foster more than wishful thinking about their return
from extinction, for the Wonka children's survival ultimately depends on their
ability to read and respond to honeybees' eusocial model of collective thinking.

Their immunity to Solon lies in their capacity to produce a rare protein
that is the same growth medium required to make Solon, as well as, in their
case, its apparent antidote. As Diana puts it, the bees highlight how the five are
"damaged in a distinct way . . . [via] our mutant protein-making genes."[99]
Initially this information is suppressed from them while technicians milk
their blood in laboratory isolation, effectively treating them like industrial-
agricultural animals and, worse, surreptitiously cloning their brain material and
feeding it to them all to see what happens to the mutant protein when ingested
in their different bodies. In this weird, techno-scientific way, they are made to
cannibalize each other, and the inadvertent result is that they become capable
of swarm power/knowledge.

Serge, a researcher gone rogue, reveals these details after he holes up with
the Wonka children on the pretext of further study. He requires them to make
and tell stories to each other, ostensibly to pass the time in their rural hide-
away, but really to speed up the process whereby the five find that their shared
proteins enable them, through the stimulus of oral storytelling, to become a
collective "superentity," smarter than the smartest individual among them.[100]
That their stories revolve around scenes of mass killing is both important to
the emergence of a collective understanding of their situation as well as to their
immediate ability to act to save their hive mind. When this capacity emerges is

The Birds and the Bees, or Life After Sex

important: in a clever plot twist, they all of a sudden deduce and thwart Serge's attempt to murder and eat them in search of the ultimate high. Where this happens also matters to the story of honeybees, Indigenous people, and oral narrative traditions.

The location of Serge's final experiment is Haida Gwaii, a western Canadian island group that includes biodiverse landscapes so rich that they have been called the "Galápagos of the North." They are also significant for their archaeological sites, dating back thirteen thousand years, and the continuous presence of Haida people there across eight millennia. In the near future of Coupland's fiction, it is also the site where the world's last known bee colony died. Due to Serge's importation of the drug, the setting serves also as a final frontier in the Haida's battle against Solon. The problem is not simply that users become addicts. The drug is particularly poisonous for the Indigenous group because it makes users quite specifically antisocial: they "stop caring about the tribe."[101]

The Wonka children, who by then have formed a "hive mind" that thwarts the evil scientist's plan,[102] also recognize in the sudden, violent disintegration of the Haida around them that someone had imported large quantities of the drug to a community that had previously banned it. They conclude that Serge more successfully pursued another mad plan, which was to use Solon, as Zack says, "to destroy a tribe—a society."[103] The historical use of alcohol as a tool of colonization is well documented in North America and has been influential to disparaging and disproportionate literary representations of Natives as addicts,[104] making this plot turn, from the global to a local story of addiction, bear some heavy settler-colonialist baggage. Only Coupland crafts an ending that, while remaining realistically bleak—the Haida prove no different from any other people besides the Wonka children in terms of their susceptibility to Solon—also intervenes in this pattern by foregrounding a collective assertion of agency.

As the remaining Haida gather at the site of the last beehive, taking the drug together in a final ceremony, one by one, they experience its alienating effects, which results in their collective self-destruction. Although Zack wants to intervene in what unfolds as a mass cultural suicide, Diana clarifies that it's the tribe's own business, "something larger than us . . . [that] played itself out."[105] Like the colonial bees before them, the novel's Indigenous humans cannot continue with the ordinary business of life in alienation from each other, but their final gesture is as collective as it is constructive. Ultimately, the swarm intelligence activated by honeybees in the growing hive mind of the Wonka children transforms them from isolated, vulnerable individuals into a self-protecting collective, and witnessing the Haida's dissolution commits them to continue to grow their own social cohesion together through continuing their storytelling sessions. Because the novel clarifies that none of the Wonka children are sexually into each other, the future of their community likewise remains uncertain, as is what exactly will be their relations to each other. But in the relational dynamic of storytelling as performance, individual desire bleeds into a collective experience of the kind of love each had been longing for before they met, securing the group's ongoing, dynamic presence in a way that Indigenous artists and scholars argue is "lifting the burden of colonialism by visioning new realities."[106]

Projecting a near-future in which honeybees' disappearance signals severe diminishments of global plant varieties, food supplies, mobility, and economies, *Generation A*'s most visible loss is a culturally specific, communal sense of connectivity shared by gynocentric animal and human communities, honeybees and Haida. Especially in comparison with the earlier fictions, in which characters' encounters with nonhuman sentience in a swarm event inspires their resistance to oppression through the embrace of indigenous knowledges, the CCD-like fate of honeybees along with a tribe—and both in their different ways guiding the Wonka children's own negotiations of collective life and death—figures a message about the practice of fiction so compelling that, at least in critical discussions of *Generation A* so far, it appears to have staved off any allegations of cultural theft. Ecocritic Jenny Kerber concludes that the novel "shows the continuing power of narrative to captivate and instruct, especially as a way of wrestling with problems that are global, multi-layered, and defiant of the impulse to determine an individual cause, antagonist, or outcome." I agree, only her qualification that "[without] an awareness of the specific forms their stories take or where they end up, the Wonka kids risk becoming little more than worker bees,"[107] from the perspective of literary animal studies illustrates a much broader and more profound underestimation of the material conditions of bee swarming for narrative.

Swarming Futures

An emerging recognition of dramatic changes to the story of bees is well under way in the twenty-first century, and one of the most profound consequences is captured in Swan's 2017 book *Where Honeybees Thrive*. A collection of true stories and "galleries" of contemporary art representations of bees, it takes risks in the form of personal criticism that I have been mapping here through literary fiction. Drawing from her own experiences as a white suburban woman teaching beekeeping in an urban African American neighborhood, Swan reflects, "I recognize the dangers of comparing an insect community with a human community, but in this historical moment, the actions taken by humans and the existence or nonexistence of nonhuman communities are necessarily, and inextricably, entwined. This is especially true of a species like the honeybee, which has a rare symbiotic relationship with the human. And some of the same historical trends that have affected the honeybee have also affected the human."[108]

Less directly, she makes the case that bees are better than birds in this respect by discussing the profoundly different experiences of teaching creative stories about them. When confronted with Chris Jordan's 2011 *Midway*—a film about the devastation of the Laysan, black-footed, and endangered short-tailed albatrosses (*Phoebastria immutabilis, nigripes,* and *albatrus*) due to plastic waste—her students express hopelessness. But the lively joy that follows from teaching her own personal bee narratives underscores how much is at stake for humans together with animals in the stories that we tell about the birds and the bees.

Entomological accounts of swarming honeybees are revealing collective, lateral negotiations that operate in mirror-image patterns to the ways in which our own brains' neurons are increasingly understood as in conversation with each other, not following a chain of command as it was previously assumed. Political scientists embrace the new model of swarming as a more "lively" and accurate baseline for the "agentic assemblages" that constitute the vibrancy of social engagements.[109] Media theorists map emerging political potentials through the sudden, noncentralized, and therefore swarm-like orchestrations of flash mobs through social media.[110] Perhaps because the cover image of Hardt and Negri's *Assembly* is a drawing of a bee swarm, I initially found it surprising that there are only a few glancing references to the swarm as a social form that appeals to contemporary understandings of how decentralized, pluralistic liberation movements like Black Lives Matter effectively operate today. Reflecting the persistence of cross-species misrepresentation, their appeals to "a swarm, moving in a coherent formation and carrying, implicitly, a threat,"[111] reveal how insidious the demonizing associations remain.

Realizing the political potentials in swarms as guided by "alternative logics of thought, organization, and sensation"[112] requires more direct engagements with the ways in which humans and animals both imagine and operate

as superorganisms, which is where animist materialism can be most helpful. Reframed as a perspective that has always been available within some
Indigenous cultural perspectives, "the power of the politically activated multitude, in the form of the swarm" becomes not so much an emancipatory guide or
radical threat as an affirmation of long-suppressed political potentials.[113] What
the fictions discussed above suggest together is that learning about what makes
swarms formally unique may have to involve unlearning our sense and sensibilities of bees as instrumental objects or individual subjects and along the way
reckoning with the settler legacies that reinforce such limited views.

Anxieties about bees' and other eusocial insects' separation from "human
will" used to result in dismissal of their radical "autonymy," what literary critic
Eric Brown elaborates as their existence "beyond our capacity for language."[114]
Identifying a potential backlash, Derrida could easily identify "the old yet mod-
ernized topos of the bee" in Lacan's discounting of honeybee communication
as "coding"—that is, as exhibiting purely mechanical or "animal" reaction without the possibility of a response[115]—despite compounding scientific evidence
that over the past century relentlessly demonstrates how bees share knowledges
at and beyond human capacities.[116] The scientific histories of Apis-industrial agriculture may be well caught up in settler histories of transporting these colonial
animals outside their native habitats and into violent scenes of confrontation
in Indigenous human histories and displacements of indigenous critters more
generally. But, in literary fiction anyway, the story appears to be changing.

Appreciated as the fulcrums of ecosystems, pollinators like honeybees are
highly effective at maintaining the genetic diversity that allows plants to adapt to
changing conditions. With bees' help in cross-pollination, flowers produce well-
formed fruits with fertile seeds, helping plants feed other pollinating insects and
birds as well as all sorts of organisms that in turn rely on them to flourish—in
some cases, even to survive. As honeybees become both mechanism of and
limit to modern-industrial mechanisms whereby people exert control over each
other and other species, the hive mind or collective-personhood intelligence
epitomized by their swarming behavior may be precisely why they are calling forth recognition of complexly indigenous knowledges of human-animal
relations.

In very different ways, Erdrich's and Coupland's novels indicate that what
bees communicate may not be so important as how they do so—that is, as
radically democratic models of and for Native North American societies. By
intimating that biopolitical power is collectively negotiated by honeybees,

Coupland suggests further that swarm intelligence may be the very source of their continued existence—and the only hope for that of our own and other species. Taking wing through the interwoven stories of multiple human narrators in each novel, honeybees inspire people to abandon the old colonialist fears in order to build multispecies communities with love as a way to reclaim still older feelings of mutual respect.

Conclusion
Taking and Making Love Stories

The fragility of loving connections has been weighing heavily on my mind throughout this project, no doubt because my father, Ed, died while I was beginning it, as did my mother, Eileen, and my canine companion Sabine as I was finishing it. Through mourning them, I have come to appreciate all the more precisely how crafting and sharing a story can do wonders to alleviate a sense of longing or loss, particularly when it extends the meaningful connections made possible—if possibly also made unsettling—by love.

Although my mother always regretted not having much of a formal education, I'm grateful to her for instilling a sense of attunement to more-than-human story potentials. In 1954, at age twenty, she immigrated to the United States from a small rural village in Ireland, where I've never lived, but she made sure that I always felt my connections, and where her kind of Catholicism still is practiced in unique ways reflective of Celtic or Insular Christianity. Prayers and holy water, dreams and uncanny occurrences, especially having to do with the dead, all materially shape our lives; it wasn't a belief to be taught but axiomatic to her way of life. Loving her provided constant glimpses of rarified pathways through which animacies can be manipulated and verily opened my mind from the start to the potentials for narration beyond human life.

Still, it has taken me a long time to appreciate how her thinking has guided my work and how it complicates my identification as Eurowestern. I'm a US-based literary scholar with no religious credentials whatsoever, motivated not so much by any reverence for literature as by an addiction to fiction acquired from my dad, who was a lifelong voracious reader (before finishing secondary school, he read the entire library of the city of Denver, Colorado). My method is to gather stories and look for patterns, only lately coming to ask myself why I've spent decades studying animal stories. I have tried to be careful throughout the preceding chapters to highlight that what I am curious about are thought-forms through which perceptions of broadly animated worlds are shared and developed and that I am primarily concerned about to what effect stories reflect and shape the lives that they reference or record. That is why so many of the stories in the previous chapters represent people and animals as they are, in their ordinary circumstances. Contemplating where and how storytelling necessarily involves storytaking, I grow increasingly concerned about the risks of imposing worlds on stories at the expense of adding stories to worlds.

But are these processes ever easily separated? Narratologist David Herman identifies how "storyworlds, or the worlds projected via storytelling practices" follow from as well as support impulses to make sense of experiences: "worlding the story, or making sense of narratives," is primarily an interpretive process, geared to "fill out" details not contained in the story, and one that is complemented by "storying the world, or using narrative as an instrument of mind," potentially an interventionist process of building a story to make sense of details.[1] If only because "so many encounters with animals are mediated through narratively organized discourse," stories that concern more-than-human worlds require close scrutiny for the ways in which they can be limiting ideas about animals and people associated with them or modeling more inclusive, expansive ways of thinking.[2] Recognizing that I must make, even as I take, human alongside animal stories across boundaries of culture and biology helps me understand the complexities of storyworlds for valuing and conserving human, animal, and human-animal relations and also take seriously the risks of failing to represent them at all.[3]

Still more enlightening to me is Herman's assertion that narrativity, or what makes stories more or less stories, can no longer be defined by an exclusive "focus on human or humanlike individuals experiencing events in storyworlds," which challenges narratology's customary exclusion of other-than-human experiences from consideration.[4] Because I have long admired Herman's work, his changing course from the mainstream perspective on this point is heartening—plus intriguing for following directly from his work on literary-narrative alternatives to Cartesian representations of mind. It is quite distinct from material-ecocritical reframings of narrative's "emanating point" from a human self to "a complex of human-nonhuman interrelated agencies," which pursue a flat ontology[5]—effectively recognizing, only then to empty out, any sense of purpose to other critters' perspectives except in relation to the human. Conversely, Herman's position allows for more-than-human intelligences to be negotiating their own worlds, on their own terms. Personally, it also drives home how my mother's storyworlds brought me to a different starting place than most scholars, jibing instead with most people worldwide in never having quite believed there could be any definitively or exclusively "rational" ways or that other species categorically can be excluded from them. As Amitav Ghosh quips, "Even the most devoted follower [of Descartes] would have no trouble interpreting the thoughts and feelings of a dog who has him backed against a wall,"[6] a visceral illustration of how we refuse others' stories at our peril.

By sharing narratives throughout this book, I have become even more aware of storytelling as a communal process and of mapping these dimensions as critical in the current political climate. Integral to the project of Indigenous regeneration and resurgence has been the growing awareness of the power of storytelling to not just relate but also instill a community's values, shaping perspectives on history.[7] Because stories are vital, especially to a persecuted people's sense of their own peoplehood,[8] they are vulnerable to the counternarratives crafted to demean, degrade, and otherwise disempower them. Amid traumatic conditions like removals of children from families to residential schools—potentially interrupting or ending a community's story—a vital concern about the TRC in Canada became how the stories of survivors of acts of cultural genocide would represent their courage, strength, and power in order to "restory" the dominant narrative of settler-colonial history.[9] As important to how these stories would be told were the issues of who would later use them and how. Storymaking and storytaking are not so easily separated either.

Yet stories are a special kind of communal property, telling about even as they become mechanisms for securing belongings, sometimes contested ones. As Ali Ahmida explains in his forthcoming book, he was only able to amass the largest collection of oral testimonies of the colonial Libyan genocide by persuading skeptical informants that he shares their stories in multiple senses: his family suffered alongside theirs, in similar and sometimes the same rural circumstances, and his point is to bring their collective memory of those events to the attention of the world, on their terms. Studying her own Blackfeet tribespeople to recover sacred and practical plant knowledges, ethnobotanist Rosalyn LaPier also recounts having to field the same questions that Ahmida told me he answered constantly: "Who are you? Who is your family? What gives you the right to write about us?"[10]

At one level, such questions push back directly against histories of exploitation through cultural theft. But stories of multispecies relationships highlight how the answers become complicated. As Daniel Heath Justice argues in the context of Indigenous literary studies, "Such questions don't just connect you to a lineage, however that may be understood—they place you in a meaningful context with your diverse relatives and the associated relationships of obligation, where you have people who claim you and who have, hopefully, trained you well in the ways of being a good human being."[11] From this standpoint, the question of to whom stories belong is not restricted to birthright. Rather stories are belongings that grow through particular practices of storytelling, bringing forth connections, acknowledgments, and enactments of relations that resist reduction to biology.

This is why so often stories that reveal this powerful effect of their own relating concern how humans become persons among so many other kinds of people, actively forging relationships with not just blood relatives and other kinds of humans but also other animals, plants, rocks, and gods, natural along with supernatural forces. Why I have collected contemporary stories in which these non/human and super/natural relationships loom large is because I agree with Justice that "relationality is always vexed if it is genuine" and, more to my point, that "it's only shallow understanding that assumes all relations with the other-than-human are necessarily benevolent."[12] Stories of human-animal bonds in a time of slaughter bear witness to the liabilities as well as benefits of staying in relationships, and more, they reveal how storytelling can both nurture connections as well as reveal in their diminishment that stories are sometimes all that we have, all that can keep us in connections with others.

In the current context of planetary-level social and ecological crisis, Indigenous stories gain heightened relevance for the ways in which, according to ecocritics Joni Adamson and Juan Carlos Galeano, they have long functioned never simply as myths or fanciful artifacts but as "thought experiments, or tools, that might be employed to build livable, sustainable futures."[13] Stories of kinship beyond the restrictive parameters of biogenetic and genealogical relating are particularly important to figuring who we are and can be in relation to others. So Donna Haraway suggests revising the questions for gatekeepers of stories: "Who lives and who dies, and how, in relation to this kinship rather than that one? What shape is this kinship, where and whom do its lines connect and disconnect, and so what? What must be cut and what must be tied if multispecies flourishing on earth, including human and other-than-human beings in kinship, are to have a chance?"[14]

To "unravel the ties of both genealogy and kin, and kin and species," all while still living as and among "the earth-bound,"[15] in Haraway's terms, is a tall order that in part is fulfilled by stories that tell of long-standing, mutually beneficial human-animal relationships and that range beyond the realm of Eurowestern rationality in order to do so. By telling of the benefits of even lost senses of multispecies communities, stories can inspire more identifications of commonalities and foster connections across differences. In their honesty about the lethality of settler colonialism to their continuance, these narratives can instill a greater sense of what apology and reconciliation, let alone regeneration and resurgence, entail. While I struggled to think of what to write in order to persuade you to share this perspective, a hummingbird just flew in circles around me, stopping to stare at my face (as they always do when they catch me out reading or writing), reminding me that I need to bring you back to my story.

Along with my parents, I lost dear dog Sabine, whose photos grace the covers of two of my previous books, while writing this one. I've been thinking and writing about dogs for years, but living with her made me realize that all people fall into one of three groups: people who love dogs, people who hate dogs, and people who love people who love dogs. Our coevolution as species has depended on people like me in the third category, working to keep the peace between the other two. Everyone I have loved has been a dog lover, and my parents were no exception, nor is my husband, Mik (who provided the cover art for those earlier books, plus this one).

Mik and I were Sabine's third and last human family that we know of, and she came into our lives knowing no human words, trusting no women, and refusing all food from human hands. In no other way resembling an Inuit sled dog, she nonetheless fit their description as "headstrong and independent," too smart to "respond well to classic obedience training and never to coercion."[16] She was a nut to be cracked only by the canine genius of my mother, whose preferred dog "training" method was to shower them with treats and expect nothing in return. All dogs think that's a good idea, and Sabine was no exception. In the end, saying "Eileen" not only guaranteed an inquisitive head-tilt from sweet old Sabine but also could lead to a great sulk if a visit wasn't immediately immanent. Sabine went downhill fast after Eileen died, and within three months, she too was dead. Coming out of the morass of the melancholy that followed for me required telling a story of why Eileen took Sabine with her.

Like many immigrants, my mother clung fiercely to all kinship ties, but I see now that there are more reasons why for her the most important questions were always, Who are you? And who are your people? Up to the end, into her eighties, my mother was always telling stories, usually of her childhood in a village where, in those days, there were no strangers because everyone was related in one way or another. Peopling Eileen's stories too were beloved dogs and cats, even the trees and bushes with the most delicious fruit (she was a wild kid). By the time my dad predeceased her, close to their fiftieth wedding anniversary, the cast of characters in her stories included figures more familiar to me, like the friends and neighbors of my childhood, her coworkers, and of course the many members of our more-than-human families.

When my mom died, it was easy to imagine her delighted to be finally introducing my lifelong US-resident dad to everyone from her old stories in the old country, all the ones whom he never knew in life and who meant so much to her formative years, all gathering at last up there in that great pub in the sky. After a while, among so many new-to-him friends and family, Ed would have to stop to ask her, "What's the story with all of the others?" After all, my dad loved us, too, and would want to know what was going on in the world of the living, especially what had happened to us in the years after he died. There would be at least one story that she would dread telling him.

There was no way my mother could have been prepared for my being diagnosed with cancer in the same week that my dad died of it. I had every reason to be optimistic (the odds are good for an otherwise healthy person in treatment for Hodgkin lymphoma, even at stage two). But she was like so many from previous generations, to whom cancer always meant a death sentence. Even seven years into my remission, our weekly meals began with questions about my health, and she never quite believed me when I said I was OK. Someone would have to tell my dad my story, but she wouldn't want to do it.

Sabine came into our life before Dad's passing, and they too had years of loving each other well. Memories of wartime rationing made him a passionate meat eater, so for her, a visit with them meant something infinitely better than our usual veg table scraps. She also was an inordinately sensitive dog. My mom was the first to notice that Sabine's initial aloofness as a pup was self-protective and that she was one of the rare dogs who comfortably returned people's gazes. With a brave face and a few white lies, I could shelter my mom from knowing the worst of my illness, but nothing could be hidden from Sabine.

Sabine would remember the times when she crept into the otherwise verboten-to-her human bed to sleep with Mik when I traveled away for radiation treatments. She could explain how happy she was when, after months of chemotherapy made our daily walks slower and shorter, everything eventually went back to ordinary patterns. Sabine loved my parents, and they thought the

world of her. I don't know if my mother had to lay a trail of treats straight to that
heavenly pub that, being Irish, now allows dogs. However she went, I do think it
was willingly, as well as for the purpose of telling my story to my dad in a way that
would reassure him and my mom that it will be a while before we all meet again.

I share this maybe too personal story not because it is exceptional but
quite the opposite: to indicate an ordinary impulse of love to imagine connections between living and dead, across species, and other states of being beyond
and between them. It is not unlike the stories grounding the previous chapters,
reweaving kinship bonds frayed by the conditions of settler colonialism. I never
understood the depths of my mother's bitterness about emigrating—"leaving
her land" was her preferred turn of phrase—until I encountered in *The Plague
of Doves* Evelina's surprise at her Anishinaabe mother's still-burning resentment
about having their land stolen by white settlers. Erdrich's novel is set in North
Dakota, and through my father I am descended of colonizers of South Dakota
who fled *an Gorta Mór*, the Irish-colonial disaster known as the Great Famine.
I know very little of those ancestors' stories and have no connections to where
they settled or to the other stolen lands where I've lived (although in my mind's
eye, my mother is already there by now, maybe with Sabine's help, tracking
down "Ed's people" in the hereafter, quizzing them about their people). Ireland,
or *Éire*—derived from *Ériu*, the name of a Celtic matron goddess of sovereignty,
the goddess of the land—is different.

My mother often told the story of her own father's family being saved by a
small patch of blight-resistant potatoes on the farm where she was raised and
her brothers still live. It's a twice-told tale, maybe not true, but one that secured
a much-needed sense of belonging not just to another country but to a specific
place. That story sustained her through her early years in the United States when
especially urban Irish Americans made fun of all the "greenhorns," and it was
also important through her final days, when she kept asking me if she should
carry her US passport because of all the make-America-great-again hate being
fired up toward immigrants. She along with nine-tenths of her generation felt
compelled to leave Ireland following the postwar economic downturn, and
living in the United States for more than sixty years after that never changed
her sense that she belonged to her people's land. Telling stories was her way of
instilling a sense of being someone from somewhere, of strengthening those
ties, of re-creating that sustaining sense of community.

In his autobiography about losing the canine companions who supported
him through the loss of his partner to an AIDS-related illness, poet Mark Doty

affirms what people are too quick to reject in stories like hers that embrace human-animal bonding: "Love, I think, is a gateway to the world, not an escape from it."[17] Writing about therapeutic narratives more generally, Herman introduces the concept of "fictive kinship" to expand its application beyond the initial anthropological designation—that is, relations beyond birth or marriage that individuals nonetheless articulate in terms of kin—to include pets and working animals. While it is tempting to go back and apply it to Miyazaki's San being mothered by a wolf god, Barclay's ekjab who is both protective grandfather and strange frigate bird, al-Koni's Cain Adam who is both unwilling killer and eager consumer of his gazelle sister, and so many other spectacular examples, I find it useful also for wrapping up the story of my dead that surrounds this project.

After Sabine died, I was talking with someone about the various dogs we have lost over the years. She told a story of coming to the realization that she probably grieved more for one particular dog than she would for one of her cousins simply because she knew the dog all her life while her cousins have always lived hundreds if not thousands of miles away, and though that was probably wrong, there it was. Suddenly I realized why I needed the story of Eileen taking Sabine with her: it doesn't have to be a competition. All kinship is fictive, all stories are possible, and in the end, love is about a story that always concerns oblivion.

Notes

Introduction

1. L. J. Gorenflo, S. Romaine, R. A. Mittermeier, and K. Walker-Painemilla, "Co-occurrence of Linguistic and Biological Diversity in Biodiversity Hotspots and High Biodiversity Wilderness Areas," *Proceedings of the National Academy of Science USA* 109.21 (2012): 8032–37.

2. Thom van Dooren, *Flight Ways: Life and Loss at the Edge of Extinction* (New York: Columbia University Press, 2014); Jamie Lorimer, *Wildlife in the Anthropocene: Conservation After Nature* (Minneapolis: University of Minnesota Press, 2015).

3. I use "human-animal studies" instead of related terms (anthrozoology, animal studies, critical animal studies, etc.) to emphasize that human-animal relationships are my central concern.

4. Margot Norris, *Beasts of the Modern Imagination: Darwin, Nietzsche, Kafka, Ernst, and Lawrence* (Baltimore: Johns Hopkins University Press, 1985); Cary Wolfe, *Animal Rites: American Culture, the Discourse of Species, and Posthumanist Theory* (Chicago: University of Chicago Press, 2003); Carrie Rohman, *Stalking the Subject: Modernism and the Animal* (New York: Columbia University Press, 2009); Michael Lundblad, *The Birth of a Jungle: Animality in Progressive-Era US Literature and Culture* (New York: Oxford University Press, 2013).

5. Jacques Derrida, *The Animal That Therefore I Am*, ed. Marie-Louise Mallet and trans. David Wills (New York: Fordham University Press, 2008), 14.

6. Wendy Woodward, *The Animal Gaze: Animal Subjectivities in Southern African Narratives* (Johannesburg: Wits University Press, 2008), 3.

7. Marion Copeland, "Animal-Centric Graphic Novels: An Annotated Bibliography," *Antennae: Journal of Nature in Visual Culture* 16.1 (2011): 82–99.

8. Marion Copeland, "*Black Elk Speaks* and *Ceremony*: Two Visions of Horses," *Critique* 24.3 (1983): 158–72.

9. Gerald Vizenor, *Fugitive Poses: Native American Scenes of Absence and Presence* (Norman: University of Oklahoma Press, 1988).

10. Graham Huggan and Helen Tiffin, *Postcolonial Ecocriticism: Literature, Animals, Environment* (New York: Routledge, 2010), 135.

11. Maneesha Deckha, "Toward a Postcolonial, Posthumanist Feminist Theory: Centralizing Race and Culture in Feminist Work on Nonhuman Animals," *Hypatia* 27.3 (2012): 527–45.

12. Jopi Nyman, *Postcolonial Animal Tale from Kipling to Coetzee* (Ocala, FL: Atlantic, 2003).

13. Philip Armstrong, *What Animals Mean in the Fiction of Modernity* (New York: Routledge, 2008). 11.

14. Philip Armstrong, "The Postcolonial Animal," *Society & Animals* 10.4 (2002): 413–19.

15. Donna Haraway, *The Companion Species Manifesto: Dogs, People, and Significant Otherness* (Chicago: Prickly Paradigm Press, 2003); Hilda Kean, *Animal Rights: Political and Social Change in Britain Since 1800* (London: Reaktion, 1998).

16. Lori Gruen, *Entangled Empathy: An Alternative Ethic for Our Relationships with*

194

Animals (Seattle: Lantern Press, 2014); Rosi Braidotti, *Nomadic Theory: The Portable Rosi Braidotti* (New York: Columbia University Press, 2012); Kathy Rudy, *Loving Animals: Toward a New Animal Advocacy* (Minneapolis: University of Minnesota Press, 2011); Josephine Donovan and Carol Adams, *The Feminist Care Tradition in Animal Ethics* (New York: Columbia University Press, 2007).

17. Ann-Sofie Lönngren, *Following the Animal: Power, Agency, and Human-Animal Transformations in Modern Northern-European Literature* (Newcastle upon Tyne: Cambridge Scholars, 2015).

18. Ann-Sofie Lönngren, "Following the Animal: Place, Space, and Literature," in *Animal Places: Lively Cartographies of Human-Animal Relations*, ed. Jacob Bull, Tora Holmberg, and Cecelia Åsberg (New York: Routledge, 2018), 213.

19. Elina Helander-Renvall, "Relationships Between Sámi Reindeer Herders, Lands, and Reindeer," in *The Routledge Handbook of Human-Animal Studies*, ed. Garry Marvin and Susan McHugh (New York: Routledge, 2014), 246–58.

20. To queer the metronormative, sociologist Scott Herring "critiques any notion of the rural as an 'empty' space removed from racial, ethnic, and socioeconomic stress or inequality" and flags such notions as "faulty representations of Native non-urbanized populations" reduced to "racial primitivisms." See Herring, *Another Country: Queer Anti-urbanism* (New York: New York University Press, 2010), 85–86.

21. Wendy Woodward, "Embodying the Feral: Indigenous Traditions and the Nonhuman in Some Recent South African Novels," in *The Routledge Handbook of Human-Animal Studies*, 220–32.

22. Wendy Woodward, "Human Masks? Animal Narrators in Patrice Nganang's *Dog Days: An Animal Chronicle* and Alain Mabanckou's *Memoirs of a Porcupine*" in *Natures of Africa: Ecocriticism and Animal Studies in Contemporary Cultural Forms*, ed. Fiona Moolla (Johannesburg: Wits University Press, 2016), 235–56. See also Jason Price, *Animals and Desire in South African*

Fiction: Biopolitics and the Resistance to Colonization (London: Palgrave, 2017).

23. The problem ranges far beyond literary animal studies. Sami Schalk laments the ongoing underdevelopment of research on "writers of color . . . who engage with magical realism, vodun/voodoo, mysticism . . . [and other] nonrealist elements" and also provides an excellent model for it. See Schalk, *Bodyminds Reimagined: (Dis)ability, Race, and Gender in Black Women's Speculative Fiction* (Durham: Duke University Press, 2018), 142.

24. In the context of queer theory, Jasbir Puar cautions against invoking "intersectionality" as a tool of "difference management," which, as it slides into "a mantra of liberal multiculturalism," can enable "the disciplinary apparatus of the state" to exclude radical political thinking in "Queer Times, Queer Assemblages," *Social Text* 23.3–4 (2005): 128. So I continue to take a cautionary approach to what Harlan Weaver pluralizes as "interspecies intersectionalities." See Weaver, "Feminisms, Fuzzy Sciences, and Interspecies Intersectionalities: The Promises and Perils of Contemporary Dog Training," *Catalyst* 3.1 (2017): 1–27.

25. Tobias Linné and Helena Pedersen, "'Expanding My Universe': Critical Animal Studies Education as Theory, Politics, and Praxis," in *Critical Animal Studies: Thinking the Unthinkable*, ed. John Sorenson (Toronto: Canadian Scholars Press, 2014), 269.

26. Laura Wright, *The Vegan Studies Project: Food, Animals, and Gender in the Age of Terror* (Athens: University of Georgia Press, 2015), 11.

27. Mel Chen, *Animacies: Biopolitics, Racial Mattering, and Queer Affect* (Durham: Duke University Press, 2012).

28. Michael Lundblad, ed., *Animalities: Literary and Cultural Studies Beyond the Human* (Edinburgh: Edinburgh University Press, 2017).

29. Claire Jean Kim, *Dangerous Crossings: Race, Species, and Nature in a Multicultural Age* (Cambridge: Cambridge University Press, 2015).

30. John Miller, *Empire and the Animal Body: Violence, Identity and Ecology in Victorian Adventure Fiction* (London: Anthem Press, 2014).

31. Vinciane Despret, "The Body We Care For: Figures of Anthropo-zoo-genesis," *Body and Society* 10.2–3 (2004): 111–34. See also her "Sheep Do Have Opinions," in *Making Things Public*, ed. Bruno Latour and Peter Wiebel (Cambridge: MIT Press, 2006), 360–70.

32. Konrad Lorenz has emerged as a flash point of such discussions. See especially the critique in Thalia Field's *Bird Lovers, Backyard* (New York: New Directions, 2010), elaborated in David Herman, *Narratology Beyond the Human: Storytelling and Animal Life* (New York: Oxford University Press, 2018), 246–47; and Boria Sax, *Animals in the Third Reich* (New York: Continuum, 2000); as well as my discussion in chapter 2.

33. Donna Haraway, *When Species Meet* (Minnesota: University of Minnesota Press, 2008); Haraway, *Companion Species Manifesto*; Haraway, *Simians, Cyborgs, Women: The Reinvention of Nature* (New York: Routledge, 1991).

34. Kim TallBear, "Why Interspecies Thinking Needs Indigenous Standpoints," *Cultural Anthropology* (2011), https://culanth.org/fieldsights/260-why-interspecies-thinking-needs-indigenous-standpoints.

35. Harry Garuba, "Explorations in Animist Materialism: Notes on Reading/Writing African Literature, Culture, and Society," *Public Culture* 15.2 (2003): 265.

36. Eduardo Kohn, *How Forests Think: Toward an Anthropology Beyond the Human* (Berkeley: University of California Press, 2013).

37. Rane Willerslev, *Soul Hunters: Hunting, Animism, and Personhood Among the Siberian Yukaghirs* (Berkeley: University of California Press, 2007).

38. Paul Nadasdy, "The Gift in the Animal: The Ontology of Hunting and Human-Animal Sociality," *American Ethnologist* 34.1 (2007): 25–43.

39. Erica Fudge, "Why It's Easy Being a Vegetarian," *Textual Practice* 24.1 (2010): 149–66.

40. Joni Adamson, "Why Bears Are Good to Think and Theory Doesn't Have to Be Another Form of Murder: Transformation and Oral Tradition in Louise Erdrich's Tracks," *Studies in American Indian Literature* 4.1 (1992): 28–48.

41. Michael Hardt, "For Love or Money," *Cultural Anthropology* 26.4 (2011): 676–82.

42. Kari Weil identifies the problem with Gary Francione's vegan abolitionism as "discounting domestic animals' agency and social complexity as well as their desire—for connection, affection, and bonding across species." See Weil, *Thinking Animals: Why Animal Studies Now?* (New York: Columbia University Press, 2012), 138. I would add that such a position paradoxically imagines into being the absolute sovereignty of human dominion that it purports to overcome.

43. The initial remark is in Gilles Deleuze and Félix Guattari, *A Thousand Plateaus: Capitalism and Schizophrenia*, trans. Brian Massumi (Minneapolis: University of Minnesota Press, 1987), 244. Haraway writes, "I am not sure I can find in all of philosophy a clearer display of misogyny, fear of aging, incuriosity about animals, and horror at the ordinariness of flesh." See Haraway, *When Species Meet*, 30.

44. Susan McHugh, *Dog* (London: Reaktion, 2004).

45. Susan McHugh, "Bitch, Bitch, Bitch: Personal Criticism, Feminist Theory, and Dog-Writing," *Hypatia: A Journal of Feminist Philosophy* 27.3 (2012): 616–35. See also Harlan Weaver, "Becoming in Kind: Race, Gender, and Nation in Cultures of Dog Fighting and Dog Rescue," *American Quarterly* 65.3 (2013): 689–709.

46. Michel Foucault, preface to *Anti-Oedipus: Capitalism and Schizophrenia*, by Gilles Deleuze and Félix Guattari, trans. Robert Hurley, Mark Seem, and Helen R. Lane (Minneapolis: University of Minnesota Press, 1983), xiv.

47. Rosi Braidotti, *Metamorphoses: Towards a Materialist Theory of Becoming* (Malden, MA: Blackwell, 2002), 69.

48. Rosi Braidotti, *Transpositions: On Nomadic Ethics* (Cambridge: Polity, 2006), 278.

49. Alice Kuzniar, *Melancholia's Dog: Reflections on Our Animal Kinship* (Chicago: University of Chicago Press, 2006), 56.

50. Kathy Rudy, "LGBTQ . . . Z?," *Hypatia* 27.3 (2012): 611.

51. Lauren Berlant, "A Properly Political Concept of Love: Three Approaches in Ten Pages," *Cultural Anthropology* 26.4 (2011): 683–91.

52. Ibid., 684–85.

53. Lauren Berlant, *Desire/Love* (New York: Punctum Books, 2012), 68.

54. Ibid., 3.

55. Elizabeth Povinelli, *The Empire of Love: Toward a Theory of Intimacy, Genealogy, and Carnality* (Durham: Duke University Press, 2006), 17.

56. Ibid., 10.

57. Berlant, *Desire/Love*, 88; bell hooks, *All About Love: New Visions* (New York: Harper, 2000).

58. Jennifer Nash, "Practicing Love: Black Feminism, Love-Politics, and Post-intersectionality," *Meridians* 11.2 (2013): 18–19.

59. Sarah Ahmed, "In the Name of Love," *Borderlands* 2.3 (2003), http://www.borderlands.net.au/vol2no3_2003/ahmed_love.htm.

60. Trinh T. Minh-ha, *Lovecidal* (New York: Fordham University Press, 2016), 250.

61. Donna Haraway, *Staying with the Trouble: Making Kin in the Chthulucene* (Durham: Duke University Press, 2016).

62. Haraway, *When Species Meet*, 19.

63. Nicole Shukin, *Animal Capital: Rendering Life in Biopolitical Times* (Minneapolis: University of Minnesota Press, 2009).

64. Weil, *Thinking Animals*, 133.

65. Brian Massumi, *What Animals Teach Us About Politics* (Durham: Duke University Press, 2014).

66. Zakiyyah Iman Jackson, "Losing Manhood: Animality and Plasticity in the (Neo)Slave Narrative," *Qui Parle* 25.1–2 (2016): 95–136; Colleen Glenney Boggs, *Animalia Americana: Animal Representations and Biopolitical Subjectivity* (New York: Columbia University Press, 2013); Christopher Peterson, *Bestial Traces: Race, Sexuality, Animality* (New York: Fordham University Press, 2012).

67. Wolfe, *Animal Rites*, 1. For a more positively framed version of the implicit origin story of animal studies as "a continuing extension of the exploration of alterity" following on the heels of 1960s-era politics, see Jane Desmond, *Displaying Death, Animating Life: Human-Animal Relations in Art, Science, and Everyday Life* (Chicago: University of Chicago Press, 2016), 12.

68. Shukin, *Animal Capital*, 11.

69. Nicole Shukin, "The Biopolitics of Animal Love: Two Settler Stories," in *The Palgrave Handbook of Animals and Literature*, ed. Susan McHugh, Robert McKay, and John Miller (London: Palgrave, forthcoming).

70. Achille Mbembe, "Necropolitics," trans. Libby Meintjes, *Public Culture* 15.1 (2003).

71. Roberto Esposito, *Bíos: Biopolitics and Philosophy*, trans. Timothy Campbell (Minneapolis: University of Minnesota Press, 2008).

72. Cary Wolfe, *Before the Law: Humans and Other Animals in a Biopolitical Frame* (Chicago: University of Chicago Press, 2012), 43.

73. Lauren Berlant, "Slow Death (Sovereignty, Obesity, Lateral Agency)," *Critical Inquiry* 33.4 (2007): 754–80. An extension of her earlier work on the construction of fatness as a problem, this essay offers a rare glimpse of how biopower, as a reshaping rather than replacement of sovereign power, becomes enlisted in the management of the slow processes of dying endemic to human (I would add quite a lot more nuclear-age) life. Although Chris Breu likewise stops short of considering other species, I find his tracking of materiality and embodiment through postmodern literary narratives an intriguing contribution to the discussion, in part because it is inspired by Michael Hardt and Antonio Negri's connection of these convergences in the global appearance of the posthuman and in part because, like Berlant's analysis, it helps historicize what Fredric Jameson once termed "the logic of late capitalism." See Breu, *Insistence of the Material: Literature in an Age of Biopolitics* (Minneapolis: University of Minnesota Press, 2014), 17–18.

74. On animal studies' purported racism, see Alexander Weheliye, *Habeas Viscus: Racializing Assemblages, Biopolitics, and Black Feminist Theories of the Human*

(Durham: Duke University Press, 2014). On its speciesism, see Jeffrey Nealon, *Plant Theory: Biopower and Vegetable Life* (Stanford: Stanford University Press, 2015). On its neocolonialism, see Huggan and Tiffin, *Postcolonial Ecocriticism*. And on its insufficient environmentalism, see Ursula Heise, *Sense of Place and Sense of Planet: The Environmental Imagination of the Global* (Oxford: Oxford University Press, 2008).

75. Jacques Derrida, *Spectres of Marx: The State of the Debt, the Work of Mourning, and the New International*, trans. Peggy Kamuf (New York: Routledge, 1994).

76. Lauren Berlant, *Cruel Optimism* (Durham: Duke University Press, 2011).

77. Lydia Millet, *Magnificence* (New York: Norton, 2012), 255.

78. Deborah Bird Rose, *Wild Dog Dreaming: Love and Extinction* (Richmond: University of Virginia Press, 2011).

79. Vinciane Despret, "Introduction: Les Morts Utiles," *Terrain* 62 (2014).

80. Saidiya Hartman, "Venus in Two Acts," *small axe* 12.2 (2008), 3.

81. Steve Baker, *Artist | Animal* (Minneapolis: University of Minnesota Press, 2013); Robert McKay, "BSE, Hysteria, and the Representation of Animal Death: Deborah Levy's *Diary of a Steak*," in *Killing Animals*, ed. The Animal Studies Group (Champaign: University of Illinois Press, 2005), 145–69.

82. Kath Weston, *Animate Planet: Making Visceral Sense of Living in a High-Tech Ecologically Damaged World* (Durham: Duke University Press, 2017); Bron Taylor, "From the Ground Up: Dark Green Religion and the Environmental Future," in *Ecology and the Environment: Perspectives from the Humanities*, ed. Donald Swearer (Cambridge: Harvard University Press, 2008), 89–107; Nurit Bird-David, "'Animism' Revisited: Personhood, Environment, and Relational Epistemology," *Current Anthropology* 40 (1999): 67–91.

83. Kári Driscoll and Eva Hoffman, "Introduction: What Is Zoopoetics?," in *What Is Zoopoetics? Texts, Bodies, Entanglements*, ed. Kári Driscoll and Eva Hoffman (London: Palgrave, 2018), 6–7. See also Kári Driscoll,

"The Sticky Temptation of Poetry," *Journal of Literary Theory* 9 (2015): 212–29.

84. Catherine Parry, *Other Animals in Twenty-First Century Fiction* (London: Palgrave, 2017); David Herman, "Introduction: Literature Beyond the Human," in *Creatural Fictions: Human-Animal Relationships in Twentieth- and Twenty-First-Century Literature*, ed. David Herman (London: Palgrave, 2016); Diane Davis, "Creaturely Rhetorics," *Philosophy and Rhetoric* 44.1 (2011): 88–94; Anat Pick, *Creaturely Poetics: Animality and Vulnerability in Literature and Film* (New York: Columbia University Press, 2011); Eric Santner, *On Creaturely Life: Rilke, Benjamin, Sebald* (Chicago: University of Chicago Press, 2006).

Chapter 1

1. Alexandra-Mary Wheeler, "The Porosity of Human/Nonhuman Beings in Neil Gaiman's *American Gods* and *Anansi Boys*," in *Indigenous Creatures, Native Knowledges, and the Arts: Human-Animal Studies in Modern Worlds*, ed. Wendy Woodward and Susan McHugh (New York: Palgrave, 2017), 128.

2. Graham Huggan and Helen Tiffin, *Postcolonial Ecocriticism: Literature, Animals, Environment* (New York: Routledge, 2010), 135.

3. Before the publication of *American Gods*, Gaiman was involved in a long process of reworking the *Mononoke* script for Anglophone audiences, as detailed in "Neil Gaiman's Film Work," Neil Gaiman, n.d., http://www.neilgaiman.com/Cool_Stuff/Essays/Essays_About_Neil/Neil_Gaiman %27s_Film_Work.

4. Wendy Woodward, "Embodying the Feral: Indigenous Traditions and the Nonhuman in Some Recent South African Novels," in *The Routledge Handbook of Human-Animal Studies*, ed. Garry Marvin and Susan McHugh (New York: Routledge, 2014), 220.

5. Marilyn Ivy, "Revenge and Recapitation in Recessionary Japan," *South Atlantic Quarterly* 99.4 (2000): 834.

6. Jeffrey Williams, "Science Stories: An

Interview with Donna J. Haraway," *Minnesota Review* 73–74 (2009–10): 139.

7. John Berger, *About Looking* (London: Writers and Readers, 1980), 22.

8. Akira Lippit, *Electric Animal: Toward a Rhetoric of Wildlife* (Minneapolis: University of Minnesota Press, 2000), 197.

9. Ibid., 161.

10. Nicole Shukin, *Animal Capital: Rendering Life in Biopolitical Times* (Minneapolis: University of Minnesota Press, 2009), 38 (emphasis added).

11. Helen McCarthy, *Hayao Miyazaki, Master of Japanese Animation* (Berkeley, CA: Stone Bridge Press, 1999), 185.

12. Amy Davis, *Good Girls and Wicked Witches: Changing Representations of Women in Disney's Feature Animation, 1937–2001* (New Barnet: John Libbey, 2011), 227.

13. Saito Tamaki, *Beautiful Fighting Girl*, trans. J. Keith Vincent and Dawn Lawson (Minneapolis: University of Minnesota Press, 2011), 139. In his translator's introduction, Vincent notes that by reading Miyazaki's career-long obsession with the beautiful fighting girl figure through Lacanian-inflected auteur theory, Saito concludes that it is both "feminist and misogynist" (13). For a more focused analysis of the film's queer elements, see Michelle Smith and Elizabeth Parsons, "Animating Child Activism: Environmentalism and Class Politics in Ghibli's *Princess Mononoke* (1997) and Fox's *Fern Gully* (1992)," *Continuum: Journal of Media and Cultural Studies* 26.1 (2012): 25–37.

14. Tamaki, *Beautiful Fighting Girl*, 150.

15. McCarthy, *Hayao Miyazaki*, 188.

16. Susan Napier, "Confronting Master Narratives: History as Vision in Miyazaki's Cinema of De-assurance," *Positions* 9.2 (2001): 476.

17. John Tucker, "Animé and Historical Inversion in Miyazaki Hayao's *Princess Mononoke*," *Japan Studies Review* 7 (2003): 66.

18. Napier, "Confronting Master Narratives," 478.

19. Richard M. Siddle, "The Ainu: Indigenous People of Japan," in *Japan's Minorities: The Illusion of Homogeneity*, ed. Michael Weiner (New York: Routledge, 2009), 22.

20. Tucker, "Animé and Historical Inversion," 68.

21. Eriko Ogihara-Shuck, *Miyazaki's Animism Abroad: The Reception of Japanese Religious Themes by German and American Audiences* (Jefferson, NC: McFarland, 2014), 42.

22. Ibid., 98.

23. Ibid., 42.

24. Andrea Arai deduces that Miyazaki's neologism "*tatarigami*" is intended "to create an obvious verbal link between the curse and its source at the *tataraba* (bellows)" of Iron Town's forge, which is fired with wood taken from the animal gods' primeval forest. See Arai, "The 'Wild Child' of 1990s Japan," *South Atlantic Quarterly* 99.4 (2000): 859 n. 10.

25. Following the traditional interpretation of *mononoke* as "possession by a human spirit," Susan Napier translates the title as "possessed princess," though conceding that the girl in this story is instead "clearly possessed by the fearsome spirits of nature." See Napier, *Animé from* Akira *to* Princess Mononoke (Houndmills: Palgrave Macmillan, 2001), 480.

Connecting the film directly to ancient Japanese literary traditions, Tucker's etymology clarifies that this term bears deep associations with people's possession by all sorts of spirits, particularly "as a means of taking revenge on those who have wronged them," so the title might better be translated as "Princess of the Wrathful, Raging Spirits of Nature." See Tucker, "Animé and Historical Inversion," 74.

26. Although the dubbed translation uses the word "gun," the Japanese version uses the compound term "flint-firearrow" only "because Japanese had no word for 'gun' until the Portuguese arrived in the sixteenth century," according to McCarthy, *Hayao Miyazaki*, 188.

27. Deleuze and Guattari articulate this potential in their triangulated model of representing animals, which adds to the conventional human ego-projection and iconic options a recognition of the other potentials that proceed from acknowledging how animals at times operate as "demonic . . . multiplicity." See Gilles Deleuze and Félix

Guattari, *A Thousand Plateaus: Capitalism and Schizophrenia*, trans. Brian Massumi (Minneapolis: University of Minnesota Press, 1987), 240.

28. Naoko Matsumoto, "Changing Relationship Between the Dead and the Living in Japanese Prehistory," *Philosophical Transactions of the Royal Society B* 373.1754 (2018).

29. Napier, "Confronting Master Narratives," 474.

30. Ivy, "Revenge and Recapitation," 837.

31. More precisely focused on "the dying CGI god," Sean Cubitt reads the ending as a "passage from history into myth, from linear to circular, from abstraction back to the ground and round again," in *Eco Media* (New York: Rodopi, 2005), 35.

32. Arai, "'Wild Child,'" 844.

33. Jeff Testerman, "Seminoles Sack Chairman James Billie," *St. Petersburg Times*, 19 March 2003.

34. Linda Hogan, "An Interview with Linda Hogan," by Phoebe Davidson, *Writer's Chronicle* 31.4 (1999).

35. Linda Hogan, "Of Panthers and People: An Interview with American Indian Author Linda Hogan," by John Murray, *Terrain: A Journal of the Built and Natural Environments* 5 (1999).

36. Helen Makhdoumian, "Rewriting *Billie* and Asserting Rhetorical Sovereignty in Linda Hogan's *Power*," *Studies in American Indian Literatures* 28.4 (2016): 80–110.

37. Hogan, *Power* (New York: Norton, 1998), 85.

38. See Ernest Stromberg, who argues, against the essentialism of these critiques, that partiality is important to the "indigenist" or "Indian-determined" world view that Hogan articulates through all of these fictions. See Stromberg, "Circles Within Circles: Linda Hogan's Rhetoric of Indigenism," in *From the Center of Tradition: Critical Perspectives on Linda Hogan*, ed. Barbara J. Cook (Boulder: University Press of Colorado, 2003), 104–5.

39. Michael Hardin reads *Taiga* here alternately as signaling the erasure of distinct ecosystems (150), and the "extreme displacement of American Indians." See Hardin, "Standing Naked Before the Storm: Linda Hogan's *Power*
and the Critique of Apocalyptic Narrative," in *From the Center of Tradition*, 153 n. 16.

40. Hogan, *Power*, 111.

41. Ibid.

42. Critics of the novel who dwell on the deadlocked outcomes of the first two overlook this third trial of the woman by the animal god. See, for instance, Buell's assertion that the woman is "tried twice" (*Writing for an Endangered World: Literature, Culture, and Environment in the US and Beyond* [Cambridge, MA: Belknap, 2003], 238), which is echoed almost a decade later by Pascale McCullough Manning, "A Narrative of Motives: Solicitation and Confession in Linda Hogan's *Power*," *Studies in American Indian Literatures* 20.2 (2008): 3. See also Makhdoumian, "Rewriting *Billie*."

43. Hogan, *Power*, 111.

44. Ibid., 16.

45. Ibid., 190.

46. Hilary Thompson concludes that because "supposedly sacrificial deaths are held up to scrutiny and final judgements are left open-ended," *Power* "lets the animal have a richly equivocal and evocative power" in *Novel Creatures: Animal Life and the New Millennium* (New York: Routledge, 2018), 9.

47. Ibid., 192.

48. According to the Florida Fish and Wildlife Conservation Commission (FWC), by the early 1980s, their numbers had dwindled to 30, the count cited in *Power* (58). FWC approximates the current population to be 120–230 adults, who since 2008 have become the target of a multimillion-dollar restoration program. See *Florida Panthers: Next Steps*, 5 September 2012.

49. Hogan, *Power*, 192.

50. Ibid., 190.

51. Ibid., 233.

52. Fredric Jameson, "Postmodernism and Consumer Society," in *The Norton Anthology of Theory and Criticism*. ed. Vincent B. Leitch (New York: Norton, 2001), 1974.

53. Roland Walter, "Pan-American (Re)visions: Magical Realism and Amerindian Cultures in Susan Power's *The Grass Dancer*, Gioconda Belli's *La Mujer Habitada*, Linda Hogan's *Power*, and Mario Vargas

200

Llosa's *El Hablador*," *American Studies International* 37.3 (1999): 66.

54. Buell, *Writing for an Endangered World*, 240–41.

55. Manning, "Narrative of Motives," 2.

56. Catherine Rainwater, "Who May Speak for the Animals? Deep Ecology in Linda Hogan's *Power* and A. A. Carr's *Eye Killers*," in *Figuring Animals: Essays on Animal Images in Art, Literature, Philosophy, and Popular Culture*, ed. Mary Sanders Pollok and Rainwater (New York: Palgrave, 2005), 268.

57. Dan Wylie, "//Kabbo Sings the Animals," in Woodward and McHugh, *Indigenous Creatures*, 50.

58. Vine Deloria, Jr., "American Indian Metaphysics," in *Power and Place: Indian Education in America*, ed. Deloria and D. R. Wildcat (Golden, CO: Fulcrum, 2001), 1–6.

59. Kim TallBear, "Why Interspecies Thinking Needs Indigenous Standpoints," *Cultural Anthropology* (2011), https://culanth.org/fieldsights/260-why-interspecies-thinking-needs-indigenous-standpoints.

60. Paul Nadasdy, "The Gift in the Animal: The Ontology of Hunting and Human-Animal Sociality," *American Ethnologist* 34.1 (2007): 25–43.

61. Susan McHugh, "One or Several Literary Animal Studies?," H-Net: Humanities & Social Sciences Online, 17 July 2006, https://networks.h-net.org/node/16560/pages/32231/one-or-several-literary-animal-studies-susan-mchugh#_ednref22.

62. Alexander Wilson, *The Culture of Nature: North American Landscape from Disney to the Exxon Valdez* (Cambridge, MA: Blackwell, 1992), 13.

63. Ibid., 151.

64. Marian Scholtmeijer claims that late twentieth-century extinction novels are "historically accurate" in the sense that there is "no need to invent the animal's tragedy." See Scholtmeijer, *Animal Victims in Modern Fiction: From Sanctity to Sacrifice* (Toronto: University of Toronto Press, 1993), 120. Her discussion of examples from the 1960s to 1970s retrospectively also seems to set up how animal gods have proven useful subsequently in overcoming conceptual divides between human and animal environmental tragedies: "Whereas humans have history out of which to construct narratives, the natural animal seems to have only myth to legitimate its place and meaning in culture" (218), a point that fictions of Indigenous animal gods increasingly appear to problematize in the decades that have followed.

65. Donna Haraway, *The Companion Species Manifesto: Dogs, People, and Significant Otherness* (Chicago: Prickly Paradigm Press, 2003), 17.

Chapter 2

1. Michiko Kakutani, "From *Life of Pi* Author, Stuffed-Animal Allegory About the Holocaust," *New York Times*, 12 April 2010. For an overview of the novel's deeply mixed critical reception, see Janis Haswell, "Students, Teachers, and the Aftermath of the Horrors: Reflections on Teaching Martel's *Beatrice and Virgil*," *English Language and Literature Studies* 3.3 (2013): 28–47.

2. Yann Martel, *Beatrice and Virgil* (New York: Spiegel and Grau, 2010), 174.

3. Ibid., 134–35.

4. Ibid., 178.

5. Ibid., 190.

6. The spectacle of a major metropolitan European taxidermy shop on fire mirrors that of the widely reported remains of the Deyrolle shop in Paris, the world's oldest, best-known, and continuously operated taxidermy company, which went down in flames two years before the novel's publication. The news coverage of the Deyrolle fire, according to Giovanni Aloi, "exposed an abrasive animal materiality" in the very form of taxidermy that is "capable of subverting photography's sometimes idiomatic inability to tell the living from the dead." Aloi, *Speculative Taxidermy: Natural History, Animal Surfaces, and Art in the Anthropocene* (New York: Columbia University Press, 2018), 15.

7. Jenni Adams, "A Howl and a Black Cat: Allegory, Nonsense, and Ethics in Yann Martel's *Beatrice and Virgil*," *Journal of Literature and Trauma Studies* 1.2 (2012): 31–63.

8. Danielle Sands, "On Tails and Tales: Animals, Ethics, and Storytelling in Yann Martel's *Beatrice and Virgil*," *Critique* 57.1 (2016): 41–51.

9. Martel, *Beatrice and Virgil*, 98.

10. Ibid., 7. See also Catherine Parry, *Other Animals in Twenty-First Century Fiction* (New York: Palgrave, 2017), 139.

11. Ibid., 29.

12. Ibid., 194.

13. Stephanie Turner, "Relocating 'Stuffed' Animals: Photographic Remediation of Natural History Taxidermy," *Humanimalia* 4.2 (2013): 1–32.

14. Steve Baker, *The Postmodern Animal* (London: Reaktion Books, 2000), 54.

15. Aloi, *Speculative Taxidermy*, 34.

16. Sarah Bezan and Susan McHugh, "Introduction: Taxidermic Forms and Fictions," *Configurations* 27.2 (2019).

17. Martel, *Beatrice and Virgil*, 7. On Martel's strategic uses of human-centered discourse, see Stewart Cole, "Believing in Tigers: Anthropomorphism and Incredulity in *The Life of Pi*," *Studies in Canadian Literature* 29.2 (2004): 22–36. On his emphasis on human animality in the earlier novel, see also Hilary Thompson, "Animal Worlds and Anthropological Machines in Yann Martel's Millennial Novel *The Life of Pi*," in *Creatural Fictions: Human-Animal Relationships in Twentieth- and Twenty-First Century Literature*, ed. David Herman (New York: Palgrave, 2016), 171–92.

18. Pauline Wakeham, *Taxidermic Signs: Reconstructing Aboriginality* (Minneapolis: University of Minnesota Press, 2008), 6.

19. Alexander Weheliye, *Habeas Viscus: Racializing Assemblages, Biopolitics, and Black Feminist Theories of the Human* (Durham: Duke University Press, 2014), 24.

20. Wakeham, *Taxidermic Signs*, 25.

21. Samuel J. M. M. Alberti, "Introduction: The Dead Ark," in *The Afterlives of Animals: A Museum Menagerie*, ed. Alberti (Charlottesville: University of Virginia Press, 2011), 2–3; Liv Emma Thorsen, *"Elephants Are Not Picked from Trees": Animal Biographies in Gothenberg Natural History Museum* (Aarhaus: Aarhaus University Press, 2014), 10.

22. Geoffrey Swinney, "An Afterword on Afterlife," in Alberti, *Afterlives of Animals*, 230.

23. Aloi, *Speculative Taxidermy*, 77.

24. Anna Samuelsson, "Zoo/mbie Spaces: Museums as Humanimal Places," in *Animal Places: Lively Cartographies of Human-Animal Relations*, ed. Jacob Bull, Tora Holmberg, and Cecelia Åsberg (New York: Routledge, 2018), 136–61.

25. Pat Morris, in *A History of Taxidermy: Art, Science, and Bad Taste* (Ascot: MPM, 2012), avers that seven full taxidermy mounts of people presently exist, amid stories of several others that cannot be confirmed because "museum curators are somewhat secretive on this issue" (90).

26. Wakeham, *Taxidermic Signs*, 5.

27. My essay "Taxidermy's Literary Biographies" examines representations by many canonical authors—including Charles Dickens, H. G. Wells, Ernest Hemingway, Roald Dahl, Gustave Flaubert, and Julian Barnes, among others—to make the case that the literary history of taxidermy influenced the shift in perceptions of human taxidermy as no longer acceptable for public display. In *Animal Biography*, ed. Mieke Roscher and André Krebber (New York: Palgrave, 2018), 141–60.

28. Rachael Poliquin, *The Breathless Zoo: Taxidermy and the Cultures of Longing* (University Park: Pennsylvania State University Press, 2012), 34.

29. Jane Desmond, "Postmortem Exhibitions: Taxidermied Animals and Plastinated Corpses in the Theaters of the Dead," *Configurations* 16.3 (2008): 347–77.

30. Poliquin distinguishes taxidermy from "most other processes of bodily preparation" precisely through this "distinction between the palpable world of materials and the spiritual otherworld of material forces" (*Breathless Zoo*, 23).

31. Turner, "Relocating 'Stuffed' Animals," 8.

32. Poliquin, *Breathless Zoo*, 39.

33. Anna Linderholm et al., "A Novel *MC1R* Allele for Black Coat Colour Reveals the Polynesian Ancestry and Hybridization Patterns of Hawaiian Feral Pigs," *Royal Society Open Science* 3.9 (2016): 1–7.

34. Téa Obrecht, *The Tiger's Wife* (New York: Random House, 2011), 242.

35. Morris, *History of Taxidermy*, 359.

36. Donna Haraway, *Primate Visions: Gender, Race, and Nature in the World of Modern Science* (New York: Routledge, 1989).

37. Jeffrey Niesel, "The Horror of Everyday Life: Taxidermy, Aesthetics and Consumption in Horror Films," *Journal of Criminal Justice and Popular Culture* 2.4 (1994): 61–80.

38. Jack (published Judith) Halberstam, *Skin Shows: Gothic Horror and the Technology of Monsters* (Durham: Duke University Press, 1995).

39. Cary Wolfe and Jonathan Elmer, "Subject to Sacrifice," in *Animal Rites: American Culture, the Discourse of Species, and Posthumanist Theory*, by Cary Wolfe (Chicago: University of Chicago Press, 2003), 103.

40. Kate Mosse, *The Taxidermist's Daughter* (London: Orion, 2014), 14. On the roles specific to girls and women in Victorian taxidermy shops, see Morris, *History of Taxidermy*, 210.

41. Alissa York, *Effigy* (Toronto: Vintage Canada, 2007), 17.

42. Ibid., 416.

43. Ibid., 429.

44. L. Frank Baum, *The Marvelous Land of Oz* (Chicago: Reilly and Britton, 1904).

45. Garry Marvin, "Enlivened Through Memory: Hunters and Hunting Trophies," in Alberti, *Afterlives of Animals*.

46. Poliquin, *Breathless Zoo*, 151.

47. Richard Connell, "The Most Dangerous Game," *Collier's*, 19 January 1924.

48. Aloi, *Speculative Taxidermy*, 160.

49. Ibid., 140.

50. On the subject of Konrad Lorenz's advocacy for eugenics for animals and people, see Boria Sax, "What Is a 'Jewish Dog'? Konrad Lorenz and the Cult of Wildness," *Society and Animals* 5.1 (1997): 3–21.

51. Armen Avanessian, "(Co)Present Tense: Marcel Beyer Reads the Past," *Germanic Review* 88 (2013): 363–74.

52. Hannelore Mundt, "From *Erkunde* to *Kaltenburg*: Marcel Beyer's Never-Ending Stories About the Past," *Gegenwartsliteratur: Ein germanistisches Jahrbuch (A German Studies Yearbook)* 12.1 (2013): 334.

53. Marcel Bayer, *Kaltenburg*, trans. Alan Bance (Boston: Houghton Mifflin Harcourt, 2012), 89.

54. Ibid., 226.

55. Ibid., 227.

56. Alan Bance tracks how, through the ornithological collection, the novel as a whole marks the difference made by a "true homage to history" in contrast to a metaphorical "national taxidermy"—that is, a dynamic narrative of life in its many forms versus a "'preserving' [of] a national identity through a stylized narrative about the past," in "'Die Tierszenen beleuchten die Menschenszenen und die Menschenszenen die Tierszenen': Marcel Beyer's novel *Kaltenburg* and Recent German History," *Publications of the English Goethe Society* 80.2–3 (2011): 192.

57. Poliquin, *Breathless Zoo*, 218.

58. Lydia Millet, *Magnificence* (New York: Norton, 2012), 247.

59. Ibid., 248.

60. Poliquin, *Breathless Zoo*, 164.

61. Millet, *Magnificence*, 182.

62. Ibid., 149.

63. Ibid., 254.

64. Ibid., 253.

65. Ibid.

66. Ibid., 255.

67. Ibid., 250.

68. Sarah Ahmed clarifies, "Happiness does not reside in objects; it is produced through proximity to certain objects." In "Multiculturalism and the Promise of Happiness," *New Formations* 63 (2007–8): 125.

69. Ursula K. Heise, *Imagining Extinction: The Cultural Meanings of Endangered Species* (Chicago: University of Chicago Press, 2016), 60–61.

70. See, for instance, Heise's characterization of Susan's "acceptance of a much broader accountability for extinction on a global scale," ibid.

71. Millet, *Magnificence*, 255.

72. Heise, *Imagining Extinction*, 17.

73. Lydia Millet, *How the Dead Dream* (New York: Counterpoint, 2008), 139.

74. Ibid., 197.

75. Ella Soper, "Grieving Final Animals and Other Acts of Dissent: Lydia Millet's *How the Dead Dream*," *ISLE: International Studies of Literature and the Environment* 20.4 (2013): 752.

76. Millet, *Magnificence*, 85.

77. Ibid., 194.

78. For a similar argument about zoos,

see curator Nato Thompson's interview with artist Mark Dion in *Becoming Animal: Contemporary Art in the Animal Kingdom* (Cambridge: MIT Press, 2005), 53.

79. Henrietta Rose-Innes, *The Green Lion* (Cape Town: Umuzi, 2015), 34.

80. Ibid., 14.

81. Sandra Swart, "Zombie Zoology: History and Reanimating Extinct Animals," in *The Historical Animal*, ed. Susan Nance (Syracuse: Syracuse University Press, 2015), 54–117.

82. Ibid. Rose-Innes's acknowledgments indicate that the fictional zoo project is based on the efforts of "the late John Spence of the now-defunct Tygerberg Zoo," who identified and obtained Cape lions from Siberia's Novosibirsk Zoo archival and brought them to the Western Cape to attempt a local breeding program (263).

83. Ibid., 169.

84. Invoking ancient human-animal connections, Mark invites comparison with the "feral" character Katya in Rose-Innes's earlier novel *Nineveh* whose "openness to the nonhuman as well as interconnectedness with" them "echo traditional African beliefs in" the interconnectedness and co-constitution of all life, according to Wendy Woodward, "Embodying the Feral: Indigenous Traditions and the Nonhuman in Some Recent South African Novels," in *The Routledge Handbook of Human-Animal Studies*, ed. Garry Marvin and Susan McHugh (New York: Routledge, 2014), 223.

85. Rose-Innes, *Green Lion*, 253.

86. Ibid., 19.

87. Ibid., 20.

88. Ibid., 141.

89. Ibid., 37.

90. Ibid., 41.

91. Wendy Woodward adds, "Not only is the body of the lion parodied in taxidermy but it emblematises the instrumentalisation of wild creatures, both in colonial times and the present, in hunting and in an appropriation of the animal's being" for Mark's desires in "Returning to the Animals' Gazes: Reading the Lionesses Marah and Sekhmet," in *The Palgrave Handbook of Animals and Literature*,

ed. Susan McHugh, Robert McKay, and John Miller (London: Palgrave, forthcoming).

92. Ibid., 55.

93. Ibid., 258.

94. Jane Desmond, *Displaying Death, Animating Life: Human-Animal Relations in Art, Science, and Everyday Life* (Chicago: University of Chicago Press, 2016), 33.

95. Brett Bailey, personal communication, 20 February 2016.

96. Brett Bailey, "Exhibit B," Third World Bunfight, accessed 5 June 2017, http://thirdworldbunfight.co.za/exhibit-b/.

97. Ibid.

98. The most recent literary representation of Soliman's life is Gergely Péterfy's award-winning 2014 historical novel, *Kitömött Barbár* (*The Stuffed Barbarian*), and it was preceded by Robert Musil's final and unfinished novel, *Der Mann ohne Eigenschaften* (*The Man Without Qualities*; 1940); Conny Hannes Meyer's play *Die Schwarze Bekanntschaft oder Angelo Soliman* (*The Black Acquaintance or Angelo Soliman*; 1983); Ludwig Fels's tragic play *Soliman* (1991), which in turn inspired a ballet choreographed by Bert Gstettner titled *Angelo Soliman, ballet d'action* (1996); and Andreas Pflüger and Lukas Holliger's comic opera *Der Schwarze Mozart* (*The Black Mozart*, 2005).

99. Bailey, "Exhibit B."

100. Rosi Braidotti, *Nomadic Theory: The Portable Rosi Braidotti* (New York: Columbia University Press, 2012), 232–33.

101. Ibid., 352.

Chapter 3

1. Amitav Ghosh, *The Hungry Tide* (Boston: Houghton Mifflin, 2005), 253.

2. On the multispecies implications of Ghosh's "valorization of subaltern environmental knowledges," see Neel Ahuja, "Species in a Planetary Frame: Eco-cosmopolitanism, Nationalism, and *The Cove*," *Tamkang Review* 42.2 (2012): 29.

3. Ursula Heise, *Imagining Extinction: The Cultural Meanings of Endangered Species* (Chicago: University of Chicago Press, 2016), 167. Ben de Bruyn complicates Heise's

characterization of the novel as split by the two species, between violent visions of tigers competing for resources and anthropomorphic sympathies for dolphins that foster community-building, by pointing to the significant roles of other critters, especially the mud crabs that Fokir fishes to eat, that literally undermine people's efforts to hold back rising seas, and that Piya comes to recognize as keystone species to the ecosystem. See Bruyn, *Animal Sounds* (forthcoming), 6–7.

4. Achille Mbembe, "Necropolitics," trans. Libby Meintjes, *Public Culture* 15.1 (2003): 34.

5. Rosi Braidotti, *Nomadic Theory: The Portable Rosi Braidotti* (New York: Columbia University Press, 2012), 333.

6. Ibid., 328.

7. Amitav Ghosh, *The Great Derangement: Climate Change and the Unthinkable* (Chicago: University of Chicago Press, 2016), 30.

8. Ibid., 64, 66.

9. Frank Zelko, "From Blubber and Baleen to Buddha of the Deep: The Rise of the Metaphysical Whale," *Society and Animals* 20.4 (2012): 104.

10. Deborah Bird Rose, "In the Shadow of All This Death," in *Animal Death*, ed. Jay Johnston and Fiona Probyn-Rapsey (Sydney: Sydney University Press, 2013), 1–20.

11. Philip Armstrong, "The Whale Road," in *A New Zealand Book of Beasts: Animals in Our Culture, History and Everyday Life*, ed. Philip Armstrong, Annie Potts, and Deidre Brown (Auckland: Auckland University Press, 2013), 79. See also Lawrence Buell, *Writing for an Endangered World: Literature, Culture, and the Environment in the US and Beyond* (Cambridge, MA: Belknap, 2001), 204.

12. Jonathan Steinwand, "What the Whales Would Tell Us: Cetacean Communication in Novels by Witi Ihimaera, Linda Hogan, Zakes Mda, and Amitav Ghosh," in *Postcolonial Ecologies: Literatures of the Environment*, ed. George Handley and Elizabeth DeLoughrey (New York: Oxford University Press, 2011), 195.

13. Thom van Dooren and Deborah Bird Rose, "Storied-Places in a Multispecies City," *Humanimalia* 3.2 (2012): 1–27.

14. Jamie Lorimer, "Multinatural Geographies for the Anthropocene," *Progress in Human Geography* 36.5 (2012): 593–612.

15. Thomas King, *The Truth About Stories* (Minneapolis: University of Minnesota Press, 2003).

16. See also Steve Baker, "Beyond Botched Taxidermy," in *Dead Animals, or The Curious Occurrence of Taxidermy in Contemporary Art* (Providence: David Winton Bell Gallery, 2016), 43–57, in which he proposes an alternate emerging aesthetic that involves respect for and identifies beauty within animal bodies.

17. Sune Borkfelt, "Reading Slaughter: Heterotopias, Empathy, and Abattoir Fictions" (PhD diss., Aarhus University, 2018).

18. Linda Hogan, *People of the Whale: A Novel* (New York: Norton, 2008), 285.

19. Ibid.

20. Ibid., 99.

21. Joni Adamson, "Whale as Cosmos: Multi-species Ethnography and Contemporary Indigenous Cosmopolitics," *Revista Canaria de Estudios Ingleses* 64 (2012): 29–15.

22. Hogan, *People of the Whale*, 98.

23. Teresa Shewry, *Hope at Sea: Possible Ecologies in Oceanic Literature* (Minneapolis: University of Minnesota Press, 2015).

24. Barbara Rose Johnston and Holly M. Barker, *Consequential Damages of Nuclear War: The Rongelap Report* (Walnut Creek, CA: Left Coast Press, 2008). As ground zero for a hydrogen bomb, Bikini Atoll remains uninhabitable due to radiation pollution.

25. Robert Barclay, *Meḷaḷ: A Novel of the Pacific* (Honolulu: University of Hawai'i Press, 2002), 222.

26. Michelle Balaev, *The Nature of Trauma in American Novels* (Evanston: Northwestern University Press, 2012), 111.

27. Anthony Carrigan, "Postcolonial Disaster, Pacific Nuclearization, and Disabling Environments," *Journal of Literary and Cultural Disability Studies* 10.3 (2010): 255–72.

28. Barclay, *Meḷaḷ*, 130.

29. Hogan, *People of the Whale*, 284.

30. Hester Blum, "The Prospect of Oceanic Studies," *PMLA: Publication of the Modern Language Association* 125.3 (2010): 670–77.

31. Christopher Bear and Jacob Bull, "Water Matters: Agency, Flows, and Frictions—Guest Editorial," *Environment and Planning A* 43 (2011): 2261–66.

32. Philip Steinberg, "Of Other Seas: Metaphors and Materialities in Maritime Regions," *Atlantic Studies* 10.2 (2013): 157.

33. Christopher Tilley, *A Phenomenology of Landscape: Places, Paths, and Monuments* (London: Berg, 1994), 59.

34. Ann Finkbeiner, "The Great Quake and the Great Drowning," *Hakai Magazine*, 14 September 2014.

35. Alan McMillan and Ian Hutchinson, "When the Mountain Dwarfs Danced: Aboriginal Traditions of Paleoseismic Events Along the Cascadia Subduction Zone of Western North America," *Ethnohistory* 49.1 (2002): 44.

36. Hogan, *People of the Whale*, 108.

37. The quote is attributed to an unnamed "official" on the US Atomic Energy Commission, and "the commission's attitude toward residents of [contaminated areas is] not unlike that of a plantation owner toward slaves." See Stephanie Cooke, *In Mortal Hands: A Cautionary History of the Nuclear Age* (New York: Bloomsbury, 2009), 159.

38. Eve Grey, *Legends of Micronesia* (Honolulu: Department of Education of the Trust Territory of the Pacific Islands, 1951).

39. Simone Oettli-Van Delden, "Problematizing the Postcolonial: Deterritorialization and Cultural Identity in Robert Barclay's *Meḷaḷ*," *World Literature Written in English* 39.2 (2002): 38–51.

40. Shewry, "Sea of Secrets: Imagining Illicit Fishing in Robert Barclay's *Meḷaḷ* and Rob Stewart's *Sharkwater*," *Journal of Postcolonial Writing* 49.1 (2011): 47–59.

41. Glen Alcalay, "Human Radiation Experiments in the Pacific," Nuclear Age Peace Foundation, 21 March 2014, https:// www.wagingpeace.org/human-radiation -experiments-in-the-pacific/.

42. Greg Dvorak, "The Martial Islands: Making Marshallese Masculinities Between American and Japanese Militarism," *Contemporary Pacific* 20.1 (2008): 55–79.

43. Barclay, *Meḷaḷ*, 71.

44. Ibid., 70, ellipsis in original.

45. Paul Nadasdy, "The Gift of the Animal: The Ontology of Hunting and Human-Animal Sociality," *American Ethnologist* 34.1 (2007): 25–43; Tim Ingold, *The Perception of the Environment: Essays on Livelihood, Dwelling, and Skill* (London: Routledge, 2000); Elizabeth Kolson, *The Makah Indians: The Study of an Indian Tribe in Modern American Society* (Minneapolis: University of Minnesota Press, 1953).

46. Elizabeth DeLoughrey, *Roots and Routes: Navigating Caribbean and Pacific Island Literature* (Honolulu: University of Hawai'i Press, 2010). DeLoughrey's identification of a "dead reckoning," or accounting for the presence of ancestors, in late twentieth-century Aotearoa (New Zealand) fiction indicates how this aspect alone proves vital as a decolonizing strategy for Maori and other Native Pacific peoples.

47. Hogan, *People of the Whale*, 10.

48. Barclay, *Meḷaḷ*, 14.

49. Virginia Richter, "'Where Things Meet in the World Between Sea and Land': Human-Whale Encounters in Littoral Space," in *The Beach in Anglophone Literatures and Cultures: Reading Littoral Space*, ed. Ursula Kluwick and Richter (Burlington, VT: Ashgate, 2015), 166.

50. Donelle Gadenne, "Fishing in Fiction: A Critical Animal Studies Analysis of Fishing in Two Examples of Popular Fishing Literature," *Journal for Critical Animal Studies* 12.4 (2014): 54–78; Jacob Bull, "Watery Masculinities: Fly-Fishing and the Angling Male in the South West of England," *Gender, Place, and Culture* 16.4 (2009): 445–65; Barbara Louise Endemaño Walker and Michael Robinson, "Economic Development, Marine Protected Areas, and Gendered Access to Fishing Resources in a Polynesian Lagoon," *Gender, Place, and Culture* 16.4 (2009): 467–84.

51. The "nuclear colonization" of the Marshall Islands is the example through which ecocritic Rob Nixon introduces his call to supplement the geographies, symbolisms, and above all, stories of fast-track capitalist violence with others that are geared to address "the slow violence of delayed effects that structure so many of our most

consequential forgettings," such as the experience of horrific birth defects continuing into the 1980s among the Marshallese. See Nixon, *Slow Violence and the Environmentalism of the Poor* (Cambridge: Harvard University Press, 2011), 7.

52. Zol de Ishtar, *Daughters of the Pacific* (Melbourne: Spinifex, 1994).

53. Lauren Berlant, "Slow Death (Sovereignty, Obesity, Lateral Agency)," *Critical Inquiry* 33.4 (2007): 754.

54. Barclay, *Meļaļ*, 283.

55. Hsinya Huang, "Trans-Pacific Ecological Imaginary," in *Comparative Indigenous Studies*, ed. Mita Bannerjee (Heidelberg: Universitäatsverlag Winter, 2016), 190.

56. Gadenne, "Fishing in Fiction," 60–62.

57. Hogan, *People of the Whale*, 95.

58. See Shepard Krech, *The Ecological Indian: Myth and History* (New York: W. W. Norton, 2000), and its review by Kim Tall-Bear, "Shepard Krech's *The Ecological Indian*: One Indian's Perspective," Institute for Indigenous Resource Management, September 2000, http://www.iiirm.org/publications/Book%20Reviews/Reviews/Krech001.pdf. The parallels of this figure with Frank Zelko's "metaphysical whale" are revealing: "a sublime, mystical, ecologically harmonious and super-intelligent aquatic being representing a supreme form of power and intelligence rooted in a oneness with nature, a state that humans, in their dangerous and pathetic struggles to conquer the natural world, could never achieve" (104–5).

59. Barclay, *Meļaļ*, 191.

60. Graham Huggan and Helen Tiffin, *Postcolonial Ecocriticism: Literature, Animals, Environment* (New York: Routledge, 2010), 61.

61. See Carrigan, "Postcolonial Disaster"; Shewry, "Sea of Secrets"; and Hanna Straß, "'A Living Death, Life Inside-Out': The Postcolonial Toxic Gothic in Robert Barclay's *Meļaļ: A Novel of the Pacific*," in *Globalizing Literary Genres: Literature, History, Modernity*, ed. Jernej Habjan and Fabienne Imlinger (London: Routledge, 2016), 228–40.

62. Barclay, *Meļaļ*, 272–73.

63. Ibid., 300.

64. Ibid., 41.

65. Hogan, *People of the Whale*, 18–19.

66. Claire Jean Kim, *Dangerous Crossings: Race, Species, and Nature in a Multicultural Age* (Cambridge: Cambridge University Press, 2015), 212.

67. Hogan, *People of the Whale*, 132.

68. Giovanni Aloi, *Art & Animals* (London: I. B Tauris, 2011).

69. Johnston and Barker, *Consequential Damages*.

70. Joe Roman, *Whale* (London: Reaktion Books, 2006).

71. Huggan and Tiffin, *Postcolonial Ecocriticism*, 62.

72. Adamson, "Whale as Cosmos," 43.

73. Kim, *Dangerous Crossings*, 246–47.

74. Ruth Jacobs et al., *The Sockeye Salmon Oncorhynchus nerka Population in Lake Ozette, Washington, USA* (Washington, DC: National Parks Service, 1996), 1; Kolson, *Makah Indians*.

75. James Terry and Frank Thomas, *The Marshall Islands: Environment, History, and Society in the Atolls* (Suva: University of the South Pacific, 2008).

76. Antoine Traisnel, "Huntology: Ontological Pursuits and Still Lives," *Diacritics* 40.2 (2012): 20.

77. Val Plumwood, "Human Exceptionalism and the Limitations of Animals: A Review of Raimond Gaita's *The Philosopher's Dog*," *Australian Humanities Review* 42 (2007), http://www.australianhumanitiesreview.org/archive/Issue-August-2007/EcoHumanities/Plumwood.html.

78. Melissa Reggente et al., "Social Relationships and Death-Related Behavior in Aquatic Mammals: A Systematic Review," *Philosophical Transactions of the Royal Society B* 373.1754 (2018).

79. André Gonçalves and Dora Biro, "Comparative Thanatology, an Integrative Approach: Exploring Sensory/Cognitive Aspects of Death Recognition in Vertebrates and Invertebrates," *Philosophical Transactions of the Royal Society B* 373.1754 (2018).

80. Hogan, *People of the Whale*, 39.

81. Ibid., 126.

82. Barclay, *Meļaļ*, 130.

83. Ibid., 133.

84. Regina Rudrud et al., "The Sea Turtle

Wars: Culture, War, and Sea Turtles in the Republic of the Marshall Islands," *SPC Traditional Marine Resource Management and Knowledge Information Bulleting* 21 (2007): 17.

85. Regina Rudrud, "Sea Turtles of the Republic of the Marshall Islands" (Manoa: University of Hawai'i, 2008), http://www.reefbase.org/pacific/pub_A0000005000.aspx. The novel does not clarify this point nor specify which of the several species native to the Marshall Islands it is, which include leatherback (*Dermochelys corichea*), hawksbill (*Eretmochylys imbricate*), and most commonly, green turtles (*Chelonia mydis*).

86. Hsinya Huang, "Toward Transpacific Ecopoetics: Three Indigenous Texts," *Comparative Literature Studies* 50.1 (2013): 120–47.

Chapter 4

1. Ibrahim al-Koni's (ابراهيم الكوني) surname is also translated from Arabic to English as al-Kawnī or Kūnī, and Tuareg is variously translated also as Tawāriq or Touareg.

2. Roger Allen, "Rewriting Literary History: The Case of the Arabic Novel," *Journal of Arabic Literature* 38 (2007): 254. See also his *The Arabic Novel: An Historical and Critical Introduction* (Syracuse: Syracuse University Press, 1995), 258.

3. Wen-chin Ouyang, *Poetics of Love in the Arabic Novel: Nation-State, Modernity and Tradition* (Edinburgh: Edinburgh University Press, 2012), 19.

4. Charis Olszok, "Creaturely Memory: Animal Tales and Deep History in Modern Libyan Fiction," *Middle Eastern Literatures* 19.3 (2016): 261.

5. Ibid., 261.

6. E. E. Evans-Pritchard, *The Sanusi of Cyrenaica* (Oxford: Oxford University Press, 1949), 189.

7. Ali Abdullatif Ahmida, *We Died Because of Shur, Evil: Italian Fascist Genocide in Colonial Libya* (forthcoming). Inviting comparison with Miyazaki's non/Shinto representations, al-Koni's oblique references to the death camps skirt the fascist politics

through which these sites later became powerful symbols of oppression and protest under both the dictatorship of Muammar al-Qadhdhafi and the Sanusi monarchy that it overthrew.

8. Three highly endangered species of gazelle (*Gazella leptoceros, Gazella dorcas*, and *Gazella dama*) are all that remain in Libya, and al-Koni's novels do not distinguish between them.

9. Roger Allen, "A Different Voice: The Novels of Ibrahim al-Kawnī," in *Tradition and Modernity in Arabic Literature*, ed. Issa J. Boullata and Terri DeYoung (Fayetteville: University of Arkansas Press, 1997), 154.

10. Ibrahim al-Koni, *The Bleeding of the Stone*, trans. May Jayyusi and Christopher Tingley (Northampton, MA: Interlink, 2002), 125.

11. Melinda Cooper, "The Silent Scream: Agamben, Deleuze, and the Politics of the Unborn," in *Deleuze and Law: Forensic Futures*, ed. Braidotti, Claire Colebrook, and Patrick Hanafin (New York: Palgrave, 2009), 142–62.

12. Cary Wolfe, *Before the Law: Humans and Other Animals in a Biopolitical Frame* (Chicago: University of Chicago Press, 2012).

13. Timothy Campbell, "Translator's Introduction," in *Bíos: Biopolitics and Philosophy*, by Roberto Esposito, trans. Timothy Campbell (Minneapolis: University of Minnesota Press, 2008), xxx.

14. See Susan McHugh, *Animal Stories: Narrating Across Species Lines* (Minneapolis: University of Minnesota Press, 2011).

15. Esposito, *Bíos*, 194.

16. Ibid.

17. Ibid.

18. Campbell, "Translator's Introduction," xxxi.

19. Michael Hardt and Antonio Negri, *Commonwealth* (Cambridge, MA: Belknap, 2009), 105.

20. Ibid., 125.

21. Campbell, "Translator's Introduction," xxviii.

22. Rane Willerslev, *Soul Hunters: Hunting, Animism, and Personhood Among the*

208

Siberian Yukaghirs (Berkeley: University of California Press, 2007), 3.

23. Steve Baker, *Artist | Animal* (Minneapolis: University of Minnesota Press, 2013), 2.

24. Ibrahim al-Koni, author's note to *Anubis: A Novel of Desert Life*, trans. William M. Hutchins (New York: American University in Cairo Press, 2005), xv.

25. Ibid., xvi.

26. Ibid., xvi–xvii.

27. Ibid., 180.

28. Ibid., 74.

29. Ibid., 27, 32.

30. Ibid., 55.

31. Ibid., 56–57.

32. Ibid., 56.

33. Allen, "A Different Voice," 154–55.

34. Ali Abdullatif Ahmida, *The Making of Modern Libya: State Formation, Colonization, and Resistance* (Albany: State University of New York Press, 2009), 3. On storytelling as the preferred mode of theorizing for women and traditional minorities, see Barbara Christian, "The Race for Theory," in *Making Face, Making Soul: Creative and Critical Perspectives by Women of Color*, ed. Gloria Anzaldúa (San Francisco: Aunt Lute Books, 1990), 335–45.

35. Stefan Sperl, "'The Lunar Eclipse': History, Myth and Magic in Ibrāhīm al-Kawnī's First Novel," *Middle Eastern Literatures* 9.3 (2006): 248.

36. Sabry Hafez, "The Novel of the Desert, Poetics of Space and Dialectics of Freedom," in *La Poétique de l'Espace dans la Littérature Arabe Moderne*, ed. Boutros Hallaq, Robin Ostle, and Stefan Wild (Paris: Presses Sorbonne Nouvelle, 2002), 55.

37. Elliott Colla, "Ibrahim al-Koni's Atlas of the Sahara," in *Bridges Across the Sahara: Social, Economic, and Cultural Impact of the Trans-Sahara Trade During the 19th and 20th Centuries*, ed. Ali Abdullatif Ahmida (Newcastle upon Tyne: Cambridge Scholars, 2009), 188.

38. Al-Koni, *Bleeding*, 73–74.

39. Ali Abdullatif Ahmida, *Forgotten Voices: Power and Agency in Colonial and Postcolonial Libya* (New York: Routledge, 2005), 43–54.

40. Al-Koni, *Bleeding*, 74.

41. Ibid., 136 n. 2.

42. Elliott Colla, translator's afterword to Ibrahim al-Koni, *Gold Dust*, trans. Elliott Colla (New York: American University in Cairo Press, 2008), 169.

43. Ahmida, *Making of Modern Libya*, 169.

44. Allen, *Arabic Novel*, 247.

45. Steve Baker, *The Postmodern Animal* (London: Reaktion Books, 2000), 156; and *Artist | Animal*, 14.

46. Al-Koni, *Gold Dust*, 156–57.

47. Ibid., 157–58.

48. Al-Koni, *Bleeding*, 133.

49. Ibid., 134.

50. Ibid., 135.

51. Al-Koni, *Bleeding*, 44, 46.

52. Robert Irwin, *Camel* (London: Reaktion, 2010), 20. Irwin confirms that "drinking camel urine" is a plausible, but not desirable, way of surviving without water in the desert, 53.

53. Al-Koni, *Bleeding*, 55.

54. Ibid., 131.

55. Ibid., 61.

56. Al-Koni, *Gold Dust*, 49.

57. Ibid.

58. Ibid., 51.

59. Ibid., 50.

60. Al-Koni, *Anubis*, 19, 21.

61. Ibid., 22.

62. Ahmida, *Making of Modern Libya*, 18.

63. Ibid., 16.

64. Meike Meerpohl, "Camels as Trading Goods: The Transformation from a Beast of Burden to a Commodity in the Trans-Saharan Trade Between Chad and Libya," in Ahmida, *Bridges Across the Sahara*, 168.

65. Ibid., 174.

66. Irwin, *Camel*, 173–74.

67. Al-Koni, *Gold Dust*, 105.

68. Susan McHugh, "Bitch, Bitch, Bitch: Personal Criticism, Feminist Theory, and Dog-Writing," *Hypatia: A Journal of Feminist Philosophy* 27.3 (2012): 616–35.

69. Rudy, *Loving Animals*, 35–36.

70. Although not named by them as such, human-animal love thus conceivably instantiates "the encounter of singularities" that, as Hardt and Negri argue, serves as an "antidote" to the "corrupt identitarian love" that in contrast values sameness and unity,

motivating persecution of those unlike yourself and your kind and ultimately exterminationism, 181–86.

71. Al-Koni, *Bleeding*, 43.

72. Ibid., 44.

73. Ibid., 24–25.

74. Al-Koni, *Gold Dust*, 14, 75.

75. Ahmida, *Making of Modern Libya*, 1.

76. Al-Koni, *Bleeding*, 97.

77. Al-Koni, *Gold Dust*, 147.

78. Ibid., 50, 194.

79. Ibid., 162.

80. Al-Koni, *Gold Dust*, 157.

81. On the modern literary history of animal mothers' tales and their potential for biopolitical critique, see Robert McKay, "James Agee's 'A Mother's Tale' and the Biopolitics of Animal Life and Death in Post-war America," in *Against Life*, ed. Alastair Hunt and Stephanie Youngblood (Evanston: Northwestern University Press, 2014), 143–60.

82. Sharif S. Elmusa, "The Ecological Bedouin: Toward Environmental Principles for the Arab Region," *Alif: Journal of Comparative Poetics* 33 (2013): 24. While I agree with Elmusa's identification that Asouf has many traits of the "ecological Indian," like Hogan's Marco, his torture and death at the hands of his own people dispel any sense of romance or nostalgia.

83. Al-Koni, *Bleeding*, 104.

84. Ibid., 45.

85. Ibid., 39.

86. Ibid., 37.

87. Steven L. Monfort et al., *Sahelo-Saharan Antelope Survey in Chad*, 5 October 2011, http://www.kbinirsnb.be/cb/antelopes/Survey/2001_chad_antelope_survey_1.htm.

88. Seraj Essul and Reem Tombokti, "Libya's Desert Gazelles Under Threat of Extinction," *Saudi Gazette*, 11 August 2013.

89. Al-Koni, *Bleeding*, 14.

90. Ibid., 111.

91. Ibid., 117.

92. Ibid., 116.

93. Ibid., 119.

94. "Ibrahim al-Koni in Discussion with Ali Abdullatif Ahmida," University of New England, 2 May 2011, https://www.une.edu/calendar/2011/book-signing-and-discussion-libyan-novelist-ibrahim-al-koni.

95. Bird Rose, *Wild Dog Dreaming*, 133.

96. Ibid., 145.

97. Al-Koni, *Anubis*, 172.

98. Donna Haraway, *The Companion Species Manifesto: Dogs, People, and Significant Otherness* (Chicago: Prickly Paradigm Press, 2003), 1.

99. Olszok, "Creaturely Memory," 261.

100. Gilles Deleuze and Félix Guattari, *A Thousand Plateaus: Capitalism and Schizophrenia*, trans. Brian Massumi (Minneapolis: University of Minnesota Press, 1987), 357.

101. Kathy Rudy, "Subjectivity and Belief," *Literature & Theology* 15.3 (2001): 231.

102. Allen, "Rewriting," 252.

103. Although it may be in the interests of the state to lay claim to conquering chaos, Deleuze and Guattari open up the perspective of "nomadology" through which the state is perpetually imperiled by "the war machine," which, because it remains external to the state apparatus and its military institutions, is the provenance of nomads (380).

104. Rosi Braidotti, *Nomadic Subjects: Embodiment and Sexual Difference in Contemporary Feminist Theory*, 2nd ed. (New York: Columbia University Press, 2011), 5–6.

105. Al-Koni, *Anubis*, 172.

Chapter 5

1. Lane Ryo Hirabayashi, "Toshio Yatsushiro," *Densho Encyclopedia*, accessed 11 November 2018, http://encyclopedia.densho.org/Toshio%20Yatsushiro/.

2. Toshio Yatsushiro, "The Changing Eskimo: A Study of Wage Employment and Its Consequences Among the Eskimos of Frobisher Bay, Baffin Island," *Beaver* 293 (1962): 22. The usage of *Eskimo* by even sympathetic witnesses speaks volumes about that particular historical moment. Officially adopted in 1977 at the Inuit Circumpolar Conference, *Inuit* literally means "the people" and is preferred by them to the vague, colonialist, and otherwise objectionable term *Eskimo*, according to Geneviève Montcombroux, *The Canadian Inuit Dog: Canada's Heritage* (Imwood: Whippoorwill, 2002), 5.

3. Lisa Stevenson, "The Psychic Life of

Biopolitics: Survival, Cooperation, and Inuit Community," *American Ethnologist* 39.3 (2012): 600, unbracketed ellipsis in original.

4. Unless otherwise specified, all translations of Inuktitut terms are from the Qikiqtani Inuit Association, *QTC Final Report: Achieving Saimaqatigiingniq Thematic Reports and Special Studies, 1950–75* (Iqaluit: Inhabit Media, 2013), and unless otherwise noted, all informants cited are Inuit.

5. Francis Lévesque, "Sixty Years of Dog Management in Nunavik," *Medicine Anthropology Theory* 5.3 (2018): 199–200.

6. Frédéric Laugrand and Jarich Oosten, "Canicide and Healing: The Position of the Dog in the Inuit Cultures of the Canadian Arctic," *Anthropos* 97.1 (2002): 90. They elaborate, "The *inua* of a dog and his dog belong together. The closeness of the relationship is expressed in the account of Iqallijuq where the dog represents the penis of the man," an analogy troubled by the fluidity of Inuit concepts of gender but nonetheless illustrative of how conceptually "the dog and his owner constitute a physical whole" (101).

7. Freely accessible online, the QTC's *Community Histories, 1950–1975* include thirteen separate volumes each devoted to a particular municipality. Significantly, of the ten *Thematic Reports and Special Studies, 1950–1975*, one focuses exclusively on qimmiit.

8. Laugrand and Oosten, "Canicide and Healing," 92.

9. Qikiqtani Inuit Association, *QTC Final Report*, 24.

10. On the transformation of qimmiit from cultural to commodity form, see Frank James Tester, "Can the Sled Dog Sleep? Postcolonialism, Cultural Transformation, and the Consumption of Inuit Culture," *New Proposals* 3.3 (2010): 7–19.

11. Gilles Deleuze and Félix Guattari, *A Thousand Plateaus: Capitalism and Schizophrenia*, trans. Brian Massumi (Minneapolis: University of Minnesota Press, 1987), 241.

12. This is not to say that Deleuze and Guattari's model is thus proven wrong. As I argue in *Animal Stories*, they reject from the start the animal's exclusion from language and representation, for such positions

ultimately submit to the problem of being a human animal as it is posited by language. Many misinterpret becoming-animal as a defining property internalized by the human, but taken at its word, their formulation of animality instead pervades all forms of agency, permeating language, literature, and every living thing potentially engaged with processes of becoming. See Matthew Calarco, *Thinking Through Animals: Identity, Difference, Indistinction* (Stanford: Stanford University Press, 2015), 59.

13. Laugrand and Oosten, "Canicide and Healing," 101.

14. Nicole Shukin, *Animal Capital: Rendering Life in Biopolitical Times* (Minneapolis: University of Minnesota Press, 2009), 138.

15. Ibid., 232.

16. The Qikiqtani Inuit Association focuses on gathering the voices of communities in Nunavut, an Inuit-majority territory now formally separated from Canada's Northwest Territories, and the Makivik Corporation represents Inuit in the Arctic Québec region of Nunavik.

17. Mr. George Koneak (Elder, Makivik Corporation), 38th Parliament of Canada, 1st session, Standing Committee on Aboriginal Affairs and Northern Development, Evidence, 8 March 2005, 1115, http://www.parl.gc.ca/HousePublications/Publication.aspx?DocId=1682867&Language=E&Mode=1.

18. Peter Shawn Taylor, "The Myth of the Sled Dog Killings: The RCMP Probes a Clash Between Native Lore and White History," *Maclean's*, 1 January 2007, http://www.macleans.ca/canada/national/article.jsp?content=20070101_138986_138986.

19. Royal Canadian Mounted Police (RCMP), *Final Report: RCMP Review of Allegations Concerning Inuit Sled Dogs*, 30 May 2006, http://publications.gc.ca/site/eng/389331/publication.html.

20. Qikiqtani Inuit Association, *QTC Final Report*, 39.

21. Qikiqtani Inuit Association, *Qimmiliriniq: Inuit Sled Dogs in Qikiqtaaluk. Thematic Reports and Special Studies, 1950–75* (Iqaluit: Inhabit Media, 2013), 50.

22. Qikiqtani Inuit Association, *QTC Final Report*, 6.

23. Keavy Martin, *Stories in a New Skin: Approaches to Inuit Literature* (Winnipeg: University of Manitoba Press, 2012), 8.

24. Alisa Henderson, *Nunavut: Rethinking Political Culture* (Vancouver: University of British Columbia Press, 2007), 67.

25. Michael Asch and Norman Zlotkin, "Affirming Aboriginal Title: A New Basis for Comprehensive Claims Negotiations," in *Aboriginal and Treaty Rights in Canada*, ed. Michael Asch (Vancouver: University of British Columbia Press, 1997), 211.

26. Glen Coulthard, *Red Skin, White Masks: Rejecting the Colonial Politics of Recognition* (Minneapolis: University of Minnesota Press, 2014), 127.

27. Nicole Shukin, "Materializing Climate Change: Images of Exposure, States of Exception," in *Material Cultures in Canada*, ed. Thomas Allen and Jennifer Blair (Waterloo: Wilfrid Laurier University Press, 2015), 189–208. On specific ways in which "Arctic warming . . . undermine[s] global efforts to reduce environmental and human exposure to . . . toxic chemicals," see Jianmin Ma, Hayley Hung, Chongguo Tian, and Roland Kallenborn, "Revolatilization of Persistent Organic Pollutants in the Arctic Induced by Climate Change," *Nature Climate Change* 1 (2011): 255–60.

28. Qikiqtani Inuit Association, *Qimmiliriniq*, 31.

29. Popular environmental writer Farley Mowat interviewed survivors of an Ihalmiut Inuit community who explained how the generational loss of knowledge of caribou hunting following the switch to trapping for fur export made the collapse of the fox-fur economic bubble calamitous for Inuit, who had amassed more dogs in order to run trap lines and so suffered mass starvation when traders abandoned their posts. See Mowat, *People of the Deer* (1951; repr., Toronto: Seal Books, 1980).

30. Makivik Corporation, *Regarding the Slaughtering of Nunaviik "Qimmit" (Inuit Dogs) from the Late 1950s to the 1960s*, January 2005, http://pubs.aina.ucalgary.ca/makivik/CI232.pdf.

31. Leslie Sharpe, "Voices, Lines, Cracks, and Data Sets: Formations of a New 'Idea of the Canadian North,'" in *Far Field: Digital Culture, Climate Change, and the Poles*, ed. Jane D. Marsching and Andrea Polli (Chicago: Intellect, 2012), 203.

32. Elisapee Karetak's documentary films *Kikkik* (2000 English; 2002 Inuktitut) tell the horrific story of her father's murder, sister's death due to exposure, and mother's subsequent exoneration of charges in their deaths, all of which directly followed from governmental relocation, and of how she and her surviving siblings only learned their story as adults, after the passing of their mother Kikkik, by reading Mowat's 1957 account of it in *The Desperate People*.

33. Pauktuutit Inuit Women of Canada, *The Inuit Way: A Guide to Inuit Culture* (Ottawa: Pauktuutit Inuit Women of Canada, 2006), 43. Daniel Heath Justice notes a broader pattern: "Indigenous peoples are vastly overrepresented in all negative social indicators in Canada, the US, and other settler states, and grossly underrepresented in the positive ones." See Justice, *Why Indigenous Literatures Matter* (Waterloo: Wilfrid Laurier University Press, 2018), 3.

34. See *Looking Forward, Looking Back*, vol. 1 of *Report of the Royal Commission on Aboriginal Peoples* (Ottawa: Canada Communication Group, 1996).

35. Scott Richard Lyons, *X-marks: Native Signatures of Assent* (Minneapolis: University of Minnesota Press, 2010), 34.

36. Pauktuutit Inuit Women of Canada, *Inuit Way*, 16.

37. Contributions to Inuit family life traditionally fall along gendered lines that nonetheless remain porous in order to allow tasks to fall to those best suited to them, a uniqueness capitalized on by European and US authors. For example, Rockwell Kent's memoir details how the sewing and embroidery of Greenland Inuit Olabi was prized in his community, even if his mother is "the only woman who will ever have loved him in all his life" (295). The mother of Peter Høeg's titular character is a well-respected hunter, whose death is explained by "the remains of her kayak, which led them to conclude that it must have been a walrus . . . [among] the swiftest and most meticulous killers

in the ocean." See Høeg, *Smilla's Sense of Snow*, trans. Tiina Nunnally (1992; repr., New York: Farrar, Straus, and Giroux, 1993), 39.

38. Lee Guemple, "Gender in Inuit Society," in *Women and Power in Native North America*, ed. Laura Klein and Lillian Ackerman (Norman: University of Oklahoma Press, 1995), 27.

39. Qikiqtani Inuit Association, *Qimmiliriniq*, 15.

40. Laugrand and Oosten, "Canicide and Healing," 92.

41. Sharpe, "Voices, Lines, Cracks," 201.

42. On this history and the potential for academics to correct the damage, see especially John Steckley's unpacking of three major "white lies" told by major anthropologists like Franz Boas in *White Lies About the Inuit* (Toronto: University of Toronto Press, 2008).

43. Qikiqtani Inuit Association, *QTC Final Report*, 21.

44. Rachael Slocum, "Polar Bears and Energy-Efficient Lightbulbs, Strategies to Bring Climate Change Home," *Environment and Planning D: Society and Space* 22.3 (2004): 413–38. On the environmentalist iconicity of the polar bear as shaped by their presence in zoos, see Guro Flinterud, "Polar Bear Knut and His Blog," in *Animals on Display: The Creaturely in Museums, Zoos, and Natural History Display*, ed. Liv Emma Thorsen, Karen Rader, and Adam Dodd (University Park: Pennsylvania State University Press, 2013), 192–213.

45. Debunking recent identifications of some extant dog populations as native to the Americas, researchers in the most comprehensive study to date identify "modern American arctic dogs" (a group that also includes Alaskan huskies) as a sister taxon to pre-Columbian dogs through the latter's genome, which is preserved most comprehensively today in that of the canine transmissible venereal tumor, a contagious cancer associated with modern American arctic dogs. See Máire Ní Leathlobhair et al., "The Evolution of Dogs in the Americas," *Science* 361.6397 (2018): 81–85. They note the absence of samples from Thule archaeological sites because it makes unclear in

their study whether the ancestors of modern American arctic dogs arrived six thousand or one thousand years ago (83). Their most shocking finding is that the dogs of other First Peoples of the Americas disappeared immediately following European contact.

46. Sarah K. Brown, Christyann M. Darwent, and Benjamin N. Sacks, "Ancient DNA Evidence for Genetic Continuity in Arctic Dogs," *Journal of Archaeological Science* 40 (2013): 1279–88.

47. Harriet Ritvo, *The Animal Estate: The English and Other Creatures in the Victorian Age* (Cambridge: Harvard University Press, 1987). See also Martin Wallen, *Whose Dog Are You? The Technology of Dog Breeds and Aesthetics of Modern Human-Canine Relationships* (Ann Arbor: University of Michigan Press, 2017).

48. Kalpana Seshadri, *HumAnimal: Race, Law, Language* (Minneapolis: University of Minnesota Press, 2012), xvi.

49. I discuss *The Last Dogs of Winter* in more detail in Susan McHugh, "One or Several Dogs? Gathering Canine Stories and Filming Multispecies Multitudes in Contemporary Cinema," *Antennae* 42 (2017): 118–30.

50. Montcombroux, *Canadian Inuit Dog*, 13.

51. Canadian Eskimo Dog Foundation, 5 May 2016, https://web.archive.org/web/20160515020321/http://www.canadianeskimodogfoundation.ca/.

52. Francisco Varela, *Ethical Know-How: Science, Wisdom, and Cognition* (Stanford: Stanford University Press, 1999).

53. Qikiqtani Inuit Association, *Qimmiliriniq*, 57.

54. Otto Sverdrup, *New Land: Four Years in the Arctic Region* (London: Longmans, 1904), 18. Detouring from his history of Sverdrup's successful dog handling, Gerard Kenney cites Danish anthropologist Peter Freuchen's account of the difficulty of even defecating in the company of ravenous qimmiit. See Kenney, *Ships of Wood and Men of Iron: A Norwegian-Canadian Saga of Exploration in the High Arctic* (Toronto: Natural Heritage / Natural History, 2004), 12–13.

55. Canadian Kennel Club, "Canadian Eskimo Dog," in *Official Breed Standards. Group 3: Working Dogs*

(January 2014), III-7.1, https://www.ckc
.ca/CanadianKennelClub/media/Breed
-Standards/Group%203/Canadian-Eskimo
-Dog.pdf.

56. Martin, *Stories in a New Skin*, 123. Earlier she cautions that etymologically, the terms are more complexly aligned, but "practically speaking," *sila* indicates how "wisdom is based on a knowledge of one's environment" (5).

57. Makivik Corporation, *Regarding the Slaughtering*, 3.

58. Ibid., 12.

59. Justice, *Why Indigenous Literatures Matter*, 2.

60. Kerrie-Ann Shannon, "An Examination of Traditional Knowledge: The Case of the Inuit Sled Dog," *Fan Hitch: Journal of the Inuit Sled Dog International* 12.1 (2009), http://thefanhitch.org/V12N1/V12 ,N1TraditionalKnowledge.html.

61. D. L. Guemple, "Saunik: Name Sharing as a Factor Governing Inuit Kinship Terms," *Ethnology* 4.3 (1965): 323–35.

62. Lisa Stevenson, "The Psychic Life of Biopolitics," 605–6.

63. Alexander Zahara and Myra Hird, "Raven, Dog, Human: Inhuman Colonialism and Unsettling Cosmologies," *Environmental Humanities* 7 (2015): 169–90.

64. Shannon, "Examination of Traditional Knowledge."

65. Rockwell Kent, *Salamina* (1935; repr., Middletown: Wesleyan University Press, 2003), 182.

66. Qikiqtani Inuit Association, *Qimmiliriniq*, 11.

67. Shannon, "Examination of Traditional Knowledge."

68. Kent, *Salamina*, 192.

69. Susan McHugh, *Animal Stories: Narrating Across Species Lines* (Minneapolis: University of Minnesota Press, 2011), 53.

70. "A team working harmoniously will often react as one mind," explains Geneviève Montcombroux. "In fact, all the teams I have ever driven could act in this manner. They turned, or put on a burst of speed, as one." Montcombroux, *The Inuit Dog of the Polar North* (Middletown, DE: Whippoorwill Solitude, 2015), 130.

71. Montcombroux offers several examples of sled dogs refusing to advance over thin ice, overriding wrong directions in a blizzard, and generally exhibiting "a certain independent stubbornness [that] makes [each dog] evaluate an order as if he was really weighing the pros and cons before obeying it." She credits such behavior as evidence of the intelligence that distinguishes qimmiit. Ibid., 73, 136.

72. Victor Frankenstein's dire situation is evident as soon as he enters the story, floating on an ice floe with a sled and "only one dog [who] remained alive," in Mary Shelley's *Frankenstein, or The Modern Prometheus* (1818; repr., New York: Dover, 1994), 9.

73. Main canine character Buck is saved by his final master John Thornton from abusive, inexperienced musher Hal, only then to witness Hal force his dogs onto rotten ice, consequently drowning his own wife, brother, and the dogs. See Jack London, *The Call of the Wild* (1903; repr., Norman: University of Oklahoma Press, 1995), 48–49.

74. Kent, *Salamina*, 288.

75. Ibid., 332.

76. Peter Freuchen, *Field Notes and Biological Observations*, in *Mammals,* vol. 2 of *Report of the Fifth Thule Expedition 1921–24* (Copenhagen: Gyldendalske Boghandel Nordisk Forlag, 1935), 144.

77. Qikiqtani Inuit Association, *QTC Final Report*, 21.

78. Makivik Corporation, *Regarding the Slaughtering*, 12.

79. Samuel King Hutton, *By Eskimo Dog-Sled and Kayak: A Description of a Missionary's Experiences and Adventures in Labrador* (London: Seeley, Service, 1919), 178.

80. Makivik Corporation, *Regarding the Slaughtering*, 12.

81. Qikiqtani Inuit Association, *Qimmiliriniq*, 48.

82. Nelson Graburn, *Eskimos Without Igloos: Social and Economic Development in Sugluk* (Boston: Little, Brown, 1969), 129.

83. Kent, *Salamina*, 190.

84. London, *Call of the Wild*, 50. On London's depictions of man-dog love as "painful" and "shameful" experiences except when shared at the margins of settler culture, see

Keridiana Chez, *Victorian Dogs, Victorian Men: Affect and Animals in Nineteenth-Century Culture* (Columbus: Ohio State University Press, 2017).

85. Graburn, *Eskimos Without Igloos*, 38.

86. Kent, *Salamina*, 190.

87. Noting that "Greenland Inuit need their sled dogs to continue their traditional way of life," Montcombroux explains the threat as constant: "Regrettably, almost every year brings a report of a tragic accident when a child or an elderly person wanders among the dogs. If that person happens to fall, especially if wearing caribou clothing, the dogs paw and tear at it, often severely injuring the person." See Montcombroux, *Inuit Dog*, 53.

88. In a warm winter when the ice takes too long to form, people facing starvation "are driven to devour their dogs," according to Kent, *Salamina*, 154.

89. Hutton, *By Eskimo Dog-Sled*, 63.

90. Qikiqtani Inuit Association, *QTC Final Report*, 28.

91. Anat Pick, *Creaturely Poetics: Animality and Vulnerability in Literature and Film* (New York: Columbia University Press, 2011), 50–51.

92. Qikiqtani Inuit Association, *QTC Final Report*, 16.

93. Qikiqtani Inuit Association, *Qimmiliriniq*, 21.

94. Lévesque, "Sixty Years of Dog Management," 207.

95. Qikiqtani Inuit Association, *Qimmiliriniq*, 21.

96. Ibid., 13.

97. Ibid., 22.

98. Ibid., 22.

99. RCMP, *Final Report*, 14.

100. Ibid., 15.

101. Qikiqtani Inuit Association, *Qimmiliriniq*, 19.

102. Ibid., 24.

103. For instance, the *QTC Final Report* notes that requiring dog handlers to have surpassed "the age of maturity, 16, was meaningless . . . [because] for Inuit, maturity was measured by abilities, not age" (23).

104. See, for instance, Robert Gordon, "Fido: Dog Tales of Colonialism in Namibia,"

in *Canis Africanis: A Dog History of Southern Africa*, ed. Lance von Sittert and Sandra Swart (Boston: Brill, 2008), 173–92. Gordon's account of the 1922 Bondelswarts Rebellion in colonial Namibia as sparked by the imposition of a dog tax of "more than the equivalent of a month's salary" on African "herders employed on a settler farm" exemplifies similar accounts discussed throughout the collection (179).

105. Qikiqtani Inuit Association, *QTC Final Report*, 24.

106. Makivik Corporation, *Regarding the Slaughtering*, 11.

107. Qikiqtani Inuit Association, *QTC Final Report*, 23.

108. Ibid., 23.

109. Qikiqtani Inuit Association, *Qimmiliriniq*, 31.

110. RCMP, *Final Report*, 19.

111. Makivik Corporation, *Regarding the Slaughtering*, 15.

112. Ibid., 19.

113. Qikiqtani Inuit Association, *QTC Final Report*, 20.

114. Ibid., 23.

115. Ibid., 6.

116. Henderson, *Nunavut*, 168.

117. RCMP, *Final Report*, 19.

118. Graburn, *Eskimos Without Igloos*, 162.

119. Montcombroux, *Inuit Dog*, 36.

120. RCMP, *Final Report*, 44. Montcombroux elaborates instances of piblokto, "a disease, or possibly a condition," also referred to as "pibloqtok, problokto, and Arctic Hysteria" or simply "dog-madness," possibly an encephalitis or prion disease. See Montcombroux, *Inuit Dog*, 146–48.

121. Qikiqtani Inuit Association, *QTC Final Report*, 8.

122. Colin Dayan, *The Law Is a White Dog: How Legal Rituals Make and Unmake Persons* (Princeton: Princeton University Press, 2011), 248.

123. Sue Hamilton, "From the Editor," *Fan Hitch: Journal of the Inuit Sled Dog International* 7.4 (2005), http://thefanhitch.org/V7N4/V7,N4Front.html.

124. Makivik Corporation, *Regarding the Slaughtering*, 24.

125. Ibid., 17.

126. Dory Nason, "We Hold Our Hands Up: On Indigenous Women's Love and Resistance," *Decolonization*, 12 February 2013, https://decolonization.wordpress .com/2013/02/12/we-hold-our-hands -up-on-indigenous-womens-love-and -resistance/.

127. Coulthard, *Red Skin, White Masks*, 177.

128. Nason's position contrasts the ending of Naomi Klein, "Dancing the World into Being: A Conversation with Idle No More's Leanne Simpson," *Yes! Magazine*, 5 March 2013, https://www.yesmagazine.org/peace -justice/dancing-the-world-into-being-a -conversation-with-idle-no-more-leanne -simpson.

129. Laugrand and Oosten, "Canicide and Healing," 95.

130. Leanne Simpson, "Not Murdered, Not Missing: Rebelling Against Colonial Gender Violence," on Leanne Betasamosake Simpson's official website, originally published by *Nations Rising* (blog) on 5 March 2014, https://www.leannesimpson.ca/writings/not -murdered-not-missing-rebelling-against -colonial-gender-violence.

131. Eileen Joy identifies such work in a Foucauldian frame as the "cultivating [of] new relational modes and the company of misfits (an agonistic yet joyful venture, to be sure, in which we exult in the exquisite difficulties of becoming-with-others)." See Joy, "Improbable Manners of Being," *GLQ* 21.2–3 (2015): 221–24.

Chapter 6

1. Samuel Taylor Coleridge, "Work Without Hope," quoted in William and Mary Morris, *Morris Dictionary of Word and Phrase Origins* (New York: Harper & Row, 1977). Tracking the origin of the catchphrase, "Birds do it / Bees do it," from Cole Porter's 1928 song "Let's Fall in Love," the Morrises' lexicography traces the pattern of birds and bees as signifiers of sex back to Coleridge.

2. Writing more generally about how the 1998 film *A Bug's Life* pioneered CGI technology's visualization of animal "crowds,"

Halberstam concludes that it thus enables "animal realities and animal logic [to] creep into human worlds and change the way in which we think and inhabit sociality." See Jack (published Judith) Halberstam, "Animal Sociality Beyond the Hetero/Homo Binary," *Women and Performance* 20.3 (2010), 324.

Through a reading of Miyazaki's 2008 film *Ponyo*, Chen elaborates that Halberstam "suggests that if mainstream animation filmmakers did study the actual lives of bees, bee fiction would do much better than its currently middling job at representing feminist and other progressive politics." See Mel Chen, *Animacies: Biopolitics, Racial Mattering, and Queer Affect* (Durham: Duke University Press, 2012), 228.

3. S. L. Buchmann and G. P. Nabhan, *The Forgotten Pollinators* (Washington, DC: Island Press, 1996). Gabriela Chavarria clarifies that the crop estimate is too low, "since bees also pollinate alfalfa and other forage plants" for meat and dairy industries. See Chavarria, "Pollinator Conservation," *Renewable Resources Journal* (Winter 1999–2000).

4. In this way my approach differs from that taken by Jeff Karnicky in *The Scarlet Experiment: Birds and Humans in America* (Lincoln: University of Nebraska Press, 2016), who shows how twenty-first-century writers explore the "population management" and other biopolitical interventions into wild bird life work "for better and for worse, depending on the species and the situation" (xix).

5. On the spectacle of avian flocks wavering between heteronormative ideal and menace that ultimately unfolds to unknowable communities in cinema, see my "Unknowing Animals: Wild Bird Films and the Limits of Knowledge," in *Animal Life and the Moving Image*, ed. Laura McMahon and Michael Lawrence (London: British Film Institute, 2015), 271–87.

6. Paul Nadasdy, "First Nations, Citizenship, and Animals, or Why Northern Indigenous People Might Not Want to Live in Zoopolis," *Canadian Journal of Political Science* 49.1 (2016): 16.

7. Giovanni Aloi, "On a Wing and a Prayer: Butterflies in Contemporary Art," in *The Routledge Handbook of Human-Animal*

216 *Studies*, ed. Garry Marvin and Susan McHugh (New York: Routledge, 2014), 68–83. On hummingbird taxidermy, see Rachael Poliquin, *The Breathless Zoo: Taxidermy and the Cultures of Longing* (University Park: Pennsylvania State University Press, 2012).

8. Susan McHugh, "Flora, Not Fauna: GM Culture and Agriculture," *Literature and Medicine* 26.1 (2007): 25–54.

9. Bloodhound Gang, "Bad Touch," quoted in Cynthia Chris, *Watching Wildlife* (Minneapolis: University of Minnesota Press, 2006), 123.

10. Catriona Sandilands, "Pro/Polis: Three Forays into the Political Lives of Bees," in *Material Ecocriticism*, ed. Serenella Iovino and Serpil Opperman (Bloomington: Indiana University Press, 2014), 161.

11. Gerald Vizenor, *Fugitive Poses: Native American Scenes of Absence and Presence* (Norman: University of Oklahoma Press, 1988), 141.

12. Mark Rifkin, *The Erotics of Sovereignty: Queer Native Writing in the Era of Self-determination* (Minneapolis: University of Minnesota Press, 2012), 84. See also Rose Stremlau, *Sustaining the Cherokee Family: Kinship and the Allotment of an Indigenous Nation* (Chapel Hill: University of North Carolina Press, 2011); and Daniel Heath Justice, "'Go Away Water!': Kinship Criticism and the Decolonization Imperative," in *Reasoning Together: The Native Critics Collective*, ed. Craig S. Womack et al. (Norman: University of Oklahoma Press, 2008).

13. Christopher Pexa, "More Than Talking Animals: Charles Alexander Eastman's Animal Peoples and Their Kinship Critiques of United States Colonialism," *PMLA* 131.3 (2016): 656.

14. Histories of the ecological effects of settler colonialism include Rebecca Woods, *The Herds Shot Round the World: Native Breeds and the British Empire, 1800–1900* (Chapel Hill: University of North Carolina Press, 2017); and Virginia DeJohn Anderson, *Creatures of Empire: How Domestic Animals Shaped Early America* (Oxford: Oxford University Press, 2006).

15. Harry Garuba, "Explorations in Animist Materialism: Notes on Reading/ Writing African Literature, Culture, and Society," *Public Culture* 15.2 (2003): 265.

16. Heather Swan, *Where Honeybees Thrive: Stories from the Field* (University Park: Pennsylvania State University Press, 2017), 20.

17. Thomas King, *A Short History of Indians in Canada* (Minneapolis: University of Minnesota Press, 2014), 2.

18. Ibid., 3.

19. Thomas Gannon, *Skylark Meets Meadowlark: Reimagining the Bird in British Romantic and Contemporary Native American Literature* (Lincoln: University of Nebraska Press, 2009), 13.

20. Nadia Berenstein, "Deathtraps in the Flyways: Electricity, Glass, and Bird Collisions in Urban North America 1887–2014," in *Cosmopolitan Animals*, ed. Kaori Nagai et al. (London: Palgrave, 2015) 79–92.

21. MariJo Moore, *Genocide of the Mind: New Native Writing* (New York: Nation Books, 2003).

22. Thomas King, *The Truth About Stories: A Native Narrative* (Minneapolis: University of Minnesota Press, 2003), 33, 57.

23. Catherine Rainwater, "Haunted by Birds: An Eco-critical View of Personhood in *The Plague of Doves*," in *Louise Erdrich: Tracks, The Last Report on the Miracles at Little No Horse, The Plague of Doves*, ed. Deborah Madsen (London: Continuum, 2011), 153. See also Joni Adamson, "Why Bears Are Good to Think and Theory Doesn't Have to Be Another Form of Murder: Transformation and Oral Tradition in Louise Erdrich's *Tracks*," *Studies in American Indian Literatures* 4.1 (1992): 28–48.

24. *Ceremony* author Leslie Silko famously denounced Erdrich's first novel as "academic, post-modernist, so-called experimental" at the cost of attending to "history or politics" in a review titled "Here's an Odd Artifact for the Fairy-Tale Shelf," first published in *Studies in American Indian Literature* 10 (1986): 179.

25. Susan Strehle, "'Prey to Unknown Dreams': Louise Erdrich, *The Plague of Doves*, and the Exceptionalist Disavowal of History,"

LIT: Literature, Interpretation, Theory 25.2
(2014): 109.

26. Daniel Payne, "Border Crossings: Animals, Tricksters and Shape-Shifters in Modern Native American Fiction," in *Indigenous Creatures, Native Knowledges, and the Arts: Human-Animal Studies in Modern Worlds*, ed. Wendy Woodward and Susan McHugh (New York: Palgrave, 2017), 199–223.

27. McHugh, "Unknowing Animals."

28. Louise Erdrich, *The Plague of Doves* (New York: Harper Perennial, 2008), 5.

29. John Gamber, "So a Priest Walks in to a Reservation Tragicomedy: Humor in *The Plague of Doves*," in *Louise Erdrich*, 143.

30. Erdrich, *Plague of Doves*, 5.

31. Jonathan Burt, "The Tumult of Integrations out of the Sky: The Movement of Birds and Film's Ornithology," in *Animal Life and the Moving Image*, 255.

32. Andrew Blechman, "Flying Rats," in *Trash Animals: How We Live with Nature's Filthy, Feral, Invasive, and Unwanted Species*, ed. Kelsi Nagy and Phillip David Johnson (Minneapolis: University of Minnesota Press, 2013), 221–42.

33. Laying the mourning dove theory to rest, the passenger pigeon was identified as "the sister taxon of all other New World pigeons (*Patageonias*)" through genetic analysis. See Kevin Johnson et al., "The Flight of the Passenger Pigeon: Phylogenetics and Biogeographic History of an Extinct Species," *Molecular Phylogenetics and Evolution* 57.1 (2010): 455–58.

34. Cary Wolfe, "Each Time Unique: The Poetics of Extinction," in *Animalities: Literary and Cultural Studies Beyond the Human*, ed. Michael Lundblad (Edinburgh: Edinburgh University Press, 2017), 22–42.

35. Erdrich, *Plague of Doves*, 19.

36. Ibid.

37. Ibid., 8.

38. Gamber, "So a Priest," 144.

39. On this point, Gamber is cited without comment by Strehle, "'Prey to Unknown Dreams,'" 116.

40. Peter Beidler, *Murdering Indians: A Documentary History of the Murders that Inspired Louise Erdrich's* The Plague of Doves (Jefferson, NC: McFarland, 2014).

41. Erdrich, *Plague of Doves*, 243.

42. Ibid., 253.

43. Ibid., 254.

44. Gannon, *Skylark Meets Meadowlark*, 203.

45. Erdrich, *Plague of Doves*, 255.

46. Rainwater, "Haunted by Birds," 158.

47. Jonathan Franzen, *Freedom* (New York: Farrar, Straus, and Giroux, 2010), 210.

48. Jesus Angel Gonzalez, "Eastern and Western Promises in Jonathan Franzen's *Freedom*," *Atlantis: Journal of the Spanish Association of Anglo-American Studies* 37.1 (2015): 24.

49. Margaret Hunt Gram, "Freedom's Limits: Jonathan Franzen, the Realist Novel, and the Problem of Growth," *American Literary History* 26.2 (2014): 295–316, esp. 312.

50. Franzen, *Freedom*, 485.

51. Thorunn Endreson, "The Paradox of Freedom in Jonathan Franzen's *Freedom*," in *Development and Environment: Practices, Theories, Policies*, ed. Kenneth Bo Nielsen and Kristian Bjørkdahl (Copenhagen: Akademisk Forlag, 2012), 173–87.

52. Erdrich, *Plague of Doves*, 292.

53. Ibid., 286.

54. Ibid.

55. Ibid., 289.

56. Ibid.

57. J. M. Coetzee, *Boyhood: Scenes from Provincial Life* (New York: Penguin, 1998), 97–98.

58. Erdrich, *Plague of Doves*, 291. Although she does not flag it as such, the image of a "skull full of honey" also seems directly to reference the Old Testament (Judg. 14:80).

59. Gina Valentino, "'It All Does Come to Nothing in the End': Nationalism and Gender in Louise Erdrich's *The Plague of Doves*," in *Louise Erdrich*, 134.

60. Erdrich, *Plague of Doves*, 115.

61. Leonard Lutwack, *Birds in Literature* (Gainesville: University Press of Florida, 1994), xi. Beryl Rowland's early structuralist study *Birds with Human Souls: A Guide to Bird Symbolism* (Knoxville: University of Tennessee Press, 1978) claims a universal association of bird representations with transcendence rather than naturalist observation

218

in literature, but her examples are all Euro-western. More recently Jeff Karnicky's *The Scarlet Experiment* along with Branka Arsic's *Bird Relics: Grief and Vitalism in Thoreau* (Cambridge: Harvard University Press, 2016) examine the material presence of birds in literary history to draw very different conclusions about the meanings of species and orders of birds for particular US authors and native North American bird species, emphasizing settler perspectives.

62. Karnicky, *Scarlet Experiment*, 38.

63. Gannon, *Skylark Meets Meadowlark*, 5.

64. Rainwater, "Haunted by Birds," 153.

65. Irene Pepperberg, *The Alex Studies: Cognitive and Communicative Abilities of Grey Parrots* (Cambridge: Harvard University Press, 2002).

66. See chapter 1 of Karnicky, *Scarlet Experiment*.

67. Seweryn Olkowicza et al., "Birds Have Primate-Like Numbers of Neurons in the Forebrain," *Publication of the National Academy of Science*, 6 May 2016.

68. Thom van Dooren, *Flight Ways: Life and Loss on the Edge of Extinction* (Columbia: Columbia University Press, 2014), 14.

69. Committee on the Status of Pollinators in North America, *The Status of Pollinators in North America* (Washington, DC: National Research Council, 2007), 203. Along with declines in bat and butterfly species, plummeting numbers of birds and bees are documented, and while comparable declines in other pollinators like flies, wasps, and beetles are likely, the report concludes that there is "insufficient data to document trends" (201–2). Incidentally, butterflies fit this pattern of pollinator species decline but are not being enlisted for the same aesthetic purpose, possibly because of the direct conflict with their long symbolic history as figures of immortality.

70. White House Office of the Press Secretary, "Presidential Memorandum Creating Federal Strategy to Promote Healthy Honey Bees and Other Pollinators," 20 June 2014, https://www.whitehouse.gov/the-press-office/2014/06/20/presidential-memorandum-creating-federal-strategy-promote-health-honey-b.

71. Connal Eardley et al., *Pollinators and Pollination: A Resource Book for Policy and Practice* (Pretoria: African Pollinator Initiative, 2006), xiii. See also Knut Faegri and Leendert van der Pijl, *Principles of Pollination Ecology* (Oxford: Pergamon, 1979), 1. Records of honeybees date back to at least 3000 BCE in Egypt, where bee products permeated the culture, used in food, cosmetics, painting, medicine, and embalming, according to Gene Kritsky, *The Tears of Re: Beekeeping in Ancient Egypt* (Oxford: Oxford University Press, 2015).

72. Richie Nimmo, "Apiculture in the Anthropocene: Between Posthumanism and Critical Animal Studies," in *Animals in the Anthropocene: Critical Perspectives on Non-human Futures*, ed. The Human Animal Research Network Editorial Collective (Sydney: Sydney University Press, 2015), 185.

73. Thomas Seeley, *Honeybee Democracy* (Princeton: Princeton University Press, 2010), 3.

74. Robyn Manley, Mike Boots, and Lena Wilfert, "Emerging Viral Disease Risk to Pollinating Insects: Ecological, Evolutionary, and Anthropogenic Factors," *Journal of Applied Ecology* 52 (2015): 331–40.

75. Buchmann and Nabhan, *Forgotten Pollinators*, 164.

76. Seeley, *Honeybee*, 237. Seeley credits the analogy as original to Bert Hölldobler and E. O. Wilson, *The Superorganism: The Beauty, Elegance, and Strangeness of Insect Societies* (New York: Norton, 2009).

77. Sean Meighoo, "Human Language, Animal Code, and the Question of Beeing," *Humanimalia* 8.2 (2017): 27.

78. Ibid., 40.

79. Rosi Braidotti, *Nomadic Theory: The Portable Rosi Braidotti* (New York: Columbia University Press, 2012), 103.

80. On "the unnamed Cherokee princess great-great-grandmother so common in the US" and "the similarly anonymous Métis great-great-grandmother increasingly encountered in Canada," see Daniel Heath Justice, *Why Indigenous Literatures Matter*

Notes to Pages 168–174

(Waterloo: Wilfrid Laurier University Press, 2018), 138. See also Justice, *Our Fire Survives the Storm: A Cherokee Literary History* (Minneapolis: University of Minnesota Press, 2006).

81. Clare Archer-Leane, "David Malouf's *Remembering Babylon* as a Reconsideration of Pastoral Idealisation," *JASAL: Journal of the Association for the Study of Australian Literature* 14.2 (2014): 5.

82. Graham Murphy, "In(ter)secting the Animal in David Malouf's *Remembering Babylon*," *Ariel* 41.2 (2011): 75.

83. David Malouf, *Remembering Babylon* (New York: Vintage, 1994), 143.

84. Seeley, *Honeybee*, 7.

85. Malouf, *Remembering Babylon*, 144.

86. Sue Monk Kidd, *The Secret Life of Bees* (Harmondsworth: Penguin, 2001), 4.

87. Laurie Grobman, "Teaching Cross-racial Texts: Cultural Theft in *The Secret Life of Bees*," *College English* 71.1 (2008): 9–26.

88. Kidd, *Secret Life of Bees*, 301.

89. Gloria Anzaldúa, *Borderlands / La Frontera: The New Mestiza* (San Francisco: Aunt Lute Books, 1987).

90. Teju Cole, *Open City* (New York: Random House, 2011), 198–99.

91. Ibid., 199.

92. Ibid., 200.

93. Douglas Coupland, *Generation A* (New York: Random House, 2009), 50.

94. See Woodward, "'The Only Facts Are Supernatural Ones': Dreaming Animals and Trauma in Some Contemporary Southern African Texts," in *Indigenous Creatures, Native Knowledges, and the Arts*, 231–48.

95. Coupland, *Generation A*, 151.

96. "Wonka children" references the equally random winners of a great prize that also proves of dubious value in Roald Dahl's novel *Charlie and the Chocolate Factory* (New York: Knopf, 1964).

97. Coupland, *Generation A*, 136.

98. Ibid.

99. Ibid., 151.

100. Ibid., 355.

101. Ibid., 173.

102. Ibid., 344.

103. Ibid., 347.

104. Nicholas Warner, "Firewater Legacy: Alcohol and Native American Identity in the Fiction of James Fenimore Cooper," in *High Anxieties: Cultural Studies in Addiction*, ed. Janet Farrell Brodie and Marc Redfield (Berkeley: University of California Press, 2002), 109–18.

105. Coupland, *Generation A*, 361.

106. Simpson, *Dancing on Our Turtle's Back: Stories of Nishnaabeg Re-creation, Resurgence, and a New Emergence* (Winnipeg: Arbeiter Ring, 2011), 34. See also Justice, *Why Indigenous Literatures Matter*, 25.

107. Jenny Kerber, "'You Are Turning into a Hive Mind': Storytelling, Ecological Thought, and the Problem of Form in *Generation A*," *Studies in Canadian Literature* 39.1 (2014): 325.

108. Swan, *Where Honeybees Thrive*, 122.

109. Jane Bennett, *Vibrant Matter: A Political Ecology of Things* (Durham: Duke University Press, 2010), 31–32.

110. Jussi Parikka, *Insect Media: An Archaeology of Animals and Technology* (Minneapolis: University of Minnesota Press, 2010), 43.

111. Michael Hardt and Antonio Negri, *Assembly* (Oxford: Oxford University Press, 2017), xxi.

112. Ibid., xix.

113. Joshua Takano Chambers-Letson, "Commentary: A New Fable of the Bees," in *Animal Acts: Performing Species Today*, ed. Una Chaudhuri and Holly Hughes (Ann Arbor: University of Michigan Press, 2014), 109.

114. Eric Brown, introduction, in *Insect Poetics*, ed. Eric Brown (Minneapolis: University of Minnesota Press, 2008), xii.

115. Jacques Derrida, *The Animal That Therefore I Am*, ed. Marie-Louise Mallet, trans. David Wills (New York: Fordham University Press, 2008), 123.

116. In turn, Derrida's use of bees as metaphors "to express his disapproval of academic feminists and to condemn our allegedly regimented and authoritarian way of thinking" is called out by Braidotti, *Nomadic Theory*, 103.

Conclusion

1. David Herman, *Narratology Beyond the Human: Storytelling and Animal Life*

220 (New York: Oxford University Press, 2018), 100–101.

2. Ibid., ix.

3. Herman's discussion of ecofeminist Val Plumwood's influential distinction of anthropocentrism from anthropomorphism serves as a reminder that there isn't anything "automatically colonizing or self-imposing" about narrative representation. Instead, Plumwood persuades, "the problems of representing another's culture or another [animal's] communication . . . pale before the enormity of failing to represent them at all, or of representing them as non-communicative and non-intentional beings." See Plumwood, *Environmental Culture: The Ecological Crisis of Reason* (London: Routledge, 2002), 60–61.

4. Herman, *Narratology*, 156.

5. Serenella Iovino and Serpil Opperman, "Introduction: Stories Come to Matter," in *Material Ecocriticism*, ed. Serenella Iovino and Serpil Opperman (Bloomington: Indiana University Press, 2014), 9.

6. Amitav Ghosh, *The Great Derangement: Climate Change and the Unthinkable* (Chicago: University of Chicago Press, 2016), 64.

7. Jeff Corntassel and Chaw-win-is, "Indigenous Storytelling: Truth-Telling, and Community Approaches to Reconciliation," *ESC: English Studies in Canada* 35.1 (2009): 137–38.

8. Daniel Heath Justice clarifies, "'Sovereignty' is a story, as are 'self-determination' and 'nationhood.' These stories challenge others like 'Manifest Destiny,' 'savage,'

'assimilation,' 'genocide.'" Justice, *Why Indigenous Literatures Matter* (Waterloo: Wilfrid Laurier University Press, 2018), 207.

9. Paulette Regan, *Unsettling the Settler Within: Indian Residential Schools, Truth Telling, and Reconciliation in Canada* (Vancouver: University of British Columbia Press, 2010), 6. See also Qwul'sih'yah'maht Robina Thomas, "Honoring the Oral Traditions of My Ancestors Through Storytelling," in *Research as Resistance*, ed. Leslie Brown and Susan Strega (Toronto: Canadian Scholars' Press, 2005), 237–54.

10. Rosalyn LaPier, *Invisible Reality: Storytellers, Storytakers, and the Supernatural World of the Blackfeet* (Lincoln: University of Nebraska Press, 2017), xl.

11. Justice, *Why Indigenous Literatures Matter*, 41.

12. Ibid., 96.

13. Joni Adamson and Juan Carlos Galeano, "Why Bears, Yakumama (Mother of All Water Beings), and Other Transformational Creatures Are Still Good to Think," in *Ecocriticism and Indigenous Studies: Conversations from Earth to Cosmos*, ed. Salma Monani and Joni Adamson (New York: Routledge, 2017), 226–42.

14. Donna Haraway, *Staying with the Trouble: Making Kin in the Chthulucene* (Durham: Duke University Press, 2016), 3.

15. Ibid., 102.

16. Montcombroux, *The Inuit Dog of the Polar North* (Middletown, DE: Whippoorwill Solitude, 2015), 200.

17. Mark Doty, *Dog Years* (New York: HarperCollins, 2007), 8.

Index